D0451576

ABOUT THE EDITORS

JEFFREY TOOBIN has been a staff writer at *The New Yorker* since 1993 and is the senior legal analyst for CNN. In 2000, he received an Emmy Award for his coverage of the Elián González case. He is the author of *The Nine: Inside the Secret World of the Supreme Court,* which spent more than four months on the *New York Times* bestseller list. Before joining *The New Yorker,* Toobin served as an Assistant United States Attorney in Brooklyn, New York. He lives in Manhattan.

OTTO PENZLER is the proprietor of the Mysterious Bookshop, the founder of the Mysterious Press, the creator of Otto Penzler Books, and the editor of many books and anthologies.

THOMAS H. COOK is the author of twenty two books, including *The Chatham School Affair,* which won the Edgar Allan Poe Award for Best Novel, and, most recently, *The Fate of Katherine Carr.*

The Best American Crime Reporting

2009

The Best American CRIME REPORTING

Editors

2002: NICHOLAS PILEGGI

2003: JOHN BERENDT

2004: JOSEPH WAMBAUGH

2005: JAMES ELLROY

2006: MARK BOWDEN

2007: LINDA FAIRSTEIN

2008: JONATHAN KELLERMAN

The Best American
CRIME REPORTING
2009

Guest Editor
JEFFREY TOOBIN

Series Editors
OTTO PENZLER AND
THOMAS H. COOK

An Imprint of HarperCollins*Publishers*

Permissions appear on pages 311–313.

THE BEST AMERICAN CRIME REPORTING 2009. Copyright © 2009 by Otto Penzler and
Thomas H. Cook. Introduction © 2009 by Jeffrey Toobin. All rights reserved. Printed
in the United States of America. No part of this book may be used or reproduced in
any manner whatsoever without written permission except in the case of brief quo-
tations embodied in critical articles or reviews. For information, address Harper-
Collins Publishers, 10 East 53rd Street, New York, NY 10022.

HarperCollins books may be purchased for educational, business, or sales promotional
use. For information, please write: Special Markets Department, HarperCollins Publishers, 10 East 53rd Street, New York, NY 10022.

FIRST EDITION

Library of Congress Cataloging-in-Publication Data is available upon request.

ISBN: 978-0-06-149084-2

09 10 11 12 13 WBC/RRD 10 09 08 07 06 05 04 03 02

Contents

Preface

IF CRIME DIDN'T PAY, as none other than G. Gordon Liddy once noted, there wouldn't be any. The varied ways in which crime can pay—at least in the short run—are amply represented in this year's edition of *The Best American Crime Reporting*.

Take dead bodies, for example. As Dan P. Lee demonstrates in "Body Snatchers," there is real money to be made in the cadaver trade. The overhead is light, just a few sharp saws and a little storage space (not necessarily refrigerated). And in terms of marketing, one only needs a few choice customers who don't ask too many questions.

Using other people's credit cards can also be quite lucrative, according to Sabrina Rubin Erdely's "The Fabulous Fraudulent Life of Jocelyn and Ed," though controlling debt is really a must when spending other people's money.

Shoplifting may undoubtedly bring in a tidy income, but as John Colapinto warns in "Stop, Thief!" the sticky-fingered must be careful of many unseen eyes.

In some cases, however, boldness wins the prize, as it does in

"Breaking the Bank," L. Jon Wertheim's story of cage fighter "Lightning" Lee Murray, mastermind of the largest cash heist in criminal history.

The preceding stories show crime at its most comic and unusual. Others in this year's edition of *The Best American Crime Reporting* show it at its most tragic.

In Mark Arax's "The Zankou Chicken Murders," a hugely successful family business drowns in a pool of blood. Blind prejudice claims a wholly innocent victim in R. Scott Moxley's aptly titled "Hate and Death," while misunderstanding of another kind claims a quite different victim in Calvin Trillin's sobering account of a Long Island murder case, "The Color of Blood."

How crime spreads is the subject of Hanna Rosin's sadly illuminating "American Murder Mystery," a tale of good intentions gone disastrously awry. How crime can be thoughtlessly imported to our shores is the disturbing lesson to be taken from Matt McAllester's "Tribal Wars."

The clever solving of a crime is the subject of David Grann's fascinating account of a bizarre cold case in "True Crime." However, a Sherlock Holmes approach has nothing to do with bringing down criminals in Alec Wilkinson's "Non-Lethal Force," though as he makes clear, there is considerable intelligence behind the increasingly innovative technology of apprehending them alive.

A whole country destroyed by crime is the subject of Charles Bowden's harrowing "Mexico's Red Days," while a crime that changed the world is brought to life again in Michael J. Mooney's "The Day Kennedy Died."

These and other stories in this year's *The Best American Crime Reporting* demonstrate that although crime itself may or may not pay, reading what the best of America's writers have to say about it is profitable indeed.

We welcome submissions from any writer, editor, publisher, agent, or other interested party for *The Best American Crime Reporting 2010*. Please send the publication or a tear sheet with the name of the publication, the date on which the story ran, and contact information for the journalist or representative. If it first appeared in an electronic format, a hard copy must be submitted.

Only material first published in the 2009 calendar year is eligible. All submissions must be received no later than December 31, 2009. Anything received after that date will not be read. This is neither arrogant nor capricious. The timely nature of the book forces very tight deadlines that cannot be met if we receive articles later than that. The earlier material is received, the more favorable will be the light in which it is perused.

Please send submissions to: Otto Penzler, The Mysterious Bookshop, 58 Warren Street, New York, New York, 10007. Regretfully, no material can be returned. If you don't trust the postal service to actually deliver your submission, please enclose a self-addressed stamped postcard.

Thank you,
Otto Penzler and
Thomas H. Cook
New York, March 2009

Introduction

IF ALL THESE CRIMES are so terrible, why do I feel so good?

It's not all murder in these pages—there is a little fraud, robbery, and even (honest!) shoplifting—but most of the stories feature untimely demise, delivered by force. Some of the bodies are floating (an advertising executive in a river in Poland and a hedge fund manager in a pool near Palm Beach); some of them are mutilated (the victims of Mexican drug gangs and the corpses at a Philadelphia funeral home, sold to the transplant industry for parts); most are obscure (the victims of a Somali gang war in, of all places, Minnesota, and a loudmouthed punk on Long Island). One is very, very famous (JFK).

Still, these stories are the unlikely vectors of good cheer because, simply, they are so fascinating and so well told. These are good days for crime (most days are), but they are also rough days for journalism, especially for publications that tell stories at some length. Newspapers and magazines are going bust or shrinking, and so, it is said, are attention spans. But these stories show that narrative journalism—a fancy term for story telling, nonfiction division—is alive and well.

Notice that verb: show. As in the most venerable, and still the most useful, advice given to writers: *show, don't tell.* There is a wonderful moment in Hanna Rosin's "American Murder Mystery" that brings home the meaning of that well-worn phrase. To be honest, the subject matter of Rosin's story could sound a little dry. She is exploring whether the decision to close down high-rise housing projects for the poor and move their residents to suburban neighborhoods—a practice that was broadly supported across the political spectrum—was in fact good public policy. Rosin tells the story through a pair of husband-and-wife researchers in Memphis; by coincidence, he studies crime and she studies housing. One day, he decided to plot his violent crime statistics (in blue) over her poor people (in red). "All of the dark-blue areas are covered in little red dots, like bursts of gunfire," Rosin writes. "The rest of the city has almost no dots." Aha, says the reader, sharing the moment of recognition.

It's great reporting, which is the constant throughout these varied stories. In "The Zankou Chicken Murders," Mark Arax recounts how Mardiros Iskenderian built a small empire of fast-food chicken restaurants in and around Los Angeles. There is family strife, and ultimately murder, but the key to the story for me was how delicious the food sounded. "How did they make the chicken so tender and juicy?" Arax asks. "The answer was a simple rub of salt and not trusting the rotisserie to do all the work but raising and lowering the heat and shifting each bird as it cooked. What made the garlic paste so fluffy and white and piercing? That was a secret the family intended to keep." You could tell this story without dwelling on the food; a narrow-minded writer (or editor) could see it as extraneous to the crime story. But it's not too much of a jump to see how the family's passion in the kitchen turned into rage of another kind—at each other. Here, the mystery of the garlic paste mattered far more than the model of the handgun.

(And the story made me want to kick myself, because I spent all those years in L.A. covering O.J. and I never tried this chicken! What was I thinking?)

One of the shames of contemporary journalism is that an opinion is sometimes more valued than an eye. In "The Color of Blood," Calvin Trillin takes on a case that was a brief tabloid phenomenon in New York, and shows the complexities and heartbreak that lay beneath the sensational facts. In short, Daniel Cicciaro Jr., who was white, threw Aaron White, a black acquaintance, out of a party near their homes on Long Island. Cicciaro and his buddies pursued White to his house, where his father, John White, shot Cicciaro dead in the driveway. Was this self-defense by a black family that was about to get lynched? Or a cold-blooded murder by a trigger-happy homeowner? Neither, it seems, at least according to Trillin, who covered John White's trial. The richly detailed portraits of the White and Cicciaro families show how stereotypes about race and class yield to the messy complexity of real life.

The simplest story in the collection is "The Day Kennedy Died" by Michael J. Mooney, an account of a speech by an elderly doctor to a group of medical students in Dallas. Dr. Robert Nelson McClelland was a young doctor at Parkland Hospital on November 22, 1963, and around lunchtime that day he was showing a film of an operation for a hiatal hernia to some medical students when he was called away for an emergency. Behind a curtain in Trauma Room One lay the young president of the United States—with parts of his brain falling out on to the gurney. More than four decades later, McClelland tells the rapt students, and us, how he tried to save him. I'm a JFK—and *JFK*—buff of sorts, and I can still never get enough about the details of that day. The wound, the Zapruder film, the injury to the cerebrum—or was it the cerebellum? And two days later, incredibly enough, Dr. McClelland was called in to Parkland to try to save Lee Harvey Oswald's life, too.

If that begins to sound too somber, there are a couple of stories here that fit squarely in the most lighthearted genre of crime reporting: the caper. "The Fabulous Fraudulent Life of Jocelyn and Ed," by Sabrina Rubin Erdely, is the story of a couple of knuckle-headed college students in Philadelphia who decided to live beyond their means. (Way beyond. Thanks to identity theft.) Perhaps it speaks ill of me, but I came to have a soft spot for Jocelyn, the star of the tale, who told friends "she was fluent in Russian, which she'd learned while growing up in Lithuania; later, she'd tell classmates she spoke eleven languages, including Turkish, Czech, and Afrikaans. She also mentioned she was an athlete who had qualified for the 2004 U.S. Olympic team. In pole-vaulting." (She had me at Afrikaans.) In a similar vein, there is the tale of "Lightning" Lee Murray, who turned from a brief career in the field known as Ultimate Fighting Championship, a kind of mixed martial arts, in Las Vegas, to engineering the biggest bank heist in the history of Great Britain. In "Breaking the Bank," L. Jon Wertheim seems to have almost as much fun as the perps did when they got their hands on fifty-three million pounds, or about a hundred million dollars, in cash. I, for one, was relieved to hear that Murray bought himself a villa and "commissioned a giant mural above the hot tub, depicting his victory in his one and only UFC fight." (He also wasted some of the money.) Alas, Murray is now in prison in—don't ask—Morocco.

For all the mayhem in this collection, there's one story that's actually about how *not* to kill people—"Non-Lethal Force," by Alec Wilkinson. It turns out that the authorities have been trying for literally hundreds of years to figure out ways to stop people from making trouble, but in a way that will not kill or permanently incapacitate them. It's harder than I thought. Through an entertaining portrait of Charles Heal, a man known as "Mr. Non-Lethal Weapons"—a title I did not know existed—Wilkinson offers a wry introduction to this curious field. (Who knew, for example, that the word Taser comes from the phrase, "Tom Swift and His Electric Rifle"?) As always, the resilience of criminals is remarkable; Heal notes that in the old days, "The non-lethal options were a baton, which all it did was get the guy mad, or tear gas, which they didn't feel and tended to work better on us." It reminded me of the line from Mel Brooks's *Blazing Saddles*. "If you shoot him, you'll just make him mad."

Ultimately, though, the highest form of crime reporting, I think, is in the creation of portraits of the criminals themselves. On hearing of a particularly awful or shocking crime, who among us hasn't asked the question, "Who could do a thing like that?" Several stories in this collection try to answer that fundamental question—again, not with stereotypes or surmise, but with painstaking reporting.

I had to remind myself of the subject of Mark Boal's "Everyone Will Remember Me as Some Sort of Monster." It was a spree killing by a kid with a gun; sadly, they all seemed to come in a jumble between Columbine and Virginia Tech. This one was in Omaha, where a skinny nineteen-year-old—"Harry Potter with an AK–47"—mowed down eight people in a shopping mall just before Christmas. As Boal writes, "It was a big story. For about a week."

But Boal does what a real journalist should—which is unpack a simple story in all its awful complexity. He writes, in essence, a mini-biography of Robert Hawkins, who had bounced from foster home to no home in his sad, short stay on the planet. As with any memorable work of journalism, it's the details that stay with you. "On Mother's Day, when patients were told to draw cards for their loved ones," Boal writes, "Robbie drew a picture of a noose for his stepmother." Robbie was such a screwup that he tried to roll joints with Post-it notes. But what turned Robbie from a sad sack into a mass murderer? That's not clear; nor could it be.

The story that best sums up the paradoxes of crime reporting is David Grann's "True Crime," which begins in 2000 with the discovery of a bound-and-gagged body in a river in Poland. For years, there are no arrests or suspects. Then, in 2003, the police are alerted to the publication of a novel by Krystian Bala, an obscure Polish writer. The book, called *Amok*, includes scenes of a homicide that bear a great deal of similarity to the unsolved crime in 2000. An intrepid police detective makes copies of the novel and hands them out to his colleagues. "Everyone was assigned a chapter to 'interpret': to try to find any clues, any coded messages, any parallels with reality."

In the confrontation between detective and author-suspect, Bala denies responsibility for the murder but admits that he drew some of the novel from real life. "Sure, I'm guilty of that. Show me an author who *doesn't* do that." The question at the heart of Grann's piece is the difference between life and art—and whether any story, of fiction or nonfiction, can ever accurately portray reality.

Grann's story culminates in a trial—and all of Poland was watching. Bala denied all. The government said his novel proved his guilt. Grann writes, "A trial is predicated on the idea that truth is obtainable." So is journalism. This collection represents the best of that compelling and imperfect profession.

—Jeffrey Toobin

The Best American Crime Reporting

2009

Calvin Trillin

THE COLOR OF BLOOD

FROM *The New Yorker*

WHAT HAPPENED AT THE FOOT of the driveway at 40 Independence Way that hot August night in 2006 took less than three minutes. The police later managed to time it precisely, using a surveillance camera that points directly at the street from a house a couple of doors to the north. The readout on the surveillance tape said that it was 23:06:11 when two cars whizzed by going south, toward the cul-de-sac at the end of the street. At 23:09:06, the first car passed back in front of the camera, going north. A minute later, a second car passed in the same direction. In the back seat of that second car—a black Mustang Cobra convertible—was a seventeen-year-old boy named Daniel Cicciaro, Jr., known to his friends as Dano. He was unconscious and bleeding profusely. He had been shot through the cheek. A .32-calibre bullet was lodged in his head.

Normally, at that time of night, not many cars are seen on Independence Way, a quiet street in a town called Miller Place. Just east of Port Jefferson, on the North Shore of Long Island, Miller Place is in the part of Suffolk County where the commuters have begun to thin out. To the east is a large swatch of the county that doesn't seem strongly connected to the huge city in one direction or to the high-priced summer resorts and North Fork wineries in the other. The house at 40 Independence Way is part of a development, Talmadge Woods, that five or six years ago was a peach orchard; it's now a collection of substantial two-story, four-bedroom houses that the developer started offering in 2003 for about half a million dollars each. The houses vary in design, but they all have an arched front door topped by the arched glass transom known in the trade as a Palladian window—a way to bring light into the double-height entry hall. When people are asked to describe the neighborhood, they tend to say "upper middle class." The homeowner with the surveillance system is an orthodontist.

Miller Place could also be described as overwhelmingly white. According to a study released a few years ago, Long Island is the single most segregated suburban area in the United States. The residents of 40 Independence Way—John and Sonia White and their youngest son, Aaron—are African-American and so are their next-door neighbors, but the black population of Miller Place is less than one-half of one per cent. The Whites, who began married life in Brooklyn in the early seventies, had moved to Miller Place after ten years in North Babylon, which is forty minutes or so closer to the city. "You want to raise your family in a safe environment," John White, a tall, very thin man in his early fifties, has said, explaining why he was willing to spend three hours a day in his car commuting. "The educational standards are higher. You want to live a comfortable life, which is the American dream." One of the Whites' sons is married, with children of his own, and a second is in college in the South. But Aaron was able to spend his senior year at Miller Place High School, which takes pride in such statistics as how many of its students are in Advanced Placement history courses. Aaron, an erect young man who is likely to say "sir" when addressing one of his elders, graduated in June of 2005. He was one of four black students in the class.

In an area where home maintenance is a priority, 40 Independence Way could hold its own. John White is a serious gardener—a nurturer of daylilies and clematis, a planter of peel-bark birch trees—and someone who had always been proud, maybe even touchy, about his property. People who have been neighbors of the Whites tend to use the word "meticulous" in describing John White; so do people who have worked with him. He has described himself as "a doer"—someone too restless to sit around reading a book or watching television. He says that he's fished from Nova Scotia to the Bahamas. He's done a lot of hunting—a pastime he was taught by his grandfather Napoleon White, whose family's migration from Alabama apparently took place after a murderous attack by the Ku Klux Klan. At the Faith Baptist Church, in Coram, Long Island, John White sang in both the men's choir and the mixed Celebration Choir. A couple of polished-wood tables in the Whites' house were made by him. He's a broadly accomplished man, and proud of it. His wife, who was born in Panama, works as a manager in a department store and has that Caribbean accent which, maybe because it's close to the accent of West Indian nurses, conveys both competence and the firm intention to brook no nonsense. The Whites' furniture tastes lean toward Stickley, Audi. Their sons dress in a style that's preppy. Sitting in his well-appointed family room, John White could be taken for middle management.

But he doesn't have the sort of education or occupation that would seem to go along with the house he lives in. After graduating from a technical program at Samuel Gompers High School, he worked as an electrician for seven or eight years and then, during a slow time for electricians, he began working in the paving industry. For the past twenty-five years, he has worked for an asphalt company in Queens, patching the potholes left by utility repair crews. He is often described as a foreman, which he once was, but he says that, partly because of an aversion to paperwork, he didn't try to reclaim that job after it evaporated during a reduction in the workforce. ("I'm actually a laborer.") On August 9, 2006, a Wednesday, he had, as usual, awakened at three-thirty in the morning for the drive to Queens, spent the day at work, and, after a stop to pick up some bargain peony plants, returned to what he calls his "dream house" or his "castle." He retired early, so that he could do the same thing the next day. A couple of hours later, according to his testimony, he was awakened by Aaron, who, with a level of terror John White had never heard in his son's voice, shouted, "Dad, these guys are coming here to kill me!" Instead, as it turned out, John White killed Daniel Cicciaro, Jr.

THERE HAD BEEN A BIRTHDAY PARTY that evening for Craig Martin, Jr., a recent Miller Place High School graduate. Craig lives with his parents and his younger sister, Jennifer, in Sound Beach— a town just to the east that grew into a year-round neighborhood from what had begun as beach lots purchased in the twenties as part of a *Daily Mirror* circulation-promotion scheme. The party was mostly in the Martins' back yard, where there was an above-ground pool, a lot of cold beer, and a succession of beer-pong games. This was not the A.P.-history crowd. Craig was connected to a number of the boys at the party through an interest in cars. Some of them were members of the Blackout car club, a loose organization of teen-agers who, in good weather, gather in the parking lot of the Stop & Shop mall in Miller Place on Thursday nights for an informal car show—displaying cars whose lights and windows are likely to have been tinted in pursuit of sleekness. Dano Cicciaro (pronounced Danno Cicero) was a regular at Stop & Shop, driving a white Mustang Mach 1 with two black stripes. Dano had grown up in Selden, a blue-collar town to the south, and finished at Newfield High School there after his family moved in his senior year to one of a half-dozen houses clustered around a cul-de-sac called Old Town Estates, in Port Jefferson Station.

His father, Daniel Cicciaro, Sr., runs an automobile-repair shop in Port Jeff Station called Dano's Auto Clinic—a two-bay operation that also has some used cars parked in its lot, their prices marked on the windshields. Dano's Auto Clinic is where Dano, Jr., spent a lot of his spare time. As a boy, he had the usual range of interests, his father has recalled, but "as he turned into a teen-ager it was all cars." Even as a teen-ager, he ran a car-detailing business out of the shop, and he'd planned to keep that up when he started at Suffolk County Community College in the fall. Dano, Jr.,'s long-term plan was to take over Dano's Auto Clinic someday and expand its services. "He did exactly as I did, in that he set goals for himself and conquered them, never sitting idle," a *Newsday* reporter was told by Daniel Cicciaro, Sr., a father who'd felt the validation of having a son who was eager to follow his calling and work by his side.

Aaron White, who had finished his first year at Suffolk County Community College, was having dinner that evening in Port Jefferson with Michael Longo, his best friend from Miller Place High School. From having attended a few of the Stop & Shop gatherings, Aaron knew some of the car crowd, and, while phoning around for something to do, he learned about the birthday party at the Martins'. Craig greeted Aaron cheerfully enough, but a few minutes later Jennifer, who was then fifteen, told her brother that, because of a past incident, she felt frightened in Aaron's presence. Dano Cicciaro was assigned to ask Aaron to leave. It isn't clear why he was given that task. It couldn't have been his size: Dano was five feet four and weighed a hundred and twenty-nine pounds. It certainly wasn't his sobriety. Dano was drunk. When his blood-alcohol content was checked later at the hospital, it was almost twice the level required to prove intoxication. Still, Dano, who thought of himself as a protective older brother to Jennifer, handled the situation smoothly, saying to Aaron something like "It's nothing personal, but you'll have to leave." Aaron later said that he was puzzled ("I never get kicked out of parties"), but he got into his car and drove back to Miller Place.

When Dano learned exactly why Jennifer felt uncomfortable around Aaron, she later testified, "he freaked out." While in an Internet chat room with a couple of other boys, Jennifer told Dano, Aaron had posted a message saying that he wanted to rape her. Obtaining Aaron's cell-phone number from Michael Longo, Dano touched off what became a series of heated calls involving several people at the party. Dano wanted to confront Aaron immediately. It didn't matter that Aaron denied having posted the message. It didn't matter that the posting had taken place nine months before and that Jennifer's real older brother, Craig, had actually forgotten about it. In court many months later, Jennifer Martin was asked if she'd eventually learned that the offending message had not, in fact, been sent by Aaron—it had grown out of something said on a MySpace account set up in Aaron's name as a prank—and she answered in the affirmative. That didn't matter, either, because by then it was much too late. On the evening of August 9th, when Jennifer told Dano about the rape posting, there were other elements involved. A lot of beer had been consumed. It was late in the evening, a time when the teenage penchant for melodrama tends to be in full flower. Dano was filled with what Paul Gianelli, one of John White's defense attorneys, called "a warped sense of chivalry" and Dano's godfather, Gregg Sarra, preferred to characterize as "valor, protecting a woman, honor." For whatever reason, Dano Cicciaro and four of his friends were soon heading toward the Whites' house in two beautifully painted and carefully polished cars that passed the orthodontist's surveillance camera when its readout said 23:06:11.

What happened when they got there remains a matter of sharp dispute. There is no doubt that the boys were displaying no weapons when they got out of their cars, although one of them, Joseph

Serrano, had brought along a baseball bat that remained in the back seat of the Mustang. There is no doubt that John White emerged from his garage carrying a pre-Second World War Beretta pistol that he kept there—part of an inheritance from his grandfather that had also included, White later said, "rifles and shotguns and a lot of advice." Aaron was a few steps behind him, carrying a 20-gauge shotgun. There is no doubt that Dano "slapped" or "whacked" or "grabbed" the Beretta. There is no doubt that, before the shot was fired, there had been shouting and foul language from both sides. The tenor of the conversation, the defense team eventually maintained, could be surmised from the tape of a 911 line that the boys did not realize was open as they rushed their friend to a Port Jefferson hospital in the black Mustang Cobra. The 911 operator can be heard saying, "Sir . . . hello . . . hello . . . sir, pick up the phone." The boys, their muffled voices almost hysterical, can be heard shouting directions to one another and giving assurances that Dano is still breathing. The operator keeps saying, "Hello . . . sir." Then the voice of Joseph Serrano, sitting in the back seat with his bleeding friend and his baseball bat, comes through clearly: "Fucking niggers! Dano, I'll get 'em for you, Dano."

Back at 40 Independence Way, John White and his son were sitting in front of their house, hugging. Sonia White was screaming, "What happened? What happened?" In the trial testimony and police reports and newspaper accounts and grand-jury minutes dealing with what occurred in the meticulous front yard of 40 Independence Way after the cars had sped away, three statements attributed to John White stand out. One was in the testimony of Officer David Murray, the first Suffolk County policeman to reach the scene, who said that John White approached him with his arms extended, saying, "I did what I had to do. You might as well put the cuffs on me." Another is what Officer Murray said he heard John White say to his son: "I told you those friends of yours would turn on you." The third is what Sonia White testified that her husband said to her as he walked back into their castle: "We lost the house. We lost it all."

A WEEK AFTER the death of Daniel Cicciaro, Jr., several hundred people turned out for his funeral, held at St. Sylvester's Roman Catholic Church, in Medford, Long Island. The gathering was heavy with symbolism. Some of the younger mourners displayed "Dano Jr." tattoos. Dano, Jr.,'s main car was there—the white Mustang that was familiar from Stop & Shop and had won Best Mach 1 Mustang in a competition at McCarville Ford. Gregg Sarra, a boyhood friend of Daniel Cicciaro, Sr., and a local-sports columnist for *Newsday*, gave the eulogy, praising his godson's loyalty and his diligence and his gift for friendship. After the burial, some of Dano, Jr.,'s car-club friends revved their engines and chanted, "Dan-o, Dan-o, Dan-o." As a tribute to his son, Daniel Cicciaro, Sr., attended the service in a Dano's Auto Clinic tank top. The Stop & Shop car show that Thursday, according to a *Newsday* piece, turned into a sort of vigil for Dano, Jr., with Jennifer Martin helping to light a ring of candles—red and white candles, for the colors of Newfield High—around his Mustang and his first car, a Mercedes E55 AMG.

The sadness was accompanied by a good deal of anger. John White found that understandable. "I know how I would feel if someone hurt my kid," he said in a *Times* interview some weeks later. "There wouldn't be a rock left to crawl under." Speaking to one reporter, Daniel Cicciaro, Sr., had referred to White as an "animal." For a while after the shooting, Michael Longo—the friend who had accompanied Aaron White to the birthday party and had, as it turned out, telephoned to warn him that there were plans to jump him if he returned—slept with a baseball bat next to his bed. Sonia White later testified that after some particularly menacing instant messages ("i need ur adress you dumb nigger"), to which Aaron replied in what sounded like a suburban teen-ager's notion of gangster talk ("u da bitch tlaking big n bad like u gonna come down to my crib n do sumthin"), the Whites decided that he was no longer safe in the house, and they sent him to live outside the area.

The mourners who talked to reporters after the service rejected the notion, brought up by a lawyer for the White family shortly after the shooting, that Dano Cicciaro and his friends had used racial epithets during the argument in front of 40 Independence Way. Daniel Cicciaro, Sr.—a short man with a shaved head and a Fu Manchu mustache and an assertive manner and a lifelong involvement in martial arts—had called any connection of his son with racism "absurd." But by the time a grand jury met, a month or so after the shooting, even the prosecutor, who would presumably need the boys as witnesses against John White, was saying that racial epithets had indeed been used. The district attorney said, though, that if John White had simply remained in his house and dialled 911, he wouldn't be in any trouble and Daniel Cicciaro, Jr., would still be alive. The grand jury was asked to indict White for murder. Grand juries ordinarily go along with district attorneys, but this one didn't. When the trial finally began, in Riverhead, fifteen months after the shooting, the charge was second-degree manslaughter.

The grand-jury decision may have reflected public opinion in Suffolk County, where there are strong feelings about a home-owner's right to protect his property and his family. Suffolk County is a place where a good number of residents are active or retired law enforcement officers, and where even a lot of residents who aren't own guns—a place where it is not surprising to come across a plaque that bears the picture of a pistol and the phrase "We Don't Dial 911." James Chalifoux, the assistant district attorney who was assigned to try the case against John White, apparently had that in mind when, during jury selection, he asked jurors if they would be able to distinguish between what might be considered morally right—what could cause you to say, "I might have done the same thing"—and what was permissible under the law. He asked jurors if they could put aside sympathy when they were considering the case—meaning sympathy for John White. Judging by comments posted online in response to *Newsday* articles, public opinion seemed muddled by the conflict between two underpinnings of life in Suffolk County—a devotion to the sanctity of private property, particularly one's home, and an assumption that the owner of the property is white.

Dano's mother—Joanne Cicciaro, a primary-school E.S.L. teacher who had grown up in Suffolk County—said she was extremely disappointed that the grand jury had declined to indict John White for murder. Daniel Cicciaro, Sr., told a reporter, "Here this man points his gun at the boys and says, 'I'm going to shoot.' He says it three times. Then he shoots my son. To me, that's intentional murder." On the other hand, some of White's strongest supporters—people like Lucius Ware, the president of the Eastern Long Island branch of the N.A.A.C.P., and Marie Michel, a black attorney who joined the defense team—believed that if a white homeowner in Miller Place had been confronted late at night by five hostile black teen-agers there would have been, in Marie Michel's words, "no arrests, no indictment, and no trial." The homeowner would have been judged to have had "a well-founded fear," they thought, and if the justice system dealt with the incident in any way it would have been to charge the boys with something like breach of the peace or aggravated harassment ("What were they doing in that neighborhood at that time of night?"). For that matter, these supporters would argue, would Dano have "freaked out" if the male accused of wanting to rape Jenny Martin hadn't been black? Wouldn't teen-agers spoiling for a fight have dispersed if a white father walked out of the house, with or without a gun, and told them in no uncertain terms to go home? In other words, before a word of testimony had been heard, some people attending the trial of John White believed that in a just world he would have been on trial for murder instead of only manslaughter, and some believed that in a just world he wouldn't have been on trial at all.

THE ARTHUR M. CROMARTY Court Complex is set apart from Riverhead, the seat of Suffolk County, on a campus that seems to be mostly parking lots—a judicial version of Long Island shopping malls. Those who were there to attend John White's trial, which began just after Thanksgiving, seemed to be roughly separated by race, on opposite sides of the aisle that ran down the center of the courtroom's spectator section. That may have been partly because the room was small and on many days the prosecution's supporters, mostly Cicciaro relatives and young friends of Dano's, nearly filled half of it. Dano, Jr.,'s parents did not sit next to each other—they had separated before their son's death—but they came together as a family in hallway huddles of supporters and in speaking to the press. The people who stood out on their side of the courtroom were a couple of friends of Daniel Cicciaro, Sr., who also had shaved heads, but with modifications that included a scalp tattoo saying "Dano Jr." Although they looked menacing, both of them could be described as designers: one is a detailer, specializing in the fancy painting of motorcycles; the other does graphic design, specializing in sports uniforms.

People on the Cicciaro side might have felt some menace emanating from the phalanx of black men, all of them in suits and ties and many of them offensive-tackle size, who escorted Aaron White (wearing a bulletproof vest) through the courthouse on the first day of his testimony and then took seats across the aisle, near some women from John White's church choir. The escorts were from an organization called 100 Blacks in Law Enforcement Who Care. On that first day, their ranks were augmented by members of the Fruit of Islam, wearing their trademark bow ties, although the black leader called to mind by John White's life would probably be

Booker T. Washington rather than Louis Farrakhan. As it turned out, there was no overt hostility between those on either side of the courtroom aisle, and, at the end of testimony, the Cicciaros made it clear that they would accept any decision the jury brought in— none of which, Joanne Cicciaro pointed out, would bring their son back. Talking to a *Newsday* reporter after the trial about prejudice, Daniel Cicciaro, Sr., maintained that bias existed toward what some people called skinheads. "Don't judge a book by its cover," he said.

The four boys who accompanied Dano Cicciaro to Aaron White's house that night are all car enthusiasts who now hold jobs that echo their high-school hobby. Alex Delgado does maintenance on race cars. Joseph Serrano is a motorcycle mechanic. Tom Maloney, who drove the Mustang Cobra, sells Volkswagens. Anthony Simeone works for his father's auto-salvage business. Among those who testified that they'd tried to prevent Dano from going to the Whites' house were Alex Delgado, who drove him there, and Joseph Serrano, who brought along a baseball bat. ("He's stubborn," Anthony Simeone had explained to the grand jury. "When he wants to do something, he wants to do it.") Although there had been testimony that Dano Cicciaro used the word "nigger" once or twice in the cell-phone exchange with Aaron White, his friends denied using racial slurs at 40 Independence Way. (With the jury out of the courtroom, Paul Gianelli brought up an incident that had been investigated by the police but not included in the notes and reports that they are required to turn over to the defense: according to two or three witnesses, Daniel Cicciaro had gone to Sayville Ford with a complaint a few weeks before he was shot and, when approached by a black salesman, had said, "I don't talk to niggers." The judge wouldn't admit that into evidence, but the headline of the next day's *Newsday* story was "ATTORNEY: COPS HID MILLER PLACE VICTIM'S RACISM.") The friends who'd gone with Dano, Jr., to the Whites' house that night testified that after John White's gun was slapped away, he raised it again and shot Dano in the face. As they described how Dano Cicciaro fell and how he'd been lifted from the street by Tom Maloney and rushed to the hospital, there were occasional sobs from both Joanne and Daniel Cicciaro.

Dano's friends had said that both of their cars were in the street facing north, but the Whites testified that one was in their driveway, with the lights shining up into the house—a contention that the defense bolstered by analyzing the headlight reflections on the orthodontist's mailbox in the surveillance tape. The boys testified that they'd never set foot on the Whites' property—that contention was bolstered by pictures showing Dano's blood and his cell phone in the street rather than in the driveway—but the Whites claimed that the boys had been advancing toward the house. "They came to my home as if they owned it," Sonia White said on the stand. "What gall!"

John White testified that, believing the young men had come to harm his family, he backed them off his property with Napoleon White's old pistol. In the frenzy that followed his abrupt awakening, he said, he had yelled, "Call the cops!" to his wife as he raced into the garage, but she hadn't heard him. He described Dano Cicciaro and his friends as a lynch mob shouting, among other things, "We could take that skinny nigger motherfucker." Recalling that evening, White said, "In my family history, that's how the Klan comes. They pull up to your house, blind you with their lights, burn your house down. That's how they come." In White's telling, the confrontation had seemed over and he was turning to go back into the house when Dano Cicciaro grabbed the gun, causing it to fire. "I didn't mean to shoot this young man," John White said. "This young man was another child of God." This time, it was John White who broke down, and the court had to take a recess. One of the jurors was also wiping away tears.

TO CONVICT SOMEONE OF SECOND-DEGREE manslaughter in the state of New York, the prosecution has to prove that he recklessly caused the death of the victim—"recklessly" being defined as creating a risk so substantial that disregarding it constitutes "a gross deviation from the standard of conduct that a reasonable person would observe"—and that he had no justification. In its decision in the case of Bernard Goetz, the white man who in 1984 shot four young black men who had approached him on the subway demanding money, the New York Court of Appeals, the highest court in the state, ruled that justification could have a subjective as well as an objective component—fears raised by the defendant's past experiences, for instance. By bringing up the history that White's family had with the Klan, the defense team raised a subjective component of justification, along with the objective component of home protection. "We are all products of our past," Paul Gianelli said of his client during one of the breaks in the trial. "He brought to that particular evening who he is." The defense was making a case for, among other things, the power of race memory.

The racial divide is obviously less overt in John White's Long Island than it was in Napoleon White's Alabama. Tom Maloney, who'd also graduated from Miller Place High School, had apparently thought of Aaron White as a friend. Alex Delgado, who drove Dano Cicciaro to Aaron's house on August 9th, had been there before as a guest. In John White's testimony, Delgado was described as Hispanic. Joanne Cicciaro, who by name and appearance and accent might be assumed to have come from one of the many Italian-American families that moved to Suffolk County in recent decades from the boroughs, is actually Puerto Rican—a fact brought up to reporters by the Cicciaros in countering any implications of racism in Dano's upbringing. ("Our family is multicultural.") Even without those complications, the case for race memory would be harder to make to white people than to black people. White people are likely to say that times have changed: these days, after all, a real-estate agent who tried to steer John White away from buying a house in an overwhelmingly white Long Island neighborhood would be risking her license.

If times have changed, black people might ask in response, how come Long Island is still so segregated? In his summation, the prosecutor asked a series of questions as a way to illustrate how White's behavior had deviated from the behavior of a reasonable person. Two of the huge black men who had been part of Aaron White's escort were sitting in the courtroom at the time, and when the D.A. asked whether a reasonable person would really be guided partly by the memory of a Ku Klux Klan attack that happened years before he was born, they both began to nod their heads.

In that closing statement, James Chalifoux said that it wasn't until the trial began that John White started talking about a lynch mob. (It's true that in a newspaper interview in September of 2006 White seemed to downplay race, but it's also true that in his grand-jury testimony, less than a month after the shooting, he spoke about a "lynch mob.") Race, Chalifoux said, was being used to distract the jurors from the simple fact that by walking down the driveway with a loaded pistol John White, a man intimately familiar with firearms, had engaged in conduct that had recklessly caused the death of Dano Cicciaro. Matching up testimony with cell-phone logs, Chalifoux argued that the Whites had more time before the arrival of the cars than their story of a panicky few minutes implied. Chalifoux acknowledged that Dano and his friends were wrong to go to the Whites' that night, that Dano was wrong to use a racial epithet when he phoned Aaron White, and that John White had found himself "in a very bad situation that night and a situation that was not his fault." But how White responded to that situation, Chalifoux said, *was* his fault.

Chalifoux's summation followed that of Frederick K. Brewington, a black attorney, active in black causes on Long Island, who was Paul Gianelli's co-counsel. "Race has so much to do

with this case, ladies and gentlemen, that it's painful," Brewington told the jury: Dano Cicciaro and his friends thought they had
a right to go to John White's house and "terrorize his family with
impunity and arrogance" because of "the false racial privilege
they felt empowered by." In Brewington's argument, John White
thought, " 'Once they see I have a gun they'll back off' . . . but they
did not take 'the skinny old nigger' seriously." While Chalifoux
presented Joseph Serrano's slur on the 911 tape as, however
deplorable, an indication that the argument at the foot of the
driveway didn't include the barrage of insults that the Whites had
testified to—if it had, he said, "you would have heard racial epithet after racial epithet after racial epithet"—Brewington saw it as
a mirror of the boys' true feelings. "What we do under cover of
darkness sometimes comes to light," he said.

Shortly after the beginning of deliberations, ten jurors, including the sole African-American, were prepared to convict John
White of having recklessly caused Dano Cicciaro's death. Two
jurors resisted that verdict for four days. Then they capitulated.
They later told reporters that they felt bullied and pressured by
jurors who were impatient to be liberated as Christmas approached. In a courtroom crowded with court officers, the jury
reported that it had found John White guilty of manslaughter and
a weapons charge. The Cicciaros and their supporters were ec-
static. Dano's parents seemed to take John White's conviction
principally as proof that the accusations of racism against their son
had been shown to be false. "My son is finally vindicated," a tear-
ful Joanne Cicciaro said, outside the courtroom. Daniel Cicciaro,
Sr., said, "Maybe now they'll stop slinging my son's name and accusing him of all this racism." Outside the courthouse, friends of
Dano, Jr., honked their horns and revved their engines and
chanted, "Dan-o, Dan-o, Dan-o." The next day, Sunday, the celebration continued with a sort of open house at Dano's Auto
Clinic, which bore a sign saying "Thank You Jurors. Thank God.
Dano Jr. Rest in Peace." In Miller Place, John White briefly

spoke to the reporters who were waiting in front of his house. "I'm not inhuman," he said. "I have very deep feelings for this young man." But before that he went to the Faith Baptist Church, in Coram, and sang in the choir.

"JOHN WHITE IS A HERO," Frederick Brewington said two weeks later, addressing a crowd of several hundred people, almost all of them black, who had gathered on a cold Saturday afternoon in front of the criminal-court building in Riverhead. He repeated, "John White is a hero." The guilty verdict had made White the sort of hero all too familiar in the race memory of African-Americans—someone held up as an example of the unjustly treated black man. On the podium were black officeholders, speakers from the spectrum of black organizations on Long Island, and two people who had come from Manhattan—Kevin Muhammad, of Muhammad Mosque No. 7, and Al Sharpton. A lot of N.A.A.C.P. people were in the audience, and so were a lot of people from Faith Baptist Church. Various speakers demanded a retrial, or called for the resignation of the district attorney, or pointed out the difference in how white homeowners in similar situations have been treated, or called for the young white men involved to be indicted. ("We will raise this to a level of national attention until these young men are brought to justice," Sharpton said.) There were chants like "No Justice—No Peace" and, loudest of all, "Free John White."

That chant was not meant literally. For the time being, John White is free—he addressed the rally briefly, mainly to thank his supporters—and his attorneys hope that, while an appeal is pending, he will be allowed to remain free after his sentencing, scheduled for March 19th. ("I think he should get as much time as possible," a Post reporter was told by Jennifer Martin, whose response to Aaron White's arrival at her house set the events of August 9th in motion. "I really do.") Until the sentencing, White is back to rising at three-thirty every morning to go into the city and patch utility holes. Everything he was quoted as saying in the aftermath of the shooting that night turned out to be true. The fatalism reflected in his statement to Officer Murray as he held out his hands to be cuffed was well founded. Aaron White accepted the fact that those friends of his had indeed turned on him. In his testimony, he said, "They have no respect for me or my family or my mother or my father. . . . They have no respect for life whatsoever. They're scum." And, of course, John White had understood the situation well when he told his wife that they had lost their dream house—a comment that, as it turned out, particularly incensed Joanne Cicciaro. (His sorrow, she said to reporters after testimony had ended, "was all for themselves—sorrow about losing their house, about their life changing. He never said, 'Oh, my God! What did I do to that boy? Oh, my God. This kid is bleeding on the driveway. What did I do to him?' He had no sympathy, no sorrow for shooting a child.") Even before the trial, 40 Independence Way was listed with a real-estate broker. Its description began, "Stately 2 year young post-modern colonial in prestigious neighborhood."

CALVIN TRILLIN *has been a staff writer for* The New Yorker *since 1963. For fifteen years, he wrote a* New Yorker *series called "U.S. Journal"—a three-thousand-word article from somewhere in the United States every three weeks. He is the author of twenty-six books, including* Killings *and* American Stories.

Coda

I was initially attracted to this story by its sheer drama. As the first sentence of my piece says, what happened at the end of John White's driveway—events that transformed the lives of so many people—happened in less than three minutes. Also, I was curious about the role of race. I've been writing about race off and on since the early '60s, when I spent a year as a newsmagazine reporter covering the civil rights movement in the South. In that time and place, the issues were pretty clear-cut. They were less so in Miller Place, Long Island, nearly half a century later, and, in a way, that made them even more interesting to me.

L. Jon Wertheim

BREAKING THE BANK

FROM *Sports Illustrated*

WITH FLASHING BLUE LIGHTS illuminating his rearview mirror, Colin Dixon pulled his car to the side of a deserted road. It
was around six on the evening of Feb. 21, 2006, and Dixon had
just clocked out from his job at the Securitas cash depot in Ton-
bridge, England, 30 miles southeast of central London. A pur-
posely nondescript, brown building tucked behind a car repair
garage, the depot serves as a regional warehouse of sorts, where
cash for the Bank of England is stored and disbursed. Dixon, 52,
was the manager.

Now, driving home, he figured he was getting pulled over by
an unmarked police car for a routine traffic stop. A tall, athletic-
looking man in a police uniform approached. Though it would
turn out that the cop was no cop at all—the uniform was fake, the
Kent police badge he flashed had been purchased on eBay, and the
guy's face had been distorted with help from a professional makeup
artist—Dixon was compliant. He got out of his Nissan sedan and
was handcuffed and placed in the back of the other car.

He would later testify that the driver, a second man in uniform, turned and said menacingly, "You will have guessed we are not policemen. . . . Don't do anything silly and you won't get hurt." When Dixon tried to adjust his handcuffs, he says the "officer" who'd apprehended him brandished a pistol and barked, "We're not f------ about. This is a nine-millimeter."

Dixon was blindfolded and transferred to a van, then taken to a remote farm in western Kent. Meanwhile, two other fake cops drove to Dixon's home in the nearby town of Herne Bay, along with accomplices in a second van. Greeted at the door by Dixon's wife, Lynn, they explained that her husband had been in a serious traffic accident. They said that Lynn and the couple's young child needed to accompany them to the hospital. Outside the home, the Dixons were placed in the back of the second van and taken to the farm, where the Dixons were reunited. At once relieved and terrified, they were bound and held at gunpoint. Colin Dixon was ordered to give the plotters information about the depot. "If you cooperate, no one will get hurt. Otherwise," one abductor warned, "you'll get a hole in you."

A group of at least seven men then drove to the Securitas depot, Colin Dixon accompanying a phony police officer in a sedan and his family bound in the back of a large, white Renault truck. By now it was after midnight on the morning of Feb. 22. Surveillance video shows Dixon being buzzed into the depot with an officer beside him. Once inside, the fake cop overpowers the security guard and buzzes in the rest of the robbers wearing ski masks and armed with high-powered weapons, including an AK-47. Dixon told the 14 staffers working the graveyard shift, "They've got my family," and instructed them not to touch the alarms. He proceeded to deactivate the security system and hand over the keys to the vault. The Dixons and the staff were then bound and placed in metal cages normally used for storing cash. The truck can be seen backing up to a loading dock.

The robbers clearly knew their way around the depot—where the doors were located and how they locked—and with good reason. One member of the gang, Ermir Hysenaj, 28, an Albanian immigrant, was the classic inside man. Months earlier, after just a 10-minute job interview, Hysenaj had been hired for roughly $11 an hour to work the evening shift at the depot. It was later revealed that in the weeks before the robbery, he had come to work wearing a small video camera hidden in his belt buckle.

For the next 40 minutes, the gang emptied the vault of its contents, wheeling metal carts filled with cash into the truck. The supply of £10 and £20 notes was so massive that by the time the truck was filled to capacity, it accounted for only one quarter of the money in the vault. Still, the conspirators absconded with a haul of £53 million, or more than $100 million.

If the caper didn't entail pyrotechnics worthy of, say, the current movie *The Bank Job*, it seemed to come off remarkably smoothly, at least from the robbers' perspective. All their discipline and meticulous preparation had paid off. There were no surprises. No one was physically injured, much less ventilated with bullets. No one had triggered the alarms. At around 3 a.m., Dixon's child was able to slither out of a metal cage and the police were summoned. By then the thieves were back at the farm divvying up the money—a bounty that one British prosecutor would later characterize as "dishonest gain almost beyond the dreams of avarice."

As investigators worked to crack the case, they began to suspect that the ringleader was Lee Murray, and that he and his pal Lea Rusha were the impostors who had first abducted Colin Dixon. Murray was no stranger to London law enforcement. He spent time in a juvenile detention center as an adolescent and later was tried and acquitted in a serious road-rage incident. Ironically, he'd also been questioned by police after a traffic stop in the area of the Securitas depot the summer before the robbery. But he was a prominent figure in pockets of the sports community as well, a fearsome British cage fighter who'd recently gone the distance against the great Brazilian champion Anderson Silva. Murray lost a decision and was paid the equivalent of a few thousand dollars for that fight. Now,

Kent police contended, he was a fugitive in Morocco, luxuriating poolside at a villa in an upscale part of Rabat. Lightning Lee was now worth a small fortune in pounds sterling, they alleged, having just orchestrated the largest cash heist in history.

Lee Murray came into the world in 1977 with his fists balled, and he never quite seemed to unclench them. The son of a British mother and a Moroccan father—his given name is Lee Lamrani Ibrahim Murray—he grew up poor in public housing in a rough-and-tumble section near London's East End.

His salvation, such as it was, came through fighting. It wasn't so much what he did as who he was. By his own reckoning, he was a veteran of hundreds of street fights, lining up his target, transferring his weight and then unloading punches that would seem to detonate on impact. After so many bare-knuckle brawls, he figured, not unreasonably, that he might as well get paid for his violence. He frequented boxing and kickboxing gyms, channeling some of his primal tendencies into mixed martial arts (MMA), the increasingly popular sport that combines the striking of boxing and Muay Thai with the ground game of wrestling and jujitsu. In particular Murray had designs on competing in the Octagon, the eight-sided cage used for bouts in the Ultimate Fighting Championship (UFC), the preeminent MMA league, which is headquartered in the U.S.

Murray recognized that while his standup fighting was exceptional, he was at a loss when a bout went to the ground. That is, he needed to improve his grappling and jujitsu, disciplines predicated less on brute strength and aggression than on technique and smarts. So in the winter of 2000 he packed a duffle bag, flew to the U.S. and made his way to gritty Bettendorf, Iowa. Pat Miletich, a former junior college wrestler and five-time UFC champion, had opened an MMA training gym in Bettendorf a few blocks from the banks of the Mississippi. Aspiring fighters came there from all over the world, making Miletich's gym to fighters what Florence was to Renaissance painters—though with bloodier canvasses.

To this day, Miletich's so-called Battlebox represents athletic Darwinism at its most brutal. Under the open-door policy, anyone is welcome to come and spar against a stable of regulars, many of whom have fought in the UFC. Self-styled tough guys show up every Monday. Those with the requisite skill and ruggedness stay. The other 95% are back on the interstate, bloodied and bruised, before sundown. Murray was one of the few who stuck it out. All bone and fast-twitch muscle, Murray was built like a sprinter. He stood 6'3" but could cut weight and fight as light as 170 pounds. One Miletich fighter likened the kid with the Cockney accent to a British greyhound. "Lee Murray had world-class punching power," recalls Robbie Lawler, a top mixed martial arts fighter who sparred frequently with Murray. "Man, he would hit the mitts—pop-pop-POP-POP—and you would stop your workout and look over because it sounded like gunfire."

Murray crashed with other Miletich fighters before getting a room at a shopworn motel not far from the gym. He wasn't averse to going out for a beer from time to time, but he'd come to America's heartland to train. When he wasn't in the gym, strip-mining Miletich for wrestling tips, he was lifting weights or going for runs under a big dome of Iowa sky. "Not one sign of trouble," says Miletich. "One of his first days, I told him, 'It's up to you how far you want to go in this sport. At your height and weight and the way you hit, you could be a champion.' It was just a question of learning what to do once the fight hit the ground."

That spring, Murray entered a four-man MMA tournament in rural Wisconsin. After winning his first bout, Murray fought a burly Canadian, Joe Doerksen, now a UFC veteran. Murray showed his inexperience and got caught in a submission hold called an arm bar. He "tapped out" (surrendered) and cursed himself the entire drive back to Iowa. Having exhausted his budget, Murray returned to England. But he kept fighting and started to win. While MMA was becoming mainstream in the U.S., the sport was still an underground pursuit in the U.K. Still, among the niche audience Murray was regarded as perhaps England's best fighter. "He was one of those guys who rose to the occasion when he fought," says Paul Ivens, an instructor at the London Shootfighters Club, where Murray often trained. "You get guys who are tough on the street but they crumble in a real fight. He was one of the fortunate ones who would bask under pressure."

In July 2002 Murray attended a UFC card at Royal Albert Hall in London. The UFC was trying to spread the gospel to the other side of the pond, and in addition to the fighters on the card, most of the organization's brightest stars were on hand, including Miletich, Tito Ortiz and Chuck Liddell. The headline bout featured a Miletich fighter, Matt Hughes, defending his welterweight title. After the card ended, the fighters repaired to a local club for an after party, a long-standing UFC tradition. At closing time the fighters and their entourages filed out. Walking down the street, Miletich felt a body on his back. It turned out to be a buddy of Tito Ortiz's. The guy was giving Miletich a playful bear hug, but suddenly Miletich felt the man getting ripped off his back. Another fighter had mistakenly believed that Miletich was being attacked. As the misunderstanding was being sorted out, Paul (the Enforcer) Allen, a longtime associate of Murray's, approached. In what he surely thought was a show of loyalty to both Miletich and Murray, Allen cold-cocked Ortiz's pal.

This triggered what might rank as the Mother of All Street Fights, a scene that's become as much a part of UFC lore as any bout inside the Octagon. A who's who of the UFC and their entourages—drunk and in street clothes—began throwing haymakers indiscriminately. One posse member was knocked into the street and his arm was run over by a cab. Liddell got cracked in the back of the head and went ballistic. "I'm hitting guys with spinning backfists, just dropping guys," says Liddell. "It was a classic street fight. 'If I don't know you, I drop you.'"

In the mayhem Ortiz and Murray backed into an alley and squared off. According to multiple witnesses, Ortiz threw a left hook. He missed, and Murray then fired off a combination that decked Ortiz. The self-proclaimed Bad Boy of the UFC fell to the pavement. (Ortiz declined to comment to SI.) Officially, Murray was still a promising up-and-comer. But as accounts of the melee rocketed through UFC circles, the rangy British kid who poleaxed the mighty Tito Ortiz became a minor legend. "He's a scary son of a bitch," says the UFC's outspoken president, Dana White. "And I don't mean fighterwise."

As for sanctioned fights, Murray continued to win those too, mostly with devastating knockouts. In July 2003, he took on the well-regarded Brazilian fighter José (Pelé) Landi-Jons at a London event. After getting pummeled for a round, Murray regrouped and starched Pelé with a right hand. "He's probably still in the ring, probably still sleeping, catchin' flies," Murray gloated in the post-fight interview, mimicking the dazed, open-mouthed look of his opponent. "I know now that . . . [the] UFC have gotta open their eyes to me, they gotta take me. There's no ifs or buts." Sure enough, six months later Murray was summoned by the UFC to fight on a Las Vegas card. Concealing the inconvenient detail that he'd recently been questioned about his involvement in a road-rage incident that left a middle-aged motorist in a coma—he was later charged with causing "grievous bodily harm," but the jury failed to reach a verdict—Murray flew to the U.S. He won the fight in the first round, trapping his opponent's head between his legs as he tried for a triangle choke, then finishing him off with an arm bar, hyperextending the man's elbow joint. He had reached the highest level, and all of his discipline and preparation had paid off: He'd won with a classic jujitsu maneuver, proving he was no one-dimensional fighter.

Murray's next bout came in the summer of 2004 in Cage Rage, a British UFC knockoff. He was pitted against Anderson Silva, the ferocious Brazilian who is currently the Zeus of MMA.

Emboldened by his recent success, Murray snarled at Silva at the weigh-in. "He talked an unbelievable amount of s---," Silva remembers. "He said, 'I'm gonna do to you what I did to your friend Pelé.'" According to Silva, at one point Murray spotted a pair of his fighting shorts hanging from a chair. Murray grabbed them, ripped off a Brazilian flag patch and tossed it at Silva. Though both fighters dispensed and withstood considerable punishment, Silva ended up winning by unanimous decision. As the two shook hands, Silva winked and pushed a gift into Murray's palm. It was the patch of the Brazilian flag. Still, Murray did himself proud, all the more so in retrospect, as Silva would go on to become one of the UFC's brightest stars.

But in September 2005, while training for an upcoming fight at Wembley Stadium, Murray attended a birthday party for a British model at Funky Buddha, a trendy club in London's Mayfair district. At around 3:15 a.m., a street brawl broke out. Murray was stabbed repeatedly in the chest, suffering a punctured lung and a severed artery. As he explained in a 2005 interview with the website MMAweekly.com, "One of my friends got involved in the fight. I tried to help him because about six or seven guys was on [him]. That's when I got stabbed. I got stabbed in the head first. I thought it was a punch. When I felt the blood coming down my face, I just wiped the blood and just continued to fight. Next, I looked down at my chest and blood was literally shooting out of my chest. . . . It was literally flying out of my chest like a yard in front of me. . . . I died three times. They said, 'Because you're an athlete and all the training you put your body through, that's what saved your life.'"

In the same interview, he casually noted that he had been stabbed outside the same club a week earlier. On that occasion, he'd "only" had one of his nipples sliced off. "It was just a minor stabbing, like these things happen every night of the week," says Andy Geer, a British promoter for Cage Rage. "He had stab wounds, bullet wounds. He was a proper from-the-streets kid."

Three weeks after the stabbing, though covered in zippers of scars, Murray had resumed his training in the gym. But realistically, his promising career was threatened. Particularly as mixed martial arts was becoming gentrified, what promoter would permit a man with such serious injuries to fight again? What if a scar opened during a fight? Murray may have realized as much, and that could have been an incentive to turn to crime.

THE THIEVES TOOK too much money. Had the Securitas gang made off with, say, a few million pounds, it might have been one thing. But the magnitude of the heist was such that overnight it became an international cause célèbre. Even the most staid British newspapers covered the case breathlessly and exhaustively. The surveillance video from the depot was televised nationally and, inevitably, made it online. Hundreds of British policemen were immediately deployed to investigate. Hefty reward money provided an incentive to anyone with any knowledge to come forward. "The gang had no chance," says Howard Sounes, the British author of a forthcoming book on the heist.

The suspects, though, also did plenty to hasten their demise. Mirroring Murray's fighting career—disciplined and methodical in MMA; arrogant and unthinking in street brawls—the same thieves who had been smooth and poised in the actual pilferage could scarcely have been sloppier in the aftermath. Some gang members boasted to friends about the heist. One of the vehicles used in the crime was set afire in the middle of a field, attracting attention. The money was poorly hidden. *Oceans 11* quickly devolved into a comedy of errors that recalled the Al Pacino classic *Dog Day Afternoon*. "That's what happens," says Bruce Reynolds, the convicted mastermind of Britain's Great Train Robbery of 1963 and now something of an armchair analyst of British crime. "All the planning goes into the robbery and none goes into what happens once you have the money."

Within 48 hours, police had made their first arrest. Acting on a tip, they apprehended Michelle Hogg, a makeup artist and the daughter of a policeman. Police found a quantity of latex they alleged Hogg had used to make prosthetic disguises for the robbers. (Under questioning, Hogg gave a statement saying she was too scared to identify the thieves.) Later that day, police found the van used to hold the Dixons. The next day, acting on another tip, they located a second van used in the robbery. When they looked inside, they found guns, ski masks, bandannas and £1.3 million in cash. Acting on still another tip the following day, police raided the homes of Murray's pal Lea Rusha, an aspiring mixed martial arts fighter, and Rusha's friend Jetmir Bucpapa. In Rusha's bedroom, police found plans of the Securitas depot, and hidden in a nearby garage was £8.6 million in cash.

All told, within 10 days, five people had been charged. Millions of pounds had been recovered. And innumerable additional leads had surfaced. "A gang of misfits and bruisers pulled off the biggest robbery ever with considerable criminal aplomb," says Sounes. "But they were also stupid. This was a brilliant caper which turned into a farce."

The fate of the accused was sealed in the fall of 2006 when Hogg "went QE" (Queen's Evidence), as the Brits say, and testified against her co-conspirators in exchange for her freedom. She explained how she created the disguises so the gang members who posed as police officers couldn't be accurately identified.

On Jan. 28, 2008, after seven months of trial during which more than 200 witnesses were called, five men—including Rusha, Bucpapa and Hysenaj, the insider—were found guilty for their part in the robbery and sentenced to a total of 140 years in jail. At the sentencing, authorities urged the public to resist romanticizing the caper. Fearing for their lives after giving extensive testimony, the Dixons entered the British equivalent of witness protection. So did Hogg, the makeup artist, who, according to multiple newspaper accounts, has a £7 million bounty on her head. "This crime was, at heart, a crime of violence," Nigel Pilkington of the Crown Prosecution Service told reporters. And with more than half the loot still unaccounted for, he vowed to continue to pursue the case. "This is not the end of the matter for these criminals," he said. "We intend to seize their ill-gotten gains, wherever they may be."

AS THE SECURITAS GANG was being rounded up systematically, Murray apparently did not stand idly by. He left the country, leaving his wife and two children behind. Accompanied by his friend Paul Allen—he of the infamous UFC street brawl—he drove from London to Dover. There, according to Kent police, the two piloted their car onto a ferry headed for France. Murray is believed to have then traveled from France to Amsterdam to Spain, where he and Allen crossed the Strait of Gibraltar by ferry before finally finding sanctuary in Morocco.

If Morocco has historically held a certain exotic allure for Europeans, Murray is believed to have gone there for more practical reasons. Because of his lineage on his father's side, Murray is considered a Moroccan national. And Morocco has no formal extradition agreement with Great Britain.

By all accounts, Murray lived lavishly in Northern Africa. He, Allen and two other friends from England, Gary Armitage and Mustafa Basar, lived in a villa in Souissi, an upscale district popular with diplomats, in Morocco's capital city, Rabat. They tooled around town in a Mercedes and spent prodigious amounts of money on clothes, jewelry, electronic equipment and jaunts to Casablanca.

After a few months, Murray reportedly spent close to $1 million on a concrete manor around the corner from a cousin of Morocco's King, Mohammed VI, outfitting it with an additional £200,000 in upgrades that include marble floors and a fully equipped gym. He also commissioned a giant mural above the hot tub, depicting his victory in his one and only UFC fight. Allen bought a property of his own nearby.

Shortly after Murray's arrival in Morocco in March '06, the Kent police and Scotland Yard officials handling the investigation contacted Moroccan authorities and conveyed their concerns. Likely unbeknownst to Murray, almost from the day he arrived in the country he was under 24-hour surveillance. On June 25, 2006, dozens of Moroccan police sealed off a portion of the Mega Mall in Rabat, where Murray, Allen, Armitage and Basar were shopping. Because some of the suspects were experts in martial arts (and were potentially carrying weapons), the small army of police officers was armed. After a physical struggle, the four men were arrested. A Kent police spokeswoman asserted that Murray was arrested "for offenses linked to the £53 million Securitas raid."

When the Moroccan police went to Murray's residence, they found cocaine and marijuana. The four men were charged with drug possession and for violently resisting when police arrested them at the mall, a crime a Moroccan judge termed "beating and humiliating members of the security forces." They were found guilty and in February 2007 received sentences ranging from four to eight months in prison. Armitage and Basar were released soon after for time served and retuned to the U.K. Allen was extradited by the British government and is currently in a British jail, awaiting trial for his alleged role in the heist.

Murray's situation was somewhat more complicated. Because of his Moroccan heritage, the U.K.'s extradition request was initially denied. "The British government has been putting a lot of pressure on Morocco," says Abdellah Benlamhidi Aissaoui, Murray's lawyer in Morocco. "But Moroccan nationals cannot be extradited [from Morocco]. That is the law, and the law should govern."

The Moroccan government discussed swapping Murray for Mohamed Karbouzi, a suspected terrorist living in London and sought for questioning in a 2003 Casablanca bombing. But the British government reportedly declined the exchange. Aissaoui says he has also heard that Britain might file a formal request to have Murray tried for the Securitas heist by Moroccan authorities in Morocco. While the extradition mess is being sorted out, Murray, at the behest of Britain, sits in a jail cell just outside Rabat, a caged cage fighter. "It's tough for him," says his lawyer. "He states that he's innocent. He has not participated in this robbery. He made money from his fights. He doesn't need to do this."

If Murray was in fact the ringleader, the Mr. Big, it wouldn't surprise Reynolds, the Great Train Robber. He compares a heist to sport. "You're challenging the authority of the state—the challenge is what it's all about," says Reynolds, now 76 and living outside London. "[Same as] Jesse James and Pancho Villa." What about the money? "It's a benchmark. Everyone wants to beat the record. It's like [Formula One] drivers want to beat Michael Schumacher's record."

Murray isn't granting interviews these days (his lawyer says that for Murray to speak to SI "is impossible right now"), much less speaking publicly about his guilt or innocence with respect to the heist. But he told a friend this story: After learning about Murray's saga—the street fights, the stabbing, the Securitas accusation—a London casino wrote him a formal letter explaining that he was no longer welcome at the establishment. That was fine by Murray. He says he wrote a quick note back: "Haven't you already heard? I hit the jackpot."

L. Jon Wertheim *is a senior writer at* Sports Illustrated *and the author of six books, including* Blood in the Cage, *which traces the rise of the UFC. He is also a licensed attorney. He lives in Manhattan with his wife, Ellie, and two children. Greg Kelly was his editor on this story.*

Coda

In the early spring of 2008, I was speaking with the mixed martial arts champion Pat Miletich for a book I was writing on the rise of the UFC. I made a casual reference to Lee Murray, a British cage fighter who had trained with Miletich in Iowa. What ever happened to that guy? "Funny guy, Lee," Pat said casually. "He supposedly helped orchestrate this big bank heist in England and is now living in Morocco." My "story alarm" didn't merely beep; it nearly woke the neighbors.

I pitched this story to my editors at *Sports Illustrated* who, to their eternal credit, encouraged me to pursue it, despite the tangential relation to sport (and marginal sport at that). While Murray declined to be interviewed on advice of his Moroccan counsel, plenty of others were happy to help me piece together the stranger-than-fiction narrative. At this writing, Murray's alleged coconspirator, Paul (the Enforcer) Allen, having been extradited back to the UK, faces a retrial for involvement in the heist, after his first trial in winter 2009 resulted in the equivalent of a hung jury. Murray remains in jail in Morocco. And only a fraction of the fifty-three million pounds has been recovered.

Dan P. Lee

BODY SNATCHERS

FROM *Philadelphia* magazine

DAN OPREA'S MOTHER, Rose, was always fiercely self-reliant.
Born in 1923, she grew up at 5th and Oxford. After graduating
from Hallahan Catholic Girls' High School, she married Daniel
Oprea Sr., with whom she had a son. When the two divorced
after seven years, Rose took it upon herself to enroll in Drexel
University, where she studied electrical engineering. She became
an engineer with RCA. With her only child, Rose Oprea carved
out a happy life. She was not afraid of aloneness.

She and her son remained close—geographically and otherwise—as he grew older, despite the fact that they were opposites
of sorts; Rose was bookish and artistic, while Dan, who took a job
with the Navy, enjoyed working with his hands. (They shared a
common interest in movies, something Rose instilled in her son
from a young age.) Dan married and had two sons, to whom Rose
was especially devoted. When Dan and his wife Mary Rose tragi-
cally lost their 26-year-old son Stephen in 2001, the mother-son
bond grew stronger.

In her later years, Rose developed her share of health problems;

she'd had a kidney removed years earlier, she suffered from angina and diverticulitis and a low iron count, and there was some slippage mentally. Dan and Mary Rose worried about her—her continued driving was of particular concern—and tried repeatedly to convince her to let them move in with her in the three-bedroom rancher in Huntingdon Valley that Rose had always said Dan would someday inherit. But Rose, who at 82 kept herself busy painting American Indian–style works and running errands in her Chrysler Concorde, would have none of it. Dan and Mary Rose lived a few miles away, and Dan visited his mother every Saturday, mowing the lawn, raking leaves, changing light bulbs, whatever she needed done. The two spoke on the phone, without fail, every day.

One day in late December 2004, Dan tried to reach his mother. She didn't answer. He figured she was out rummaging the after-Christmas sales, and wasn't immediately worried. When it turned six o'clock and they still hadn't heard from her, Dan and Mary Rose drove to her house. They found her car parked in the driveway. Dan used his key to unlock the front door. Inside, they called out, flipping lights on as they searched. In her bedroom, they discovered Rose lying contorted on the floor. Her dachshund Sparky stood vigil beside her.

At the hospital, doctors determined that Rose had suffered a stroke. She was completely paralyzed on one side, and she was disoriented. She could no longer speak, or write. As the days wore on and her condition stabilized, she regained little of what she'd lost. After two weeks, she was transferred to a nursing home.

The Opreas visited Rose at Luther Woods Convalescent Center as frequently as possible. Though she struggled to communicate, it was clear she was uncomfortable—she tried often to wiggle out of bed—and wished to be home. She once managed to express to her son her worry that she was causing trouble. He told her she was no trouble at all. Late on the night of April 18, 2005, the Opreas rushed to the nursing home after receiving a call that

Rose was deteriorating rapidly. They stood at her bedside, holding her hands, trying their best to comfort her as she lay dying.

Obsession over what happens after death—not just to the soul but also to the physical self—has always been part of the human condition; for as far back as we can discern, human beings have taken steps to care for their dead. But what was once exclusively the province of families—literally, next of kin—has morphed into a $15 billion annual business in America. Society, with the considerable influence of the funeral industry, has come to consider the way a corpse is treated as a direct, final and lasting expression of the quantity and quality of love felt. The Opreas had talked at length about what they wanted done with their bodies after their deaths. All disliked the idea of embalming and burial, and when the Opreas' son died, they had his body cremated. Dan and his mother had made a pact years earlier, inspired by one of their favorite movies, *Beau Geste*, from 1939; it features a so-called Viking funeral, in which the body is put on a ship, lit on fire, and sent out to sea. Mother and son agreed that when she died, he'd have her cremated, place her ashes on a model ship, set it on fire, and launch it from the Atlantic City beach.

From the nursing home, Mary Rose phoned Charlie Mancini of Mancini Funeral Home, on Somerset Street in South Philadelphia, whom she'd known for years and who'd handled her son's arrangements. After she hung up, she and Dan said one last good-bye, and left.

Mancini arrived some time later to take possession of Rose Oprea's body. There was little for him to do but deliver it to the crematorium. There are just four crematoria in the City of Philadelphia, and Mancini always used one called Liberty, which was owned by Louis Garzone and his brother Gerald and their partner, James McCafferty Jr. Arriving at Liberty's nondescript building in Kensington, Mancini wheeled the body of Rose Oprea inside, where it was to have been cremated following a 24-hour waiting period, in keeping with Pennsylvania law.

Two years later, when a Philadelphia detective showed up on their doorstep, the Opreas would learn what actually happened next: Once Mancini was gone, in the cloak of darkness, a shadowy figure—a man—walked across Somerset Street. He entered the crematorium, placed the body bag containing Rose Oprea's remains on a gurney, and wheeled it back across the street, to a funeral home that Lou Garzone owned, where the cutters were waiting.

THE CUTTERS DROVE DOWN from New York usually in the morning. They arrived in broad daylight. They went to work on a rusted table in a cramped, fetid, windowless, blood-encrusted embalming room one of them would later liken to the back of a butcher shop.

They slashed off the arms and legs at their joints, and then stripped the bones from them. Bones taken in complete pieces are most valuable, so femurs and other long bones were removed whole. The cutters used power tools to remove spines. They cut out Achilles and other tendons. Occasionally they took hearts. They skinned the bodies, including the faces. It was a blood-soaked, rushed operation. A proper harvesting can take four hours; the cutters could do it in 30 minutes. Appropriately removing a thin layer of skin from the body can itself take more than 30 minutes; the cutters could do it in 60 seconds. They used the same blades, wore the same gloves, cross-contaminated bodies and specimens.

They paid no mind to established protocol for harvesting postmortem tissue, which defines a suitable donor as someone under 65, without infection, serious disease or cancer, preferably felled by accident, heart attack or stroke; harvesting is to be completed within 15 hours of death. At Lou Garzone's funeral home, bodies routinely sat for days without refrigeration, often in the alleyway. The body of Philadelphia resident Diane Thomas, who died of metastatic cervical cancer, sat out for 113 hours. Joseph Pace, a 54-year-old widower from Kensington, suffered from sepsis, cancer, HIV and hepatitis C. James Herlihy, a former Naval Yard worker, also had hepatitis C and cancer. The cutters sliced apart 81-year-old Joseph Gibson, who died at the University of Pennsylvania of stomach cancer; his tissue was recovered 92 hours after he died. The eviscerated remains were rolled across the street to the crematorium, with packed towels to prevent a trail of blood. A crematorium employee said the bodies arrived disfigured, often missing limbs. Some were just torsos. The body bags that held them were full of blood. This was how the body of Rose Oprea, too, was cared for.

On forms forwarded to tissue processing companies, the cutters invented virtually everything, creating new identities for the deceased, new death certificates, subtracting decades from their ages (one 89-year-old was said to be 60), inventing next of kin, fabricating doctors, sometimes using, as a grand jury would put it, "special touches"—writing, on one form, that "Lois Glory" traveled to Mexico in 1981. As a result, authorities have been able to identify just 48 of the 244 corpses McCafferty and the Garzones handed over to the cutters; of those 48, nearly half died of cancer, sepsis, HIV or hepatitis. To circumvent compulsory blood tests, the cutters supplied the processing companies with blood from other corpses known to be clean.

ABOUT THE SAME TIME that Rose Oprea was hospitalized for her stroke, the 62nd precinct of the New York City police department, in Brooklyn, was notified of a possible case of fraud. A couple—Deborah Johnson and her husband, Robert Nelms—had recently purchased the Daniel George & Son Funeral Home. A man had come to the home wishing to bury his aunt, who had prepaid for her funeral; Johnson could not find the appropriate documentation, and noticed larger-scale accounting irregularities. The case was assigned to Detective Patricia O'Brien.

O'Brien checked the files at the funeral home, which seemed to corroborate Johnson's concern. But there was something else, Johnson told O'Brien. The detective accompanied her upstairs, to a hidden room. It was fitted out like an operating room, with hospital-style overhead lights, a hydraulic lift that rose through the ceiling of the embalming room on the floor below, a toilet with tubes into which blood and other bodily fluids were drained, scalpels, knives, saws. . . .

Back at the precinct, O'Brien began Googling addresses from forms Johnson had also shown her: All were for tissue-transplant companies, scattered around the country.

Through records from the George funeral home—many of them obviously fabricated—the investigation spread, from Brooklyn to the city's other boroughs. O'Brien was joined by members of the NYPD's prestigious major case squad, who fanned out, interviewing relatives of the deceased. The number of corpses that had been butchered at the funeral home increased first by the dozens and quickly by the hundreds. The police learned that in every case but one, permission hadn't been granted—hadn't, in fact, even been sought—for the harvesting of the dead's skin, bones and tendons. The case seemed to grow more outrageous by the day. Detectives soon discovered that among those eviscerated was 95-year-old *Masterpiece Theatre* host Alistair Cooke, who'd died of lung cancer that had spread to his bones; his daughter, who had sought a cheap, simple cremation at her father's request, would later speak of "lives torn asunder" by "these desecrations." The exhumation of an 82-year-old Queens woman who died of brain cancer revealed that most of the bones below her waist had been cut out and replaced with plastic piping. When word of the investigation finally leaked out, a year after O'Brien first arrived at George & Son, the number of unwitting donors had eclipsed 1,000. The city was, to put it mildly, scandalized. "BODY-SNATCHERS!" shrieked the *New*

York Daily News, which broke the story. Not to be outdone, "GHOUL AND THE GANG!" shouted the *Post*.

The investigation in New York was building steam, but 90 miles away as the crow flies—or in this case, a sparrow, which was flying, flitting, above the streets of Kensington, searching for a tree or some other place to perch—in Philadelphia, no one at Lou Garzone's funeral home was aware of that. The sparrow arced down on Somerset Street, over an alleyway beside Garzone's, where a mound of . . . something lay on a gurney, covered, oddly, by a large swatch of artificial turf. Later, a cutter would tell the grand jury he distinctly remembered the sparrow perched atop a human body that had been hacked to pieces and covered in fake turf— perhaps Rose Oprea's, or one of the 243 others dismembered there—then left in the alleyway. The sparrow stood on two toothpick legs. Its head bobbed up and down, like a puppet's. With its beak, it inspected the gaps between the artificial green blades of turf. Then it stared straight, fluttered its wings once, and flushed.

FINALLY, in October 2007, the Philadelphia district attorney's office announced its own indictments: of Louis Garzone; his brother Gerald; their partner James McCafferty Jr.; the mastermind behind the entire enterprise, physician Michael Mastromarino; and Lee Cruceta, Mastromarino's right-hand man. At the same time, the D.A. released a highly unusual 104-page report from the grand jury that had spent a year investigating the case. "What we found," the grand jury wrote, "was appalling."

It began with Mastromarino, handsome, cleft-chinned, a married father of two, in his early 40s, from tony Fort Lee, New Jersey. He'd worked in Manhattan and New Jersey as an oral surgeon until 2000, when he was forced to surrender his license following a string of Demerol-induced antics at his office: He'd fallen asleep while suturing a patient; he collapsed coming out of a bathroom with his scrub pants down around his ankles; after he left a patient under general anesthesia on the operating table, a nurse found him on the floor of a bathroom with a needle in his arm. Finally, according to a lawsuit he later settled, he sliced through a nerve in a patient's jaw, leaving part of her face permanently paralyzed.

Down but not out, Mastromarino regrouped in 2002 by opening Biomedical Tissues Services, or BTS, a cadaver body-parts recovery company; he had knowledge of the business through his experience as a surgeon, since he sometimes transplanted human parts into his patients. While it's illegal in the U.S. to profit from organ and tissue donation, Mastromarino would exploit a loophole that allows companies to charge for "handling" and "processing" tissue and bone. Mastromarino met Lee Cruceta, a nurse then in his early 30s who was adept with power tools and enjoyed medicine's similarities to carpentry; he also had experience working for tissue banks. Cruceta was put in charge of field operations, a position that had him overseeing a Dickensian cast of cutters. With very little practical governmental oversight, and with the extraordinary medical need for tissue, Mastromarino operated his body-snatching enterprise with breathtaking ease.

Though it's the major organs—heart, kidneys, liver—that we think of in cases of transplantation, they represent, in fact, the minority of what's harvested. Fifty times more often, bones, skin, tendons and other tissues are transplanted in operating rooms, in more than a million procedures annually. Pieces of bone can be used to repair back and spine injuries; bone can be ground into a putty to fill voids from fractures. Cadaver skin not only replaces that of burn victims; it can repair stomach linings eaten away by acid, patch holes in hearts, shore up faulty bladders as slings.

In 90 percent or more of cases, the harvesting of such materials occurs in the confines of a hospital, as with major organs. But Mastromarino knew of a lesser-tapped, though legal, source: the funeral home. He reached out to ones in lower-income urban areas, penetrating Philadelphia through an employee of the city's medical examiner's office.

Over an 18-month period ending in September 2005, the Gar-zones and McCafferty would hand over to Mastromarino and his cutters those 244 bodies—and perhaps more—entrusted to them for cremation, from which thousands of individual body parts were harvested. (In New York, the bodies taken were destined for both cremation and burial, forcing cutters to operate conservatively if a viewing was to be held; Philadelphia's bodies were taken exclusively from the cremation lot, so cutters were free, according to Cruceta, to go "whole hog.") Of the more than $3.8 million earned by BTS, Mastromarino and Cruceta from their enterprise, $1 million came from Philadelphia corpses. The Garzones and Mc-Cafferty were paid $1,000 a body, or approximately $250,000 total.

The funeral directors apparently felt little obligation to their unsuspecting customers, even failing to make sure that the ashes returned to them were actually those of their loved ones. One family held its memorial the day before the relative was actually cremated. Another conducted a service in the family home at the precise time cutters were at work on the body.

What then, exactly, is their crime? How to categorize it? Prosecutors have labeled it fraud. Theft. Fraud and theft committed upon the families who trusted the funeral directors to render the agreed-upon services. But also, implicitly, theft upon the dead, the very pilfering of their parts. Such thinking, though, not only places the dead, strangely, at the center of the victimization; it also ignores the underlying basis of what funeral directors do, which is, after all, to traffic in death.

We have given them that. Until the Civil War—when sons died far from home and needed to be preserved for transport, and when hundreds of thousands of Americans were exposed for the first time to an embalmed body vis-à-vis Abraham Lincoln's epic train journey from Washington to Philadelphia to New York to Illinois—there was no such thing as embalming here, or funeral directors. Americans took care of their dead. They stood by them when they died, washed them, built them wooden coffins, laid them out in front parlors (hence "funeral parlor"), and then buried them themselves, paying more than lip service to the axiom of "Ashes to ashes, dust to dust." Now we hand off our loved ones' bodies before they've even appreciably cooled to funeral directors charged with transforming corpses into what's called, in funerary parlance, "a memory picture," to drain them of blood, pump them full of dye and formaldehyde, glue their eyes and wire their mouths shut; to jab a metal instrument through their abdomens and pierce their vital organs, vacuuming up their discharge; to paint them with makeup and position them in coffins in mimicry of peaceful sleep. Or, in cases of cremation, to introduce their bodies into ovens heated to 1,600 degrees, and stoke their bones during an hours-long combustion. This is their job.

Yes, the dead may have been victims of a sort, but beyond them, there was what the funeral directors and cutters did to the living, and not just to the families of the dead. For once their work was finished, the cutters packed the flesh and bones into picnic coolers and headed back north with them. BTS then forwarded the bones and tissue to its client processing companies, which cleaned, handled and supposedly sterilized the parts. Next they were repacked and shipped to doctors and hospitals around the world, including Thomas Jefferson University Hospital, where on the morning of May 12, 2005, 65-year-old Betty Pfaff lay unconscious in an operating room as her surgeon tore open a plastic package containing AlloDerm—a white freeze-dried substance, derived from cadaver skin, that dissolves into a wound and stimulates rapid tissue regeneration—which he lowered into the opening stretching across the woman's abdomen.

LYING IN THE RECOVERY ROOM, draped in covers and her mind foggy, Betty Pfaff was informed that her surgery—a somewhat complicated one, due to the fact that her abdomen had been opened so many times before—had been a success. Everything went well. You're going to be fine, she was told. At this moment, these sentences were not only accurate as far as anyone knew, but provided Pfaff with great solace.

Pfaff, a sweet, plump widow who lived alone in a tiny white house across the street from a picturesque cemetery in Jenkintown, had had surgery for abdominal hernias twice before. She'd become susceptible to them as a result of having undergone two cesarean sections within one year. (After her first child, a daughter, died at three months, in 1976, she'd quickly become pregnant with a son, Philip.) Another hernia had cropped up the previous winter; she scheduled the operation for the spring, when the weather would be better. She was unaware before her surgery that she'd be receiving human tissue—she didn't recall her doctor explicitly telling her, and hadn't read the consent forms carefully— and remained unaware after, which isn't unusual, given how routinely it's used.

She was wheeled back to her room. Her wound, about eight inches long, was to remain open so that accumulating fluids could drain, and doctors came frequently over the next several days to check it, and to change the dressing. She was out of bed and sitting in a chair in one day, and walking down the hallway in three. After a week, she was doing well enough to be discharged. Instead of going home, she decided to recuperate at a nursing home, as she was worried about being alone. She intended to stay there for a month, but was so disgusted with the care she received that she left after six days, despite having developed a fever, which fluctuated seemingly without reason. Her doctor prescribed an oral antibiotic, which she supplemented with Tylenol. Overall, she felt unwell, weak.

Surrounded by the comforts of home—her favorite navy blue recliner, her books and magazines, her favorite stuffed bunny with the long floppy ears and a country dress—Betty hoped she'd begin feeling better. She did not. Visiting nurses handled the wound and monitored her fever, which continued. In early June, she began feeling particularly bad, and her temperature spiked to 100.4°. She called a friend, who drove her back to Jefferson, where she was admitted.

While examining Pfaff, her doctor discovered a tiny piece of gauze deep inside her wound. He performed a debridement—a deep cleaning of the wound. Afterward, he told her, once again, that all had gone well. He ordered a culture of the wound, and started her on a three-day course of high-potency amoxicillin. She remained in the hospital for four more days.

Her son picked her up and returned her to her home, and the visiting nurses began coming again. She felt about the same, and her temperature persisted; she remained on antibiotics, and was instructed to return to the ER if her fever broke 100.5°. On July 1st, her visiting nurse came and took her temperature: It was 104°. "We have to get you to the hospital," the nurse said, and left a message for Pfaff's son. Betty called her sister Nancy, who came over to sit with her and wait for Philip.

Betty's condition worsened. She began staring; she had trouble focusing. She rocked oddly in her chair. Nancy feared her sister was suffering a stroke. Philip arrived, and Nancy went outside to confer with him. They dialed 911.

By the time they reached Abington Hospital, Betty's fever was burning at 106°. Her heart rate had increased rapidly, along with her respiration. Nurses threaded a catheter into her hand and pumped fluids into her. A doctor ordered several intravenous medications. She appeared to be getting better. At 9 p.m. she told Nancy and Philip to go home, that she would be fine. Then, at midnight, Philip received a call to return to the hospital. His mother had been moved to intensive care. Doctors told him there was just a 20 percent chance she would survive.

Betty Pfaff was septic, meaning her entire body was ravaged by infection. When Philip saw her, a ventilator was breathing for her. She was horrifically swollen. She was hooked to a dialysis machine that was removing and purifying her blood. Philip was told to summon his family. They arrived at the hospital and surrounded Betty. A priest administered last rites.

For nine days her family stood vigil, having been assured she would die. Incredibly, on the 10th day, she opened her eyes.

All around the hospital, she became known as "the new Lazarus."

It would be, however, a long, difficult recovery. She couldn't walk, wash, or take care of herself. She spent 26 days at Abington Hospital, then two months in rehabilitation, slowly building back her strength.

Over and over, Betty Pfaff asked her doctors a single question: How could this happen? They replied with the only answer they knew: Infection is always a risk with surgery. But Betty was unsatisfied.

It wasn't until Valentine's Day 2006, almost a year after her surgery, that she opened a letter that arrived from the Food and Drug Administration via her doctor. It advised her that she'd received human tissue, stolen from a cadaver, that was now the subject of an unprecedented and, for her, utterly impossible recall.

AS OF PRESS TIME, after vehemently professing their innocence for two years, Michael Mastromarino, Lee Cruceta, several New York City funeral directors and several cutters were either in the process of accepting or already had accepted deals to plead guilty to the charges they faced in both New York City and Philadelphia. They are expected to testify against the remaining defendants, including the Garzone brothers and McCafferty, who have pleaded not guilty in Philadelphia court and are scheduled to stand trial later this year. The defense is expected to argue that these defendants did none of the actual harvesting and therefore cannot be held accountable, though the spate of plea agreements by their co-defendants obviously bodes poorly for them. In addition,

Mastromarino, having just been sentenced to 18 to 54 years in prison, will likely cooperate in implicating the tissue companies that bought from him. Those companies—which generate multimillion-dollar profits annually and are publicly traded—have claimed they had no way of knowing the documents Mastromarino prepared were fabricated, and no way of knowing the true source of the materials they received.

Then there are the civil lawsuits. Philadelphia attorney Larry Cohan has been named by the U.S. District Court in Newark, New Jersey, as lead counsel in a class-action lawsuit against all of the defendants in the criminal case as well as the tissue companies, representing so far 900 people nationwide, including Betty Pfaff, who received some of the 20,000 pieces of stolen tissue. In addition, along with his partner Melissa Hague, Cohan is representing 15 families of the unwitting donors in their suits in Philadelphia court, including the Oprea family.

The cases are, however, by no means surefire. In the first place, there seems to be little money to be wrung from many of the defendants, including Mastromarino, who's paid for legal representation in several jurisdictions, and the funeral home operators, whose insurers have maintained that their policies don't cover subscribers' criminal conduct. That leaves the tissue companies that distributed Mastromarino's stolen goods, especially Regeneration Technologies Inc., recently renamed RTI Biologies, the first-stop processing company in Florida through which all of Mastromarino's body parts flowed.

Cohan and Hague argue that it's impossible RTI didn't know what Mastromarino was up to. Parroting the prosecutors' argument, they say the paperwork—including the death certificates—forwarded to the company were almost transparently fraudulent. The numbers themselves coming out of Mastromarino's company, they say, should have raised red flags. "Normally, one particular harvesting company might get just a minimal number of donors, say one a month or maybe two or three," says Hague. "Mastromarino was getting 10 or 30 a month. He was RTI's primary supplier for human tissue implants, and they never questioned him about it. There's no way they couldn't have known."

Still, RTI—which recently announced record revenues of $94.2 million for 2007—and the other tissue companies are preparing an aggressive defense, challenging the idea that those who've developed serious diseases contracted them from the transplanted materials, given the claimed sophistication of the companies' sterilization processes.

Bob Rigney, CEO of the American Association of Tissue Banks, puts great stock in RTI's "BioCleanse" low-temperature chemical sterilization process; RTI claims to have distributed more than 500,000 BioCleansed implants "with zero incidence of infection." Rigney says furthermore that the risk of spreading infection or disease from transplanted tissue, even in cases when the tissue has not been treated as such, is exceedingly low. "Quite frankly, the safety record in terms of tissue is remarkable," he says. "In the last 20 years, we've seen only one confirmed death."

Rigney attributes that level of success in large part to the extraordinary safeguards his organization has helped build into the tissue retrieval system, from the stringent donor criteria that disqualify 90 percent of would-be donors—not only the diseased but in some cases even those with tattoos—to the multi-layered testing of donors' blood, to careful reviews of the deceased's medical records, to elaborate interviews with loved ones to ascertain the donor's lifestyle—the same safeguards, in short, that Mastromarino and his henchmen systematically ignored. And the one death that Rigney mentions is noteworthy. In 2001, a 23-year-old Minnesota man died following knee surgery to repair a torn ACL. An investigation later determined that the cadaver cartilage implanted during his surgery hadn't been recovered until 19 hours after the donor's death, during which time a deadly fungus grew in it, forming spores that withstood the sterilization process and blossomed inside the recipient into an overwhelming infection. The investigation specifically cited the 15-hour limit for safe retrieval, the same 15-hour limit authorities believe was exceeded in Philadelphia in almost every case.

Cohan will also have the testimony of these witnesses to offer to a jury: A 41-year-old Ohio man who tested positive for HIV and hepatitis C after receiving BTS bone implants in surgery for degenerative disk disease. A 30-year-old Colorado woman who had to undergo a repeat ACL replacement after her first BTS tendon failed. A 74-year-old widow from Ohio who received BTS bone for a lower-back surgery and developed syphilis.

Though he has the model ship ready, Dan Oprea hasn't yet fulfilled his promise to his mother to deliver her ashes to the sea in a Viking funeral. "I intend to do this," he says. "I've got the ship, I've got everything. I know it sounds ridiculous, but I have this feeling like . . . I'm throwing her in the trash. And I understand that's not what's happening, and I intend to do this eventually, but I'm just not ready yet."

Oprea says he's struggled to get past the news of what happened to his mother's body. His wife says she often catches him staring into space, and knows where his mind is. In many ways, Dan says, he wishes he never found out about it. "It's just like something out of a horror movie," he says. "You just can't understand how anybody could do this."

And this poses the question, again, of what the greatest crime here may be. Irish journalist Mary Kenny, whose sister Ursula was among the unwitting donors, wrote that she doesn't resent that her sister's body was dissected, only that it was done without express permission. "What is a body after death anyway? Nothing but waxwork effigy," she noted. "Her spirit remains strongly with me, hovering over so many moments in my life, and that is dearer to me than the fate of a mere anatomy."

Certainly the accused in this case may be guilty of much, of fraud, of larceny, of misleading loved ones, of taking advantage of their vulnerabilities, of falsifying records, of harvesting remains in grotesque, unsanitary settings, and of introducing potentially infectious parts into otherwise healthy bodies. Isn't that last thing, without doubt, their most egregious offense? Yet it hasn't resulted in a single criminal charge. Instead, it's the charge of "abuser of corpses"—defined by the Commonwealth as "a person who treats a corpse in a way that he knows would outrage ordinary family sensibilities"—that has given the government the most traction. That may seem, in the scheme of things, almost quaint. Except that for Dan Oprea and millions of others, it goes to the very heart of how we still look at an uncertain line, between life and death.

DAN P. LEE *writes about crime, science, and politics for* Philadelphia magazine. *Another of his stories—about two dueling forensic pathologists— appeared in* Best American Crime Reporting 2007. *He lives in Phila- delphia's Old City neighborhood.*

Coda

After pleading guilty to the thousands of charges against him, Mi- chael Mastromarino was sentenced to twenty-five to fifty-eight years in Philadelphia and eighteen to fifty-four years in New York; the sentences are to be served concurrently, and he won't be eligi- ble for parole for at least eighteen years. Appearing in a Philadel- phia courtroom, Mastromarino looked gaunt, his hair recently shaved. He apologized to his victims, saying, "I have many years to think about the wrongs I have committed, in prison."

Louis Garzone and his brother Gerald also pleaded guilty, on the day their criminal trial was to commence; each was sentenced to nine and a half to twenty years in state prison, of which they are expected to serve at least eight. Their pleas were in large part the result of Mastromarino's cooperation with Philadelphia authorities, as well as that of codefendant James McCafferty Jr. McCafferty, who claimed to have suffered from severe alcoholism, received a shorter sentence—three and a half to ten years in state prison—in exchange for agreeing to testify against the Garzone brothers and because he played a significantly smaller role in the criminal enterprise; he could be eligible for parole in as little as two years and eleven months.

The scene was emotional as the Garzones offered their pleas. About fifty people—some furious, others sobbing—packed the courtroom. Among them was Elizabeth Sparagno, who'd hired Louis Garzone to cremate her eighty-four-year-old mother Marie Lindgren's body; Lindgren had been savagely murdered by two teenage neighbors to whom she'd once fed homemade cookies. Sparagno told the *Philadelphia Inquirer* she remained tortured by the double indignity. "It's just not right," she said. "Those boys already cut her head off, her pinky finger. And then later I find out that Garzone took her to the funeral home for those cutters who came down from New York."

The civil trial against all the defendants is still pending.

Mark Boal

Everyone Will Remember Me as Some Sort of Monster

FROM *Rolling Stone*

On an overcast wednesday afternoon last December, a skinny white teenager shuffled into the Westroads Mall in Omaha, Nebraska, with an assault rifle hidden under his black hoodie. A cheery holiday atmosphere filled the aisles. Christmas trees twinkled, holiday music played softly. Nobody paid attention to the slouching teen as he got on the elevator in the Von Maur department store and rode it to Level 3.

He came out with his gun raised: an effeminate-looking, almost pretty boy with alabaster skin and cherry-red lips, holding the rifle like a pro—stock to cheek, elbow high. Harry Potter with an AK-47. He crossed the hall to the GIRLS 7-16 section, where, among the rows of dresses and frilly tops, he came across two women and shot and killed them both.

The high-decibel blasts ricocheted through the store and sent the remaining shoppers into a panicky, screaming dash for cover, and as they ran, crying out in confusion, the teen squeezed off two more rounds hitting the arm of a man lunging into a side door—then aiming at a man fleeing down an escalator, killing him before he reached the last step. The boy leaned over a balcony overlooking a central atrium, squinted down 40 feet to Level 1, where a janitor was scrambling to find a safe zone, and shot and killed him. Swiveling back to Level 3, he saw a woman ducking into an employee locker room, and he shot and killed her.

In the midst of the carnage, the boy changed magazines, loading in 30 fresh bullets. He walked over to the customer-service counter, behind which four workers were huddled. One of them, Dianne Trent, 53, had hastily called 911 and was describing a "young boy with glasses" coming toward her when the teen shot her at point-blank range, killing her instantly. He then shot the remaining three people behind the counter, wounding a man and two women. They collapsed in a squirming, bloody tangle. Then he turned around and shot and killed a 65-year-old man hiding behind a chair with his wife.

Barely five minutes had passed since the boy started shooting. Seven were now slain, four more badly wounded, bleeding into the thick-pile carpet. Behind the customer-service counter, one of the boy's victims was crying out, "I need oxygen, I need oxygen." She bled to death before help arrived. Police and ambulance sirens could now be heard approaching from the distance.

The teen shot a stuffed teddy bear. Then he turned the gun on himself: one shot, under the chin.

At that same moment, in a suburban sheriff's office miles away from the pandemonium at the mall, a 41-year-old woman named Molly Rodriguez was consulting a deputy about her son, whom she feared might be planning to kill himself. She had discovered a rifle missing from her ex-husband's house that morning, she told the deputy. She wasn't sure of the rifle's make, other than that it was black, and ugly.

As the deputy compiled his report, news came in over the radio about the shooting at the mall. "Ma'am," the deputy asked, "might that be your son?" Rodriguez said she doubted it. Ten minutes later, the shooter was positively identified as Robert A.

Hawkins, born May 17th, 1988, to Ronald Hawkins and Molly Rodriguez.

Her child.

It was a big story. For about a week. Immediately after the shooting, the media descended on the woodsy suburb of Omaha known as Bellevue (population 50,000), where Hawkins had been living, and began some hit-and-run reporting. But that soon sputtered out. After it was discovered that the shooter had a history of mental illness, the national media left town, and then when it came out that he'd recently been fired from a job at McDonald's, even the local guys dropped the story and went back to reporting on the weather. That was pretty much the extent of the digging, as if losing the opportunity to flip burgers was what drove the teen to murder.

Less than a decade ago, in the aftermath of the Columbine High School shootings, teen murder was such a horrifying novelty that it occupied the entire national conversation for months. But these days, teenage shooters come and go on TV with such regularity that their sprees hardly seem surprising anymore; on the contrary, it feels almost naive to be shocked. In the end, the Robert Hawkins mall massacre—the bloodiest episode in Nebraska since the Charles Starkweather murders of 1958, and one of the deadliest rampages in American history—amounted to just a few days' worth of news and infotainment. Within two weeks of the shooting, Von Maur was speed-cleaned and reopened, just in time for the Christmas rush. In the atrium where Hawkins had sprayed bullets and slain eight, there was no lasting marker of what he had done: no plaque for the dead on the freshly polished marble columns, no memorial fountain where the victims had fallen. The aisles were soon humming with contented customers who didn't seem to mind, or even know, that they were shopping in a former killing field. Only the presence of a new security guard, roaming the racks with a revolver on his belt, suggested that anything untoward had happened here at all.

From the very beginning of his life, Rob Hawkins was a throw-away kid. In 1982, Molly Rodriguez was working the counter at the Swiss Colony in a mall in San Angelo, Texas: a buxom, petite 16-year-old in white pants and a tube top, looking for a husband to take her away from being the seventh kid in a working-class family of nine kids. In walks Ronald Hawkins, young buck, rising star in the Air Force's electronic-warfare division, and they hit it off: marriage in a matter of months, and then a child, Cynthia. But things changed after the birth, and they changed for the worse. The infant bawling in the house turned them both off, Molly recalls, and without the bedroom to bond them, the tenderness left their relationship. Soon Ronald acted like Molly wasn't so hot anymore, calling her a "pussy life-support system." She got back at him by having affairs with soldiers at the base in Suffolk, England, where Ronald was transferred.

After that, the sex was more sadistic than loving. It seemed to Molly like Ronald enjoyed when she came home with other men's semen still inside her—at night, while she slept, he would sometimes ejaculate on her face. She got pregnant again in 1987, hoping the second kid would solve the problems of the first, but by then all they really felt for each other was hostility. Robbie was born the next spring, a normal, healthy baby, but during his fragile first months—the period when the infant nervous system soaks up every stimulus—he got wired to violence as his parents' marriage devolved into a cage fight. "Mom and Dad were on the floor slugging it out," Molly recalls. Before long, Rob's childhood became even more traumatic; several doctors would later conclude that at some point during these first years, Rob was molested. Once, when Molly was changing Rob's diapers, his older sister, Cynthia, then six, leaned forward and put her mouth on his privates. Molly pulled her off. She stared at her husband, but he said nothing. On another occasion, Rob was left alone with a relative who, Rob would later say, "tickled" him in a way that made him feel odd.

Infants are imitative: They learn by copying what they see. And by the time he was four years old, Rob had grown into an attack machine. He was a menace on the playground, punching other kids or kicking them in the groin whenever he got upset. When teachers disciplined him, he bit their hands. And he held grudges; he once came up to a teacher he disliked and slammed her head in a door. He did this when he was a preschooler, only three and a half feet tall and 34 pounds.

In 1992, after Ronald was posted to an Air Force base in Omaha, he brought his four-year-old son to the Methodist Richard Young Hospital and asked the psychiatrists what to do with the violent boy. The doctors asked Robbie why he kept hurting other kids. He lowered his eyes to the floor.

"Because I'm stupid and bad," he mumbled.

Committed to the hospital for observation, Rob behaved erratically. One minute he was playing peacefully with Matchbox cars; the next he was desperately throwing his arms around a nurse, as if asking for protection. He was diagnosed with depression and post-traumatic stress disorder—the condition usually found in battle-weary veterans—caused by his hellish family life. After a month of heavy medication, the doctors sent him home with a warning that his recovery depended on continued therapy, and more important, on having a stable, nurturing family environment.

But stability was not his fate. Robbie returned instead to a chaotic custody battle between his parents, who were now divorced and waging a *Jerry Springer*-style campaign against each other that culminated in Molly being dragged away in handcuffs and threatening Ronald's new wife, Candace. Molly herself had quickly remarried—hooking up with an Air Force friend of Ronald's named Mark Dotson—and she was anxious to start a new family that didn't have the drama and the burdens of her first big relationship. So after Candace had repeatedly called the police on

Molly with charges of child endangerment, Molly gave up and surrendered her visitation rights to Rob, hoping to cut ties with the past and start fresh.

She called her son into her room to explain the situation. By then Rob had been on regular doses of Thioridazine, the antipsychotic drug, and Ritalin, to treat attention-deficit disorder. Molly hugged him and said that she was going away. "He didn't really understand it," she recalls. "He was so young."

WHEN MOLLY'S ABANDONMENT finally sunk in, Rob turned his formidable anger against his stepmother, Candace, the only maternal figure left in his life, transferring onto her all the rage he must have felt toward his biological mother. It probably didn't help matters that while Rob was always getting in trouble for smoking and fighting, Candace's own son, Zachary, four years Rob's junior, seemed to skate smoothly along. Nor did her response to his tantrums help. Rob's father preferred to handle his outbursts by pinning him on the floor, sometimes for as long as an hour, until he would calm down. But when it was her turn to control him, Candace, an Air Force vet, used the back of her hand.

Growing up on a steady diet of psychiatric medication and corporal punishment, Rob became more violent and withdrawn. When he was 13, his ongoing battle with Candace went nuclear. She searched his backpack for cigarettes, and Rob flipped out on her. In response, she slapped him across the face so hard that her ring cut his forehead. He balled up his fist and said quietly, "I'm going to kill you."

Candace believed he was capable of making good on the threat: For his 14th birthday, Rob got another hospital admission and another fistful of pills. This time he sat in the doctor's office and stared blankly, refusing to acknowledge the gravity of the situation. The doctor insisted he apologize to Candace. But Rob was in no mood to make amends with his family. "I hope they get into a car accident," he told the doctor. By now, he no longer regretted his outbursts. The four-year-old kid who thought of himself as stupid and bad for hitting people was now a teenager deep in the throes of mental illness. If the doctors returned him to his stepmother, he said, he "knew where the knives were located, and she would leave the house in a body bag." On Mother's Day, when patients were told to draw cards for their loved ones, Robbie drew a picture of a noose for his stepmother.

Not long after, his father drove to juvenile court and asked the judge to take over: His health insurance had run out, he told the court, and he couldn't afford to pay Rob's medical bills. Molly, Rob's biological mother, wasn't at the hearing—she wasn't even informed of the court date, although she lived 12 miles away—but in any case she was out of the picture by then, off raising her new family. After a hearing that lasted just eight minutes by the stenographer's clock, Judge Robert O'Neal rapped his gavel and the state department of Health and Human Services became Rob's legal guardian.

TWO YEARS LATER, the angry young man waiting in his therapist's office for his father and stepmother to show up for a counseling session looked more like a refugee from a Dickens tale than a kid from Omaha. At 16, Rob was now a veteran of institutions, having spent the last 24 months of his childhood in group homes because he resisted the reconciliation with Candace that would have allowed him to rejoin his family. He looked the part of a miserable ward of the state: painfully thin from years of undereating, nails chewed to gnarled stubs. He wore his hair long, in a thick curtain that hid much of his face and obscured his eyes. He had been molested by another resident, and was prone to suicidal despair. None of it matters, he would tell his therapists: "We're basically just numbers."

In some ways, he was even more traumatized than when he'd entered the system. He had done nine months at the Piney Ridge Center, a residential treatment center in Missouri (where he got into physical fights with other residents), before being transferred at the judge's behest to Cooper Village, a home for boys in Nebraska (where he lived under strict isolation, rarely allowed to leave the campus or make phone calls). Over the years he kept trying to buck the rules and talk to his biological mother, with whom he held out hope of a reunion, but he was never allowed to call her.

By now, his psychological profile included the darker, more exotic ailment that would lie behind his future crimes: anti-social personality disorder, a condition that makes it difficult, if not impossible, for sufferers to feel empathy for strangers. It is the underlying pathology of most serial killers. Rob drew swastikas and professed to believe in Satan. When the staff threatened to send him to another institution if he didn't reconcile with his family, this brooding young man who had spent his teen years being raised by orderlies gave them a dark warning. "If you send me there," he said, "I'll burn that motherfucking place down and all of the people in it."

But now, sitting in the therapist's office, Rob was about to surprise the doctors and social workers who had seen little evidence of change in him. After two years of round-the-clock therapy—at least two sessions a day, plus novel approaches like equine therapy, where he worked with horses—Rob was finally ready to apologize to Candace for threatening her. His therapists considered this the breakthrough they'd been working toward, and his caseworker noted in his file that he was mentally well enough to return home.

But when Rob asked her forgiveness for "saying all those hurtful things to you when I was mad," Candace refused to accept his apology. Rob, she told a caseworker, had clearly been "coached" by his therapist. What's more, she added, she would "never feel safe with Robert in the house." She threatened to divorce Ronald if he ever brought his son home.

Rob was furious. The state had spent two years coaxing and pressuring and drugging him to get him to apologize—and when he finally did, it got him nowhere. "My stepmother is evil—she has no heart," Rob told his roommate at Cooper Village, another skinny, lost kid named Dallas. As the days passed in quiet isolation, the two boys clung to each other—from the back, their long hair made them look identical—and swore an oath of brotherhood, sealed by wearing purple rubber bracelets. They called themselves the Purple Skulls. Noticing that the boys got into more trouble when they were separated, the staff made it a point to keep them together. "We were closer than brothers," Dallas recalls. "Never apart."

One day, when Dallas turned 17, Rob was given permission to go to a dollar store, where he got heaps of candy and all the soda bottles he could carry. That night, he invited the other patients on his hall over and threw Dallas a surprise birthday party. It touched his friend deeply. "Rob could be great when he loved you," Dallas says.

As the months passed and other kids came and went at Cooper Village, Rob and Dallas remained, dutifully obeying the regimen of classes and therapy, scheduled in orderly blocks from wakeup at 6:30 a.m. to lights out at 10:30 p.m. The two worked the system to the point that the staff allowed them to have guitars and video games in their room, just like regular kids, and to stay up late playing chess and drawing and talking. It was during these late-night bull sessions that Rob admitted to Dallas that he missed his mother terribly. "He talked about her a lot," Dallas recalls. "He wanted to be with her."

Rob had no idea where his mother was at that point, let alone the kind of life she was leading. By then, her marriage to

Dotson had fallen apart and she was soon in full-blast dating mode, seeing three or four guys at once, hopping from bed to bed, taking full advantage of the variety and the freedom.

In December 2004, Rob finally caught a break and was relocated to a pleasant foster home. Run by a grandmother named Marty Glass who had 10 kids of her own, and who over the years had taken in nearly two dozen more children, it was the first place where Rob felt "appreciated and understood," he told his caseworker. Glass thought he was a "joy to have around" and a "very intelligent boy with an interesting point of view." Rob spent much of that winter outdoors, helping a contractor build a new addition to Glass' front porch, and though he was still no angel— he was flunking out of Fort Calhoun High School, selling pot to seventh-graders and staging half-assed stickups at gas stations— that period, he would later tell his friends, was the happiest of his life.

It was around that time that Rob, who now had access to a telephone after years in group homes, finally connected with his mother. One day, after convincing his sister to give him the number, he picked up the phone and called his stepfather.

"Do you remember someone named Robert Hawkins?" he asked.

"Of course I do," his stepfather said. Then he handed the phone to Molly, who was over for a visit. She didn't recognize the voice on the other end of the line.

"Mommy, it's me, Robbie."

"Oh, my God, Robert!" she gasped. "How are you? Where are you?"

Molly threw herself into his life as if the separation and abandonment had just been a big misunderstanding. A few days after he called her, she was sitting on Glass' front porch, bouncing Rob on her knee as they talked. Glass objected, saying she shouldn't treat the 17-year-old like a baby. "But he is my baby," Molly shot back. "He's my baby boy."

Molly convinced Rob to clean up his appearance and cut his long hair, and then she went one better, buying him a used green Jeep in good condition and promising it to him if he finished high school. "I wanted to let him know that I believed in him, that he could do it," she recalls. "To let him know that he was troubled but he wasn't sick."

The next time Rob went to court, wearing a shirt and tie that Molly had purchased for him, Judge O'Neal was impressed. "I think you're doing a great job, and you are a sharp-dressed man today," the judge told him. "I'm very pleased, and I'm proud of you."

Despite Rob's progress, however, the judge wasn't able to send him home. His stepmother still refused to let him return—and Rob's father sided with Candace, refusing to take his own son back. "He appears to have picked his wife over his son," Judge O'Neal exploded in open court. "It's not my responsibility to raise his kid." But with nowhere else to put Rob, the judge was forced to keep him in Marty Glass' foster home.

Given how well things were going with Molly, Rob asked his caseworker if he could live with his mother. But Molly also decided that she didn't want Rob living in her house. He was using meth, and in her gut she felt he was still dangerous. "Given what his father was like, you had to be careful," she says. "I was afraid of what Rob might do to the girls."

For a second time in his life, Rob had been rejected by his own mother. He was so angry that he didn't speak to her for two years.

IN DECEMBER 2005, after Rob's stepmother divorced his father, he was finally allowed to come home. By now he was 17, practically an adult, and the judge and his father decided that he ought to get a job. For his part, Rob wanted to work. He felt like he could contribute something, even if he didn't have much to offer an employer. Four years cocooned in the state system had left him with little education and no marketable talents, and he lacked even basic life skills—such as knowing how to drive a car. Still, he wasn't stupid, and he was willing to learn.

But he soon discovered that Nebraska had become an unforgiving place for kids like him. Globalization and mechanization had winnowed away the decent jobs working in corn and soybeans, and by the time Rob went looking for work, there were 20,000 fewer farm jobs in Nebraska than there had been when he was born. The loss left an entire generation out in the cold—some 10,000 high school dropouts in the state are currently unemployed, roaming the plains with nothing to do. After looking for a while with no success, Rob gave up the job hunt. He started bumming around in a haze of marijuana smoke, got busted and was put under house arrest. Eventually, he persuaded the judge to release him from the state's supervision. The county prosecutor argued against it, but by then the state had already spent $265,000 on Rob, and, as his caseworker put it, "I'm not sure that we're benefiting him anymore."

"I know you'll do well, Robbie," O'Neal said. On August 21st, 2006, he made Rob a free man for the first time in more than four years.

A month later, Debora Maruca opened her front door one dewy morning and found Rob curled up asleep on her lawn, homeless and broke. Maruca was the mother of one of Rob's high school buddies, Will—another working-class kid who was struggling to find a place for himself—and the two friends had spent the night partying before Rob crashed on the grass. A few months earlier, Rob had stormed out of his dad's house without a plan or place to stay, and ended up sleeping in a meth head's car. Now he had nowhere else to go. So Maruca, a surgical nurse at a local hospital, took him in.

"He was like a lost puppy," she recalls. "He would follow me around with his head down. But he was really polite, and you kind of felt sorry for him." She helped him get menial jobs, and charged him only $50 a month, including three meals a day, for an air mattress in a little room in her house. For nearly a year and a half, Rob slept in that room—a space so tiny that two people lying shoulder to shoulder would be a tight fit—and tried to make a go of life on his own.

He did OK for a while. He found a social circle of partyers through Will, and they sort of adopted him as their McLovin, the dorky, awkward, inappropriate kid who would always say something funny, whether he meant to be amusing or not. "This is *sooo* badass," he liked to half-joke, a cigarette dangling from his lips as he did something stupid like roll a joint with a Post-it note. "It's rugged." He got himself a driver's license: After five spastic failures, he finally calmed down enough to stop ramming curbs and treating the car like a video game. He found a job working fast food, borrowed money from his dad to buy a used white Cadillac with a V8—the first thing he ever really owned. "Rob loved that car," a friend recalls. "He used to say that when he made it big time he was going to have it dipped in gold."

And he also got a girlfriend: a 16-year-old blond stoner chick named Kaci, who was attracted to Rob's intense oddball demeanor. "He was sexy," she recalls, "sexy and dorky." Pretty soon they were inseparable, and if they weren't getting stoned together, or watching TV, they were swooning over each other on the phone. She'd lie in bed while on the other end of the line he played Halo 3 on the Xbox, and they'd go for hours like that, with Rob whispering about his shitty childhood and his fickle mother as he mowed down virtual enemies on the screen. "We were totally co dependent," Kaci recalls, "Sometimes we wouldn't even talk, we'd just stay on the phone to hear each other breathing. Man, I really loved Rob." She pauses, then adds, "He cried all the time. It was really sad because he had, like, no family. He was the saddest about his mother."

Still, in his stoner ways, Rob seemed on the surface to be no different from a million other slacker teens, and he might have gone on like that indefinitely. But after a year of bumming around, he started wearing out his welcome at the Marucas. He was "getting cocky," as Debora puts it, blowing his raises on beer and pot, and not offering to pitch in more money for rent. "We were feeling like maybe he was just conning us," says Will, "like he could do better if he wanted to."

Everything Rob tried to do to make money failed miserably. Whenever he looked for jobs online, all he could find were minimum-wage gigs—nothing with a future. He enlisted in the Army, announcing to his friends one night that he was going to make it to general, but the recruiter rejected him on account of his record and mental-health issues. Spiraling down into depression and drinking, he tried drug dealing in earnest. He borrowed $400 worth of pot in what was supposed to be his big move, but he ended up smoking it all. "It was just so moist," he told a friend with a laugh.

Little by little, Rob began to feel like he was living a "meaningless existence," as he eventually wrote in a suicide note. As he became more lost and depressed, the volatile side of his personality emerged again. The threats started gradually—a 16-year-old girl who had the misfortune of offending him was told that she was going to be killed for crossing him—but pretty soon they were indiscriminate, just like they'd been when he was a kid, and Rob got a reputation among his friends as a sort of dorky hothead.

"Rob was going around talking about kicking everyone's ass," one friend says. "Which was kind of funny in a way, because he was such a skinny shit. But you also felt that maybe he did know how to fight, from those years at Cooper. When he got really upset, he'd say he was going to take a bunch of people out. I'd say, 'Dude, that's crazy,' and he'd be like, 'I know,' so I always thought he was kidding."

Even Dallas, his friend from the group home who had managed to get a job at Target and a fiancee, couldn't convince Rob to straighten up. "There was a side of Rob that didn't want to go the quiet route," Dallas recalls. "He was getting pretty heavy into his drugs. He wanted to deal like crazy for a few years and then retire." But when Rob tried a second stab at dealing, plunking all his cash into a cocaine buy, he ended up getting robbed, losing every gram and every dollar he had invested. "He came over to my house and was really upset," says Dallas. "He cried a lot. He owed some pretty serious people money, and he wanted to kill himself."

After a year of working and living on his own, Rob was broke. All that he really had to his name was the old Cadillac. He sunk again into his childhood depression—but this time there were no responsible adults in his life, no doctors and no parents, to help him. When he told his stoner friends he was feeling suicidal, they thought he was being Rob, talking shit, just blowing off steam. The only person who managed to keep him afloat emotionally was Kaci. She would talk him down and make him feel better about himself.

It was in this tenuous position that he reached out one last time to his mother. Last September, just as he had two years earlier, he picked up the phone and called her out of the blue.

Molly was thrilled. She plunged herself back into Rob's world and tried to help him—not realizing that in the end, all her good intentions would backfire, inadvertently magnifying his despair. "I just cried," she says of the reunion. "I really believed things were going to be better."

Things didn't get off to the best start. Right off the bat, Rob asked his mother if she would buy some magic mushrooms that he couldn't unload. "Aren't those the ones that make you sick?" she asked him. He said they could do that. "Well, I don't think your mother is going to be buying any of those from you," she said.

But that didn't mean Molly was adverse to sharing her son's

drugs. When Rob came over to her small apartment on Thanksgiving, they smoked a few bowls together. "Rob always said he wanted the kind of mom he could get high with," Molly says. "Well, OK. If you got it, pass it around."

Molly was supported by a variety of men: Her ex-husband covered her rent, and an elderly friend paid her to keep him company. To help set Rob on a better financial path, Molly insisted that he get rid of his gas-guzzling Cadillac and take the Jeep she'd bought for him instead. He offloaded the car to Dallas for $325, taking a $900 loss. Molly even bought a new stereo for the Jeep and had it installed for him.

But then his luck ran out. A few days after he put the Jeep in his name, he got busted drinking beer in it one night with his friends. Given his prior record, he was sure the judge would throw the book at him and send him to jail. Molly assured him that he could get the hearing delayed until after the holidays, but he took little comfort in her advice, telling his friends that he secretly feared she was planning to take the Jeep away. "He thought she was going to punish him," Dallas recalls.

In private, feeling alone and desperate, he wrote out a suicide note. "Nothing ever seems to work for me. And I know that nobody will ever really understand. I am always in debt, and I probably always will be. I'm not going to lie and say I'm not afraid. But whatever happens I know it can't be too bad when you die." Then he closed by begging whoever found his body to hide his suicide from Kaci. "Just please, I don't want Kaci or her family to know what I've done."

But instead of acting on the note, he shoved it in a bookcase in his bedroom at the Marucas, where it would not be found until two weeks after the shooting.

Then things got even worse. A few days earlier, he had gone on a date with a co-worker at McDonald's, where he was working the night shift. The date set in motion a chain of events that pushed Rob over the edge. When Kaci found out that he had taken the girl home, she confronted him. At first he acted guilty and distraught, but he was soon alternating between begging her forgiveness and angrily demanding that she understand his need to spread his wings. When he went to his mother for advice, saying he felt horrible for cheating on Kaci, she counseled him not to take it so seriously.

"I don't view it as cheating," she told him. "You're not really expected to be monogamous when you're 19. You're young—things are forgivable."

Emboldened by his mother's words, Rob called Kaci and told her that he was going to keep fucking the new girl. "She's a nasty bitch," he bragged. "I fuck her all over the place, and she's good to me."

Kaci burst into tears. "How can you be so mean to me?" she sobbed. Rob apologized. "This is a weird time in my life," he told her. "I don't know how much longer I'll be around." He explained that he planned to kill himself.

It was not the first time he'd said that, and Kaci was especially sensitive to the threat, since her last boyfriend had hung himself over a staircase one day after school. As it happened, this boyfriend had been the third friend of hers who'd taken his own life; suburban communities like Bellevue are the hardest-hit by teen suicides in Nebraska. But instead of confronting Rob, as she always had, she let it go. "I always used to talk him out of killing himself," she recalls. "But this time, I just didn't. I was so mad at him for breaking my heart."

That was on Tuesday afternoon, December 4th. A few hours later, as the sun was setting on the Nebraska plains and workers at Von Maur were turning on the Christmas lights at the mall, Rob drove to his mother's for dinner.

HE WAS LATE, as usual, and dressed like crap, but Molly was too overjoyed to see him to comment. So great was the gulf between them, and so thorough was her misunderstanding of his condition, that she couldn't see he was depressed when he shuffled through the front door that evening. In fact, she thought he was "doing pretty well."

Molly was in a good mood that night. She had just finished writing her autobiography, a strangely graphic confession of her sexual adventures, and she felt like celebrating. But as the dinner wound down, the conversation turned to Rob's breakup with Kaci. When he said he felt guilty about the whole affair, Molly replied, "Well, if you feel bad about it, maybe you shouldn't have done it."

Rob said he guessed she was right and returned to his food as the talk turned to other subjects. Then, toward the end of the meal, he abruptly said that he had been fired from McDonald's a few days before. The cash-register count was short on Rob's shift. "The manager made me empty my pockets," Rob complained. "He took $12 from me."

"He can't do that," Molly said. "Do you want me to go down there and get your money back?"

"No," Rob said. "It's not worth it, Mom."

After dinner, they sat in front of the computer and found a couple of online applications for low-wage job openings, including one at a nursing home. Molly tried to encourage him. Sometimes in life you have to be poor for a very long time, she told him, but you always get by. "Look at me," she said. "I think I've done pretty well for myself."

"Yeah. I guess you're right," he told her.

Then Molly went shopping, leaving Rob alone in the house. He went upstairs to the master bedroom, went into the closet, took his stepfather's AK-47 and put it in the Jeep. Then he went back inside and sat on the couch listening to his iPod. His favorite song was Judas Priest's "Hell Bent for Leather": *Screams! From a streak of fire as he strikes.* Molly had loaded the songs for him, because he couldn't figure out iTunes. When she came home half an hour later, Rob was still there, lost in his own world.

"He just got up, hugged me really tight, and left," Molly says. "He didn't say much of anything."

That evening, when he got back to the Maruca residence, Rob proudly showed the rifle to Will, saying that it was on loan from his stepfather. He invited Will to take it target-shooting the next day. The two boys often went to a homemade target range they had set up in the woods nearby, where Rob had honed his skill. But they rarely got their hands on an AK-47, and now they snapped a picture of the weapon with a cellphone and e-mailed it to a few friends. Around 11 p.m., Rob smoked a few Camels, tossing the empty butts in a bucket by his bed, and went to sleep, stone-cold sober.

Rob may have intended to use the rifle for target practice. But in the morning, he got a rude awakening. Molly had discovered the theft, and she was pissed. She called the Marucas and left a message: "Tell Rob to call his mother right away." When Will gave Rob the message, he recoiled. "Oh, man—she found out I took the gun," he told Will, who admonished him for swiping it. Rob promised to return it. But rather than face his mother, he sat down and wrote another suicide note.

"I've been a piece of shit my entire life," he wrote. "It seems this is my only option. I know everyone will remember me as some sort of monster, but please understand that I just don't want to be a burden on the ones that I care for my entire life. I just want to take a few pieces of shit with me."

Rob left the note next to his bed and drove over to see his friend Dallas. When he arrived, he slumped down on the big leather couch, flicked on the Xbox and began to play in wordless concentration. But before long, he tossed the controller on the couch and started talking, then crying.

Tears ran down his face. Everything was wrong—everything. The Marucas were going to kick him out and he'd be homeless. He'd fucked up with Kaci, the one girl he could see marrying. She hated him, and maybe rightly so. He was looking at jail time—over Christmas—for drinking beer in the Jeep, and he didn't even have the money to pay the fine, let alone a lawyer.

When his mother found out about the gun, she was likely to take back the Jeep, and then how the hell was he going to get around? Where was he going to sleep? What were they going to do to him in prison? Through tearstained eyes, he looked up at his old friend. "I'm fucked, dude."

"Dude, I love you. I'm here for you."

"I know," Rob said, getting up off the couch. "Can I borrow your phone?"

He called Will and said he was sorry for everything. Will could tell by his voice that he was on edge. "You haven't done anything yet, Rob," Will told him. "Just chill out, OK?" Putting his hand over the phone, he called out to his mom, who was getting ready for work.

"I think Rob's going to kill himself," Will said. "Can you talk to him?"

His mother got on the phone. Whatever it is, she said, it's no big deal.

"I just want to thank you for all the stuff you've done for me," Rob told her. "I'm sorry."

Rob hung up and called his mother. When Molly didn't answer, he left a message. He sent a text message to Kaci, telling her that he loved her and was sorry for everything and that he was going to go have a "standoff." Then he sent the exact same message to his new girlfriend.

Rob told Dallas he was going to take off. Standing at the door, the two friends hugged. Dallas felt like Rob wasn't really there, "like he wasn't in his body." After Rob left, Dallas grew worried. He switched on the TV. "I was thinking if Rob was going to do something, like get in a shootout, it would be on the news."

Molly, meanwhile, was looking for Rob. She thought he was going to "sell the gun to one of his druggie ex-con friends, probably as barter for some tattoo work." She was going to seriously kick his ass. She called Dallas to see if he was there. "If you see Rob, don't let him out of your sight—just tackle him," she said. Dallas was like, OK, whatever. When they hung up, he went back to the TV.

By the time Molly was on her way to the police station, Rob was in the green Jeep she had given him, going in the opposite direction, toward the mall. He was so broke that even the clothes on his back were on loan: He had scrounged a winter jacket from Will because the morning was cold.

As she raced to find her son, Molly looked down at her cellphone and noticed that there was a missed call. When she pressed the phone to her ear, she heard Rob's high-pitched, reedy voice.

"Hi, Mom," he said. "It's me. I just wanted to let you know that I love you. I'm sorry for everything. See you later."

MARK BOAL *is a producer, screenwriter, and journalist. Born and raised in New York City, he graduated with honors in philosophy from Oberlin College before beginning a career as an investigative reporter and writer of long-form nonfiction. An acclaimed series for the* Village Voice *on the rise of surveillance in America led to a position at the alternative weekly writing a weekly column, "The Monitor," when he was twenty-three. Boal subsequently covered politics, technology, crime, youth culture, and drug culture for* Rolling Stone, Brill's Content, Mother Jones, *and* Playboy. *He is currently a writer-at-large for* Playboy *and a contributor to* Rolling Stone.

Boal's 2003 article "Jailbait," about an undercover drug agent, was adapted for Fox television's The Inside, *and his piece "Death and Dishonor," the true story of a military veteran murdered by his own platoon mates, became the basis for the film* In the Valley of Elah, *for which Boal shares a story credit with Paul Haggis. Boal wrote and produced the film* The Hurt Locker, *an award-winning, critically acclaimed war thriller directed by Kathryn Bigelow and inspired by his firsthand observations of a bomb squad in Baghdad.*

Coda

After it was published, the article hit a nerve, especially in Nebraska. *Rolling Stone*'s website was slammed by angry readers who wrote that Hawkins was a monster who didn't deserve the attention of the national press. Many Omaha natives posted that their hometown had been unfairly portrayed as a wasteland for unemployed teenagers. Still, not all the write-in comments were negative, and quite a few readers praised the magazine for daring to treat the life of a mass murderer in such exacting detail.

Then, a year later, the *Omaha World-Herald* confirmed the discovery of a cluster of nine teen suicides in Sarpy County from 2005 to 2007, and the newspaper subsequently called for an official investigation into the state's handling of mentally ill youth.

At the time of this book's publication, no official action had taken place.

Sabrina Rubin Erdely

The Fabulous Fraudulent Life of Jocelyn and Ed

FROM *Rolling Stone*

SHE TOLD EVERYONE her boobs were real, which was a laugh: They were immobile and perfectly round, and looked airbrushed, even in person. She credited her violet eyes to Lithuanian genes, rather than the purple contact lenses she wore. And on this afternoon last November, sitting in a Philadelphia hair salon with a college textbook open on her lap, she told the stylist she was a University of Pennsylvania student named Morgan Greenhouse. The name was as fake as the hair now being glued onto her head.

"I love this," Jocelyn Kirsch declared, fingering her new $2,200 auburn hair extensions. "Don't you love it?"

Her boyfriend, Ed Anderton, looked on adoringly. "I love it," he echoed. The two of them returned to their murmured conversation, discussing the $400 room they planned to rent at the W hotel, once Jocelyn finished taking her final exams. After that, they planned to spend winter break vacationing in Morocco.

Jocelyn and Ed made performance art out of their extravagance.

They posted photos on Facebook of their constant travels: smooching under the Eiffel Tower, riding horses along Hawaiian beaches, sunning themselves on Caribbean sand. They lived in one of Philadelphia's most expensive neighborhoods, Rittenhouse Square, where they dined in pricey restaurants and danced on tables in the trendiest bars. Friends figured Ed must have been pulling in a big salary as a financial analyst, which seemed plausible; he was a bright recent Penn grad who'd majored in economics. Plus, Jocelyn held herself out as some kind of trust-fund baby, with a closet full of expensive clothes—for today's hair appointment, tight True Religion jeans, a navy cashmere hoodie and white Juicy Couture flats—and bore the expectant, impatient manner of the rich.

"Oh, money's not an issue," she told the Giovanni & Pileggi stylist at her consultation a week earlier. She'd put down a $500 deposit, using a credit-card number phoned in by "Mr. Greenhouse," her remarkably young-sounding father.

It was all a big, gleeful sham. Ed had actually been canned from his job four months before, and twenty-two-year-old Jocelyn was a senior at nearby Drexel University, a big step down from Penn. When Philadelphia police busted into the couple's apartment a few days later, they found an extensive identity-theft operation, complete with a professional ID maker, computer spyware, lock-picking tools and a crisp North Carolina driver's license soaking in a bowl of bleach. Though the investigation is still unfolding, this much is apparent: The lovebirds stand accused of using other people's names and Social Security numbers to scam at least $100,000, sometimes buying merchandise and selling it online to raise more cash.

What's striking about the two grifters is how determined they were to flaunt their ill-gotten gains. They acted not like furtive thieves but like two kids on a joy ride, utterly delighted by their own cleverness—as in the invitation Jocelyn e-mailed to friends not long before their arrests, announcing a surprise twenty-fifth-birthday party for Ed at an upscale tapas bar. "My treat, of course!" she'd written. Steeped in narcissism and privilege, fueled by entitlement and set in an age of consumer culture run amok, theirs is truly an outlaw romance for the twenty-first century. The *Philadelphia Daily News* immediately dubbed the photogenic couple "Bonnie and Clyde." It's a name some people take exception to. "Bonnie and Clyde, that's only because they're young and good-looking," scoffs Detective Terry Sweeney of the Philadelphia police. "These two were complete idiots. If this was two fat fucks from South Philly, it would have been Turner and Hooch."

JOCELYN KIRSCH MADE AN IMPRESSION in the fall of 2003 when she strolled onto Drexel University's campus showing off her legs in a denim miniskirt and tan Uggs, in full makeup—with a bunny rabbit named Frisbee peeking from her oversize Coach handbag.

She was a freshman but had already acquired a boyfriend on campus: a strapping ROTC senior we'll call Thomas, whose dorm suitemates would never forget the first time he brought her by. They were all lazing around watching television when Thomas led her in. Jocelyn looked different back then: ordinary pretty, with mousy-brown curls, and for a few moments she just stood there awkwardly. But in an instant, her manner became so outrageously flirtatious that no one was watching TV anymore. Jocelyn proceeded to tell them a little about herself: that she was the daughter of two high-profile plastic surgeons with homes in California and North Carolina; that she was fluent in Russian, which she'd learned while growing up in Lithuania; later, she'd tell classmates she spoke eleven languages, including Turkish, Czech and Afrikaans. She also mentioned that she was an athlete who had qualified for the 2004 U.S. Olympic team. In pole-vaulting.

"That's surprising," said Penn student Emily Heffernan, who was there visiting her boyfriend, Jason. "Drexel doesn't have a track team."

"I train with Penn," Jocelyn replied. Then with a wink at Emily, she sat on Jason's lap.

No one at Drexel knew what to make of Jocelyn. Men found her mesmerizing. Her relationships with women were another story. "She was like Regina George in *Mean Girls*," says a classmate. Jocelyn had a way of eyeing other girls—"as if you had, like, spaghetti sauce all over you"—then choosing a careful compliment. "I like your bag," she'd say, and then add, "Mine's Marc Jacobs. It cost $1,500." Still, women found themselves captivated too. "She wasn't a healthy person," says Heffernan. "But she was entertaining. We were always waiting to see what she'd say next."

The truth about Jocelyn wasn't as exciting as she advertised. She was a child of privilege and divorce, raised in affluent Winston-Salem, North Carolina. Her father, Lee, was a plastic surgeon with a standoffish demeanor but known for his community service: He gave to charity, volunteered as a doctor for the high school athletic department and hosted a Lithuanian exchange student, whom Jocelyn took to her prom. By then, Jocelyn was living with her mother, Jessica, a nurse completing her doctorate in public health. Jocelyn also had a brother, Aaron, one year older, whom she shut out so completely that friends were unaware he even existed. Few realized how the Kirschs' divorce had fractured their family: When Jocelyn went to live with their mother, Aaron stayed behind in their father's Tudor-style manse.

"I always got the sense that her home life wasn't very happy," says high school friend Kate Agnelli. Jocelyn was closemouthed about the acrimony within her family and rarely brought friends home. But her anger bled into her public life. Classmates remember their sunglasses and cellphones disappearing in her wake. She was always hungry for male attention; she'd tell a later lover that she'd cheated on every boyfriend she ever had. Each year, Jocelyn also reinvented herself, trading old friends for new ones, transforming from goth girl to Abercrombie prep to outdoorsy rock climber to frisky cheerleader wanna-be. As her high school career progressed, and Jocelyn's parents bitterly finalized their split, her behavior grew worse. Previously a good student, according to a friend, she was suspended twice for cheating. Jocelyn lied about her absences, telling friends she'd been visiting her dying grandparents (who were alive and well). Another time, she said she was battling ovarian cancer.

"This girl has been crying out for help forever," says Agnelli. "She doesn't like who she is, so she invents something she thinks is better." In college, Jocelyn leapt at the chance to create herself anew. Once in Philadelphia, she rarely went back to North Carolina, especially after her mother swiftly remarried and moved to California.

At Drexel, classmates noticed that when Jocelyn wasn't running her mouth, she didn't know what to say. But then she'd blurt out some outrageous lie—like when she returned from shopping at Urban Outfitters saying they'd asked her to be a model—and suddenly she'd seem comfortable again. But, again, little things started to disappear from friends' rooms: art supplies, kitchen utensils. Her boyfriend Thomas' suitemates started spotting Jocelyn's name in their dorm's guest log when she was nowhere to be found—only to discover she'd been visiting the brawny swimmer next door. Not that Thomas listened to his friends' warnings.

"I loved her," says Thomas now. "I thought we had a future." They made a curious pair, the glamour girl and the clean-cut ROTC engineering major. But he was graduating and heading for life in the Army, so he wanted to savor what little time they had left. He knew Jocelyn was in for a rough transition without him.

"She didn't like being alone," says Thomas.

She didn't intend to stay that way for long. That fall, Jocelyn returned to campus transformed, with bleached-blond hair, a perma-tan and a set of new breasts, all of which she insisted were natural. Her face had changed too: Her nose and cheeks were somehow more sculpted. She had reinvented herself yet again, this time as a centerfold-quality beauty with a savvier, brasher personality to match, a new, more perfect Jocelyn, ready to take on the world. Or, at least, its men.

WHILE JOCELYN WAS FAST becoming Drexel's answer to Paris Hilton, a few blocks away at the University of Pennsylvania, Edward Kyle Anderton was winding down his college career in obscurity. Most people considered Ed a good guy, if only because he had no discernible personality to dislike. Even his good looks failed to distinguish him: With dark hair atop a heart-shaped face, a disarming smile and ears that stuck out a few degrees too far, he was handsome but not overly so. Strolling the well-tended campus, Ed Anderton blended into the background, utterly forgettable.

He hadn't always been so anonymous. He grew up in Everett, Washington, where at Snohomish High School his achievements set him apart. He was a straight-A striver and a standout swimmer whom *The Seattle Times* once named "Star of the Month." Though Ed was too busy for parties, people knew who he was; he was friendly but never outgoing. "He was a little shy," says friend Danielle Newton. "But at home with his family, he'd open up."

Unlike Jocelyn's, Ed's background was middle-class. His father, Kyle, worked in circulation for *The Seattle Times* and took a second job driving for UPS to pay for his children's college tuition. His mother, Lori, was a doting stay-at-home mom. They were a wholesome clan that got silly playing board games and seemed to enjoy one another's company. When Ed was admitted to Penn on scholarship, his family couldn't have been prouder.

But at Penn, Ed was just one bright undergrad among 10,000 others. Intimidated, Ed tried assuming the confident airs of his Ivy League peers. But if he made any sort of impression, it was for the way he feigned cheer to mask something else. "His niceness didn't seem all that genuine," says a former classmate. "When you talked to him, there was a feeling of disconnect. He was a bit fake." And when Ed wasn't making the effort to be pleasant, he revealed a very different side, one that was brusque and impatient. "If you weren't on his good side, he'd make that clear," says a fraternity brother. "He just always seemed like a dick."

Still, Ed got by just fine. He studied hard, made the swim team, majored in economics and joined the frat Alpha Chi Rho. "He seemed to have his life together," recalls former housemate Joe Pahl. After graduating in 2005, Ed went to work for Johnson & Johnson and then as an analyst for the giant real estate equity firm Lubert-Adler. His hard work had come to fruition. He was twenty-four years old, working in a glass skyscraper in downtown Philadelphia, commanding a comfortable five-figure salary. All Ed needed was someone to share it with.

IN THE SEDUCTION DEPARTMENT, Jocelyn had become a steamroller. One night, at a Drexel house party, a skinny indie-rock guy, Jayson Verdibello, caught her eye. So she ran after him as he was leaving the party, pushed him against the wall and made out with him, holding him by the collar to keep him from running away.

By that time, Jocelyn had developed a fearsome dramatic streak. "What did I do?" Verdibello begged throughout their ten-month relationship. "The fact that you don't know just shows how fucked-up you are!" she'd scream back. She was forever berating him in public, and when he tried to walk away from her tantrums, she'd flail at him with her bony arms. "I was a little scared of her," admits Verdibello. "I just let her have her way." He wasn't alone. Everyone gave Jocelyn lots of leeway, because she seemed to exist in a world apart—a world of plenty. Her friends lived in dorms, but Jocelyn lived in a $1,600-a-month loft apartment with floor-to-ceiling windows and a rooftop pool. Jocelyn would take her friend Sallie Cook on her shopping sprees, using her father's credit card to blow $5,000 at, say, Neiman Marcus. "My dad's gonna be *sooo* mad," she'd say coquettishly, rearranging her oversize bags while pointedly eyeing Cook's own tiny purchase.

"Jocelyn is extremely confident," says Cook. "There's no cap to how strong she is or how arrogant she is. She wants what she wants. And she feels she's entitled to it." Even Jocelyn's own father seemed cowed. When Lee Kirsch flew to Philly to take his daughter to Cirque du Soleil—bearing $190-a-pop VIP tickets—Jocelyn treated him with utter contempt. "Dad, shut up," she kept telling him in the VIP tent, putting as much distance between them as possible, except to hand her father an armload of merchandise to buy for her.

Jocelyn tried hard to appear unflappable, but her life was unraveling. On the side, she was still dating Thomas, visiting him at Army bases all over the country. Then in March 2006—the month after she seduced Verdibello—Thomas was deployed to Afghanistan where he was injured by an IED. Jocelyn told him in their phone conversations that she was beside herself with worry. And in her moments alone, she sought comfort in old habits. In the span of a year she was arrested three times for shoplifting. When she got caught, her tough-gal act fell apart. Previously busted in a CVS and Lord & Taylor, she broke down and wept when she was arrested in a Douglas Cosmetics store with a purse full of makeup. (Two of the three charges were dropped; she pleaded guilty to the department-store theft.)

Jocelyn told Verdibello nothing about her brushes with the law, or of her other boyfriend. They made an odd couple—Verdibello was a sensitive punk who lived in his Minor Threat T-shirt—but she had a knack for snaring guys so grateful for her attention they'd let her get away with anything. "She has this magnetism," Verdibello explains. "She can make you feel like the brightest star in the sky. But she can also make you feel like nothing at all." He was convinced they were soulmates—Jocelyn proved it with each love note she wrote him in her beautiful script. And when one day Verdibello discovered her sobbing, she confided in him about her brother, a soldier who had just been hurt by an IED—her brother, Thomas, whose framed photo hung on her apartment wall.

It was a testament to Jocelyn's powerful allure that Verdibello stayed in the picture. He figured out that Thomas wasn't really her brother, but Jocelyn managed to talk her way out of it, explaining that she had both a brother and an ex-boyfriend in the Army, both named Thomas—but that the flower deliveries really were from her brother. ("Whaddya want?" says Verdibello. "She could make me believe anything.") Then one evening in the fall of 2006, spooning Jocelyn in bed, Verdibello nuzzled the plush fabric of her Juicy Couture sweatsuit, breathing in her scent. Jocelyn was distracted—busy texting someone. Verdibello looked over her shoulder in time to read her message: "My cute capitalist ;-)" He knew it could be only one person: Jocelyn's new "econ tutor," Ed Anderton.

THEY HAD CROSSED PATHS one night in September when Ed was out drinking in downtown Philadelphia. One glance at Jocelyn, and Ed was toast. Jocelyn was smitten as well. The next day she told Sallie Cook, "Oh, my God, I met this guy last night, he's *sooo* hot!" She then ran down his vitals: tall and dark-haired like Verdibello, but better-groomed, worked in finance, and, best of all, he told her he made $115,000 a year.

From the beginning, the two were always publicly making out, broadcasting their relationship to the world. Everyone noticed them, which provided the kind of attention Jocelyn had come to expect, but it was a new experience for Ed. In the light of Jocelyn's affections, Ed had turned into a somebody: important and successful. And as malleable as Jocelyn's personality was, Ed's proved to be just as plastic. He became Jocelyn's perfect sidekick, a cocky braggart who always mentioned his Ivy League education and his supposed six-figure salary (double what he actually made). Ed embraced Jocelyn's flirtatiousness, too. At clubs, they'd split up to hit on strangers, watching each other's progress from across the bar—a game Jocelyn initiated for the sexy fun of it.

Jocelyn already had a boyfriend, of course. Ed had discovered that fact one embarrassing morning when he'd come over for brunch and Verdibello had opened the door in his boxers. (Ed had just stood there frozen, clutching a bottle of Simply Orange, while Jocelyn worked her mentalist magic on both men.) But Ed divined the quickest path to her heart: He made sure he was always pulling out his wallet and that everyone noticed his largesse. Together Ed and Jocelyn made a striking—and strikingly shallow—pair.

Three months after they met, Jocelyn and Ed departed for a New Year's trip to Paris. Other travelers their age might have been backpacking, but these two spent their vacation in four- and five-star hotels, shopping at Gucci and skiing the French alpine slopes. They dressed for maximum impact: Jocelyn's wardrobe included a rabbit-fur vest, red thigh-high boots and a crotch-length strand of pearls; Ed held his own in lavender button-downs and a leather man-purse. They snapped dozens of photos, which Jocelyn posted on Facebook (to the shock and heartbreak of both Verdibello and Thomas, who each thought he was dating Jocelyn exclusively). And the pair brought home a souvenir: a sign they'd swiped from a cafe, warning PROFESSIONAL BAG THIEVES OPERATE IN THIS AREA, PLEASE KEEP A CLOSE EYE ON YOUR PERSONAL BELONGINGS AT ALL TIMES.

Their year of living fabulously had begun.

ED AND JOCELYN SWIFTLY MORPHED into nouveau-riche brats, intent upon getting the things they wanted—no, *deserved*. Like their new two-bedroom apartment in the Belgravia, a grand building owned by Ed's company. Their third-floor pad was a huge, high-ceilinged affair, decorated in ultramodern style with black lacquer and chrome furniture. Jocelyn's walk-in closet was strewn with designer clothes; in Ed's closet, everything was neatly pressed and hung. They used their second bedroom as an office—stocked with four computers, two printers, a scanner and, most curiously, an industrial machine for manufacturing ID cards. And squirreled away in their apartment was a lockbox filled with keys to many of their neighbors' apartments and to all of their mailboxes ("Is the mail here yet?" they'd ask at the front desk); police suspect that Ed managed to procure the keys through his company, since it owned the building.

Their crimes seem to have begun fairly early. "These two have only been together since September '06," says Detective Sweeney, noting that they were arrested a little over a year later. "So they managed to do a lot in that short time. Which tells me this was a perfect meeting of the minds." The police say that while neighbors were out, the pair would sneak into their apartments and steal their Social Security numbers, driver's license numbers, bank-account info and, in one case, a passport. Then they'd open credit cards and bank accounts in their victims' names, supplying a mailing address on the Penn campus—really a UPS Store, where the apartment number they'd listed ("Apt. 124") was a PO box. As a finishing touch, they made phony driver's licenses, using as a guide an article Ed clipped from Penn's student newspaper titled "How to Spot Fake IDs."

They also had Spector spyware—software that, once installed on their neighbors' computers, they may have used to glean confidential information. When police had disconnected the pair's computers, the entire building's Internet access crashed—the police suspect that the tech-savvy Ed rigged everyone's Internet accounts to run through his own computer.

Neighbors weren't the only ones at risk. Morgan Greenhouse, an '07 Penn grad, still has no clue how her identity was stolen—only that one day a credit-card company called to verify a check she'd written to herself for several thousand dollars. "I freaked out," she says. Panicked, she checked her credit online and discovered seven unauthorized credit cards, many nearly maxed out to their $2,000 or $3,000 limit.

But while some of the couple's capers seemed well-planned, others were stupidly obvious—including preying on their own friends. In the summer of 2007, the pair reportedly spent a weekend in Manhattan crashing with a Penn buddy of Ed's. Weeks later, the guy and his roommate filed a report with the NYPD, claiming $3,000 in fraudulent charges. Even Sallie Cook, Jocelyn's friend from Drexel, says she was fleeced, though in a decidedly low-tech way: Shortly after Jocelyn watched Cook punch her PIN number into a cash machine, Cook's debit card disappeared, and $600 was withdrawn from her account.

"I called Jocelyn to tell her what happened," Cook remembers. "And she was like, 'Ohhh, you called the police? Umm, well, I have your debit card here. . . . It's the same color as mine. . . . I must have accidentally used yours, and I guess our PIN numbers are the same!'" (Cook filed a police report but then let the matter drop.)

The incident didn't seem to bother Jocelyn. She was disengaging from campus anyhow, once again shucking her old life for a better one. She and Ed were always flying off somewhere—London, Montreal, Florida, Hawaii—and posting the proof online. At home she and Ed were attending black-tie events, appearing in *Philadelphia* magazine's society pages, laughing and cuddling, Jocelyn's black bra peeking from under her leopard-print dress. They became fixtures at the hookah bar Byblos, where Jocelyn would come in wearing a bustier and a miniskirt, then spend the night getting hammered, dancing on tables and vamping it up with a hookah pipe between her lips—all while photographing herself and Ed, who'd be nibbling on her neck.

Other criminals might have made themselves inconspicuous, but for Jocelyn and Ed, conspicuousness was the point. The high life didn't mean squat unless people were watching, envying, validating them. They went about their glamorous lives as if there was nothing else to life, nothing beyond the acquisition and flaunting of goods—and in that they were true believers.

In July 2007, they took a long weekend at Turks and Caicos' ritzy Regent Palms resort and made spectacles of themselves. "Especially her," says a patron. "She worked it." Sunning by the infinity pool in matching red bathing suits, while hotel staff fluffed their towels and misted them with water, Ed and Jocelyn were in their element: Ed chatted with other guests about his favorite Philly restaurants while Jocelyn basked silently behind silver aviators, looking utterly content.

"Take our picture?" Jocelyn asked a couple lounging beside them. Ed and Jocelyn stood at the pool's edge, wrapping their arms around each other, and smiled.

OCCASIONALLY, reality intruded in unpleasant ways—like when Ed brought Jocelyn home to meet his parents. Jocelyn barely masked her distaste for their home and provincial sensibilities. At a gathering of family and friends, Jocelyn refused to play their board games, choosing instead to sit at Ed's elbow, sipping wine while everyone else drank soda, her blouse undone a few buttons too many, her face arranged in a careful, lipsticked smile. "She made us feel like she was the outsider watching us do our silly things," remembers Ed's friend Danielle Newton. "It was uncomfortable."

Back at home, the couple also had the minor inconvenience of shoehorning their "real" lives into their jet-set schedules. Jocelyn had now declared a major in international studies, telling people she hoped to become a U.N. ambassador. Decked out in fur and stiletto boots, Jocelyn continued attending her classes, where she dominated the discussion in her assertive, know-it-all tone. But she showed so much promise, in fact, that a professor helped place

her on a panel discussion on the Penn campus about globalization—
where she sat near special guest Prince Charles.

"Hi, my name is Jocelyn Kirsch," she introduced herself, as the
crowd and Britain's future heir to the throne looked on. "I'm
originally from Vilna, Lithuania." She went on to speak eloquently
about the way globalization is stratifying societies around the
world.

Ed, on the other hand, wasn't faring so well. His boss had taken
one look at Ed's tan, after the couple's return from Turks and Caicos, realized the "sick days" had been bogus, and fired him. All
the things Ed had worked for had fallen apart, leaving nothing but
the sham.

Ed told few people about his unemployed status. Instead, he
and Jocelyn kept up appearances, going harder than ever. Jocelyn
planned a birthday party for Ed, reserving a table for ten at Tinto,
one of the most exclusive restaurants in town; afterward, they
were going to vacation in Morocco. They had enough cash to get
by—stowed in their apartment was $17,500 rubber-banded in
stacks. Meanwhile, Ed's world had narrowed to just one person,
and he now ministered to Jocelyn's every need. He fetched her
lunches. He came with her to class, even reportedly taking an
economics midterm for her. And he accompanied her on errands—
like when, in November 2007, she treated herself to hair extensions. It was an indulgence the couple would regret.

HAIRDRESSER JEN BISICCHIA STARED furiously at two bogus checks from Tacoma, Washington. She had finished weaving
in "Morgan Greenhouse's" extensions, ending a seven-hour appointment. Morgan had been pleased with the results; she'd stared
at her reflection with approval as she reapplied her makeup. Then
she'd flashed a Georgia driver's license and got out of there fast,
leaving behind $1,900 in what Bisicchia assumed were phony
checks—since it made little sense that a girl from Georgia would

have a Tacoma bank account. Just then the phone rang. It was a woman calling to find out why she'd been charged $500 a week earlier.

"Oh, my God!" Jen Bisicchia shouted; the charge had been "Morgan's" deposit. The victim told Bisicchia her tale: She had just moved to Philly—as it turned out, across the hall from Jocelyn and Ed—and weeks later various credit-card companies notified her of a batch of new accounts in her name. She told Bisicchia that the thieves had been using a West Philly mailing address.

That's all Bisicchia needed to hear. She jumped in her car and found the UPS Store. Then she started calling the cell number "Morgan" had left with the salon. She dialed all night until, at 11:30 p.m., a man picked up.

"Is Morgan there?" Bisicchia asked.

"Uh, she's not available."

"Oh, is this Mr. Greenhouse?" she said. Bisicchia told the guy that Morgan had left her textbook behind. "You can come by tomorrow and pick it up. Or I could drop it off to you," she suggested. The man offered to meet her at a Starbucks. "I don't feel comfortable giving Morgan's book to someone that's not Morgan," Bisicchia said, enjoying herself now. "But you know what's funny? Her name's not Morgan! And I know what's going on, and I want my money." The man hung up.

At 3:30 that morning, Bisicchia received a text message—from Morgan. It read:

"Hello Jen Bisicchia. You don't know my name but I know yours. I also know ur nice place on wolf st and how u get home at night. youre the one who should be worried . . . you seem like a smart girl, walk away now or you will regret it."

Shaken, Bisicchia turned the message over to the police the next morning. Things unfolded quickly from there. The police discovered a package of lingerie waiting for Box 124 at the UPS Store, addressed to the across-the-hall victim. So the police sat back. Explains Detective Sweeney, "There was a chance these two idiots might come back and pick up the stuff." Which they did later that same morning, pushing through the glass doors, Jocelyn wearing a red beret, though with tired rings beneath her eyes, then waiting patiently while the clerk pretended to have trouble locating their package. And there beside the packing-tape display, Jocelyn Kirsch and Edward Anderton's joy ride came to an end.

Even after her arrest, Jocelyn clung to her fictions as long as she could. In a holding cell, her mascara smeared from crying, she tucked her long locks into her collar and insisted it was her real hair—no way could she be the hair-extension thief. Police had to call in a stylist to fish around in her hair and confirm its fakeness, while Jocelyn sat stunned, her huge violet eyes open wide. It wasn't until after her mug shot that she removed her colored contacts, revealing the brown irises underneath.

JOCELYN AND ED'S TALE could end only one way: with their parents bailing them out of jail. Despite prosecutors' arguments that the pair posed a flight risk, Ed and Jocelyn were released into the custody of their families. Ed is now sulking in his childhood bedroom in Washington, while Jocelyn is holed up at her mom's Marin County house. Their first court date is scheduled for May 12th. They hope to negotiate a plea deal.

Jail seems a certainty for the duo, given the laundry list of criminal charges, including identity theft, terroristic threats, conspiracy and unlawful use of a computer. If convicted on all counts, Ed and Jocelyn could face decades in prison. So far, the police have turned up five alleged victims, and estimate the crime spree at $100,000. But the investigation is expected to turn up more victims and money. And now that the FBI is looking into the case, federal charges loom on the horizon.

Today Jocelyn is semifamous—though, perhaps, not in the way she'd hoped. When she plunged through the reporters outside the courthouse, she pulled her hoodie over her face; Ed snuck out a back door. Jocelyn's friends, meanwhile, rushed to exact revenge on the woman who had been a source of fascination and resentment. One Drexel classmate put up a vitriolic Facebook page: "She goin' to jaaail!" And they wasted no time trashing Jocelyn in the media. Chief among her detractors was Sallie Cook, who, moments after hearing of Jocelyn's arrest, texted her, "How was jail?"

The only words from Jocelyn herself have been meek e-mails to her soldier-boyfriend, Thomas, apologizing for any embarrassment she caused. "From her tone, she's hurting," Thomas says. As for Ed, he can't stop crying. "He's disgusted with himself," says Newton.

Still, someone as resourceful as Jocelyn could use this as a launching point, and parlay the whole episode into—who knows?—a nude magazine spread, maybe a reality-TV show. Jocelyn can dream. This is, after all, not just the land of second acts. It's a land in which notoriety and celebrity are one and the same. Where, with a little ingenuity, a woman with looks, brains and a rap sheet can really cash in. And speaking of cashing in:

"*Dr. Phil* is flying me out for a taping," says Sallie Cook, taking a pull off her three-foot hookah. "The media coverage is insane." She's sitting in her Marlton, New Jersey, living room, her fifty-inch TV tuned to Jerry Springer while she looks through her trove of Jocelyn photos—all of which have suddenly become valuable. "Ugh, look at this one, what a slut!" she says.

Cook's no dope; she's hoping to turn this into something more tangible. "My agent's telling me we can get, like, $5,000 a picture!" she says. "They can get me, like, fifty grand!" Her eyes twinkle at the prospect, and the sheer unending possibility of it all.

SABRINA RUBIN ERDELY *is a freelance journalist living in Philadelphia. She is a regular contributor to* Rolling Stone, *a contributing editor at* SELF, *and a writer-at-large at* Philadelphia *magazine; her work has also appeared in* GQ, The New Yorker, Reader's Digest, *and* Mother Jones. *She has earned many awards for her feature writing and reporting, including a National Magazine Award nomination. Her writing previously appeared in* Best American Crime Writing 2003.

Coda

This story had everything a reporter could want—a terrific narrative, a larger-than-life character, loads of sexy details—and was great fun to work on. But what drew me to this story was the commentary it offered on our times. Jocelyn and Ed's lust for the high life spoke to America's culture of runaway materialism, and to the perverse degree to which we feel validated by our purchases. Their sense of entitlement, and their dedication to living beyond their means, wasn't far removed from the values so many of us shared by the close of the go-go free-market experiment of the Bush era. In some ways, Jocelyn and Ed's caper was a last (criminal) hurrah for that gluttonous consumer culture, before we plunged into the current recession.

The feds took over "Bonnie and Clyde's" case. Ed Anderton pleaded guilty and was sentenced to four years. He'd spent his time out on bail working as a landscaper, putting his earnings toward the restitution he now owes. In his appearance before the judge, Ed looked like a man still shocked at what he'd discovered himself capable of. I'm told Ed has cut off contact with Jocelyn, a rejection she finds crushing.

As for Jocelyn Kirsch, her story just got weirder—because, while out on bail and working as a Starbucks barista, she had continued in her theatrical, outrageous crimes. She was accused of stealing a coworker's credit card, which she used for a spree at Ikea and a drugstore. The Marin County DA's office charged Jocelyn with making a phony 911 call to report screams coming from her mom and stepdad's house. One day Jocelyn strolled into a local bike shop and asked to test-drive a two-thousand-dollar bicycle, leaving her car keys as collateral; she never returned, and naturally her keys didn't open any cars in the lot.

By the time Jocelyn appeared in U.S. District Court in July 2008 to enter her guilty plea, she was already wearing a green prison uniform, having opted to start the clock on her eventual prison sentence. In a memo to the judge, her lawyer painted a picture of a damaged and mentally ill young woman coping with the aftermath of a difficult childhood—and revealed, among other things, the nauseating fact that Jocelyn's breast-implant surgery had been performed by her own father. The judge ordered psychological treatment and sentenced Jocelyn to five years.

David Grann

TRUE CRIME

FROM *The New Yorker*

IN THE SOUTHWEST CORNER OF POLAND, far from any
town or city, the Oder River curls sharply, creating a tiny inlet.
The banks are matted with wild grass and shrouded by towering
pine and oak trees. The only people who regularly trek to the
area are fishermen—the inlet teems with perch and pike and sun
bass. On a cold December day in 2000, three friends were casting
there when one of them noticed something floating by the shore.
At first, he thought it was a log, but as he drew closer he saw what
looked like hair. The fisherman shouted to one of his friends,
who poked the object with his rod. It was a dead body.

The fishermen called the police, who carefully removed the
corpse of a man from the water. A noose was around his neck, and
his hands were bound behind his back. Part of the rope, which
appeared to have been cut with a knife, had once connected his
hands to his neck, binding the man in a backward cradle, an ex-
cruciating position—the slightest wiggle would have caused the
noose to tighten further. There was no doubt that the man had

been murdered. His body was clothed in only a sweat-shirt and underwear, and it bore marks of torture. A pathologist determined that the victim had virtually no food in his intestines, which indicated that he had been starved for several days before he was killed. Initially, the police thought that he had been strangled and then dumped in the river, but an examination of fluids in his lungs revealed signs of drowning, which meant that he was probably still alive when he was dropped into the water.

The victim—tall, with long dark hair and blue eyes—seemed to match the description of a thirty-five-year-old businessman named Dariusz Janiszewski, who had lived in the city of Wroclaw, sixty miles away, and who had been reported missing by his wife nearly four weeks earlier; he had last been seen on November 13th, leaving the small advertising firm that he owned, in downtown Wroclaw. When the police summoned Janiszewski's wife to see if she could identify the body, she was too distraught to look, and so Janiszewski's mother did instead. She immediately recognized her son's flowing hair and the birthmark on his chest.

The police launched a major investigation. Scuba divers plunged into the frigid river, looking for evidence. Forensic specialists combed the forest. Dozens of associates were questioned, and Janiszewski's business records were examined. Nothing of note was found. Although Janiszewski and his wife, who had wed eight years earlier, had a brief period of trouble in their marriage, they had since reconciled and were about to adopt a child. He had no apparent debts or enemies, and no criminal record. Witnesses described him as a gentle man, an amateur guitarist who composed music for his rock band. "He was not the kind of person who would provoke fights," his wife said. "He wouldn't harm anybody."

After six months, the investigation was dropped, because of "an inability to find the perpetrator or perpetrators," as the prosecutor put it in his report. Janiszewski's family hung a cross on an oak tree near where the body was found—one of the few reminders of what the Polish press dubbed "the perfect crime."

ONE AFTERNOON IN THE FALL OF 2003, Jacek Wroblewski, a thirty-eight-year-old detective in the Wroclaw police department, unlocked the safe in his office, where he stored his files, and removed a folder marked "Janiszewski." It was getting late, and most members of the department would soon be heading home, their thick wooden doors clapping shut, one after the other, in the long stone corridor of the fortresslike building, which the Germans had built in the early twentieth century, when Wroclaw was still part of Germany. (The building has underground tunnels leading to the jail and the courthouse, across the street.) Wroblewski, who preferred to work late at night, kept by his desk a coffeepot and a small refrigerator; that was about all he could squeeze into the cell-like room, which was decorated with wall-sized maps of Poland and with calendars of scantily clad women, which he took down when he had official visitors.

The Janiszewski case was three years old, and had been handed over to Wroblewski's unit by the local police who had conducted the original investigation. The unsolved murder was the coldest of cold cases, and Wroblewski was drawn to it. He was a tall, lumbering man with a pink, fleshy face and a burgeoning paunch. He wore ordinary slacks and a shirt to work, instead of a uniform, and there was a simplicity to his appearance, which he used to his advantage: people trusted him because they thought that they had no reason to fear him. Even his superiors joked that his cases must somehow solve themselves. "Jacek" is "Jack" in English, and *wróbel* means "sparrow," and so his colleagues called him Jack Sparrow—the name of the Johnny Depp character in "Pirates of the Caribbean." Wroblewski liked to say in response, "I'm more of an eagle."

After Wroblewski graduated from high school, in 1984, he began searching for his "purpose in life," as he put it, working variously as a municipal clerk, a locksmith, a soldier, an aircraft mechanic, and, in defiance of the Communist government, a union organizer allied with Solidarity. In 1994, five years after the Communist regime collapsed, he joined the newly refashioned police force. Salaries for police officers in Poland were, and remain, dismal—a rookie earns only a few thousand dollars a year—and Wroblewski had a wife and two children to support. Still, he had finally found a position that suited him. A man with a stark Catholic vision of good and evil, he relished chasing criminals, and after putting away his first murderer he hung a pair of goat horns on his office wall, to symbolize the capture of his prey. During his few free hours, he studied psychology at a local university: he wanted to understand the criminal mind.

Wroblewski had heard about the murder of Janiszewski, but he was unfamiliar with the details, and he sat down at his desk to review the file. He knew that, in cold cases, the key to solving the crime is often an overlooked clue buried in the original file. He studied the pathologist's report and the photographs of the crime scene. The level of brutality, Wroblewski thought, suggested that the perpetrator, or perpetrators, had a deep grievance against Janiszewski. Moreover, the virtual absence of clothing on Janiszewski's battered body indicated that he had been stripped, in an attempt to humiliate him. (There was no evidence of sexual abuse.) According to Janiszewski's wife, her husband always carried credit cards, but they had not been used after the crime—another indication that this was no mere robbery.

Wroblewski read the various statements that had been given to the local police. The most revealing was from Janiszewski's mother, who had worked as a bookkeeper in his advertising firm. On the day that her son disappeared, she stated, a man had called the office at around 9:30 A.M., looking for him. The caller made an urgent request. "Could you make three signs, quite big ones, and the third one as big as a billboard?" he asked. When she inquired further, he said, "I will not talk to you about this," demanding again to speak to her son. She explained that he was out of the office, but she gave the caller Janiszewski's cell-phone number. The man hung up. He had not identified himself, and Janiszewski's mother had not recognized his voice, though she thought that he sounded "professional." During the conversation, she had heard noise in the background, a dull roar. Later, when her son showed up at the office, she asked him if the customer had called, and Janiszewski replied that they had arranged to meet that afternoon. According to a receptionist in the building, who was the last known person to see Janiszewski alive, he departed the office at around four o'clock. He left his car, a Peugeot, in the parking lot, which his family said was very unusual: although he often met with customers away from the office, he habitually took his car.

Investigators, upon checking phone records, discovered that the call to Janiszewski's office had come from a phone booth down the street—this explained the background noise, Wroblewski thought. Records also indicated that, less than a minute after the call ended, someone at the same public phone had rung Janiszewski's cell phone. Though the calls were suspicious, Wroblewski could not be certain that the caller was a perpetrator, just as he could not yet say how many assailants were involved in the crime. Janiszewski was more than six feet tall and weighed some two hundred pounds, and tying him up and disposing of his body may have required accomplices. The receptionist reported that when Janiszewski left the office, she had seen two men seemingly trailing him, though she could not describe them in any detail. Whoever was behind the abduction, Wroblewski thought, had been extremely organized and shrewd. The mastermind—Wroblewski assumed it was a man, based on the caller's voice—must have studied Janiszewski's business routine and known how to lure him out of his office and, possibly, into a car.

Wroblewski pored over the materials, trying to find something more, yet he remained stymied. After several hours, he locked the file in his safe, but over the next several days and nights he took it out again and again. At one point, he realized that Janiszewski's cell phone had never been found. Wroblewski decided to see if the phone could be traced—an unlikely possibility. Poland lagged behind other European countries in technological development, and its financially strapped police force was only beginning to adopt more sophisticated methods of tracking cellular and computer communications. Nevertheless, Wroblewski had taken a keen interest in these new techniques, and he began an elaborate search, with the help of the department's recently hired telecommunications specialist. Although Janiszewski's telephone number had not been used since his disappearance, Wroblewski knew that cell phones often bear a serial number from the manufacturer, and his men contacted Janiszewski's wife, who provided a receipt containing this information. To Wroblewski's astonishment, he and his colleague soon found a match: a cell phone with the same serial number had been sold on Allegro, an Internet auction site, four days after Janiszewski disappeared. The seller had logged in as ChrisB[7], who, investigators learned, was a thirty-year-old Polish intellectual named Krystian Bala.

It seemed inconceivable that a murderer who had orchestrated such a well-planned crime would have sold the victim's cell phone on an Internet auction site. Bala, Wroblewski realized, could have obtained it from someone else, or purchased it at a pawnshop, or even found it on the street. Bala had since moved abroad, and could not be easily reached, but as Wroblewski checked into his background he discovered that he had recently published a novel called "Amok." Wroblewski obtained a copy, which had on the cover a surreal image of a goat—an ancient symbol of the Devil. Like the works of the French novelist Michel Houellebecq, the book is sadistic, pornographic, and creepy. The main character, who narrates the story, is a bored Polish intellectual who, when not musing about philosophy, is drinking and having sex with women.

Wroblewski, who read mostly history books, was shocked by the novel's contents, which were not only decadent but vehemently anti-Church. He made note of the fact that the narrator murders a female lover for no reason ("What had come over me? What the hell did I do?") and conceals the act so well that he is never caught. Wroblewski was struck, in particular, by the killer's method: "I tightened the noose around her neck." Wroblewski then noticed something else: the killer's name is Chris, the English version of the author's first name. It was also the name that Krystian Bala had posted on the Internet auction site. Wroblewski began to read the book more closely—a hardened cop turned literary detective.

FOUR YEARS EARLIER, in the spring of 1999, Krystian Bala sat in a café in Wroclaw, wearing a three-piece suit. He was going to be filmed for a documentary called "Young Money," about the new generation of businessmen in the suddenly freewheeling Polish capitalist system. Bala, who was then twenty-six, had been chosen for the documentary because he had started an industrial cleaning business that used advanced machinery from the United States. Though Bala had dressed up for the occasion, he looked more like a brooding poet than like a businessman. He had dark, ruminative eyes and thick curly brown hair. Slender and sensitive-looking, he was so handsome that his friends had nicknamed him Amour. He chain-smoked and spoke like a professor of philosophy, which is what he had trained, and still hoped, to become. "I don't feel like a businessman," Bala later told the interviewer, adding that he had always "dreamed of an academic career."

He had been the equivalent of high-school valedictorian and, as an undergraduate at the University of Wroclaw, which he attended from 1992 to 1997, he was considered one of the brightest philosophy students. The night before an exam, while other

students were cramming, he often stayed out drinking and ca-
rousing, only to show up the next morning, dishevelled and hung
over, and score the highest marks. "One time, I went out with
him and nearly died taking the exam," his close friend and former
classmate Lotar Rasinski, who now teaches philosophy at another
university in Wroclaw, recalls. Beata Sierocka, who was one of
Bala's philosophy professors, says that he had a voracious appetite
for learning and an "inquisitive, rebellious mind."

Bala, who often stayed with his parents in Chojnow, a provincial town outside Wroclaw, began bringing home stacks of
philosophy books, lining the hallways and filling the basement.
Poland's philosophy departments had long been dominated by
Marxism, which, like liberalism, is rooted in Enlightenment no-
tions of reason and in the pursuit of universal truths. Bala, however, was drawn to the radical arguments of Ludwig Wittgenstein,
who maintained that language, like a game of chess, is essentially
a social activity. Bala often referred to Wittgenstein as "my master." He also seized on Friedrich Nietzsche's notorious contention
that "there are no facts, only interpretations" and that "truths are
illusions which we have forgotten are illusions."

For Bala, such subversive ideas made particular sense after the
collapse of the Soviet Empire, where language and facts had been
wildly manipulated to create a false sense of history. "The end of
Communism marked the death of one of the great meta-narratives,"
Bala later told me, paraphrasing the post-modernist Jean-François
Lyotard. Bala once wrote in an e-mail to a friend, "Read Wittgenstein and Nietzsche! Twenty times each!"

Bala's father, Stanislaw, who was a construction worker and
a taxi-driver ("I'm a simple, uneducated man," he says), was proud
of his son's academic accomplishments. Still, he occasionally
wanted to throw away Krystian's books and force him to "plant
with me in the garden." Stanislaw sometimes worked in France,
and during the summer Krystian frequently went with him to
earn extra money for his studies. "He would bring suitcases stuffed

with books," Stanislaw recalls. "He would work all day and study through the night. I used to joke that he knew more about France from books than from seeing it."

By then, Bala had become entranced by French postmodernists such as Jacques Derrida and Michel Foucault. He was particularly interested in Derrida's notion that not only is language too unstable to pinpoint any absolute truth; human identity itself is the malleable product of language. Bala wrote a thesis about Richard Rorty, the American philosopher, who famously declared, "The guise of convincing your peers is the very face of truth itself."

Bala interpreted these thinkers idiosyncratically, pulling threads here and there, and often twisting and turning and distorting them, until he had braided them into his own radical philosophy. To amuse himself, he began constructing myths about himself— an adventure in Paris, a romance with a schoolmate—and tried to convince friends that they were true. "He would tell these tall stories about himself," Rasinski says. "If he told one person, and that person then told someone else, who told someone else, it became true. It existed in the language." Rasinski adds, "Krystian even had a term for it. He called it 'mytho-creativity.'" Before long, friends had trouble distinguishing his real character from the one he had invented. In an e-mail to a friend, Bala said, "If I ever write an autobiography, it will be full of myths!"

Bala cast himself as an enfant terrible who sought out what Foucault had called a "limit-experience": he wanted to push the boundaries of language and human existence, to break free of what he deemed to be the hypocritical and oppressive "truths" of Western society, including taboos on sex and drugs. Foucault himself was drawn to homosexual sadomasochism. Bala devoured the works of Georges Bataille, who vowed to "brutally oppose all systems" and who once contemplated carrying out human sacrifices; and William Burroughs, who swore to use language to "rub out the word"; and the Marquis de Sade, who demanded, "O man! Is it for you to say what is good or what is evil?" Bala boasted about his drunken visits to brothels and his submission to temptations of the flesh. He told friends that he hated "conventions" and was "capable of anything," and he insisted, "I will not live long but I will live furiously!"

Some people found such proclamations juvenile, even ridiculous; others were mesmerized by them. "There were legends that no woman could resist him," one friend recalled. Those closest to him regarded his tales simply as playful confabulations. Sierocka, his former professor, says that Bala, in reality, was always "kind, energetic, hardworking, and principled." His friend Rasinski says, "Krystian liked the idea of being this Nietzschean superman, but anyone who knew him well realized that, as with his language games, he was just playing around."

In 1995, Bala, belying his libertine posture, married his high-school sweetheart, Stanislawa—or Stasia, as he called her. Stasia, who had dropped out of high school and worked as a secretary, showed little interest in language or philosophy. Bala's mother opposed the marriage, believing Stasia was ill-suited for her son. "I thought he should at least wait until he had finished his studies," she says. But Bala insisted that he wanted to take care of Stasia, who had always loved him, and in 1997 their son Kacper was born. That year, Bala graduated from the university with the highest possible marks, and enrolled in its Ph.D. program in philosophy. Although he received a full academic scholarship, he struggled to support his family, and soon left school to open his cleaning business. In the documentary on Poland's new generation of businessmen, Bala says, "Reality came and kicked me in the ass." With an air of resignation, he continues, "Once, I planned to paint graffiti on walls. Now I'm trying to wash it off."

He was not a good businessman. Whenever money came in, colleagues say, instead of investing it in his company he spent it. By 2000, he had filed for bankruptcy. His marriage also collapsed. "The basic problem was women," his wife later said. "I knew that he was having an affair." After Stasia separated from him, he seemed despondent and left Poland, travelling to the United States, and later to Asia, where he taught English and scuba diving.

He began to work intensively on "Amok," which encapsulated all his philosophical obsessions. The story mirrors "Crime and Punishment," in which Raskolnikov, convinced that he is a superior being who can deliver his own form of justice, murders a wretched pawnbroker. "Wouldn't thousands of good deeds make up for one tiny little crime?" Raskolnikov asks. If Raskolnikov is a Frankenstein's monster of modernity, then Chris, the protagonist of "Amok," is a monster of postmodernity. In his view, not only is there no sacred being ("God, if you only existed, you'd see how sperm looks on blood"); there is also no truth ("Truth is being displaced by narrative"). One character admits that he doesn't know which of his constructed personalities is real, and Chris says, "I'm a good liar, because I believe in the lies myself."

Unbound by any sense of truth—moral, scientific, historical, biographical, legal—Chris embarks on a grisly rampage. After his wife catches him having sex with her best friend and leaves him (Chris says that he has, at least, "stripped her of her illusions"), he sleeps with one woman after another, the sex ranging from numbing to sadomasochistic. Inverting convention, he lusts after ugly women, insisting that they are "more real, more touchable, more alive." He drinks too much. He spews vulgarities, determined, as one character puts it, to pulverize the language, to "screw it like no one else has ever screwed it." He mocks traditional philosophers and blasphemes the Catholic Church. In one scene, he gets drunk with a friend and steals from a church a statue of St. Anthony—the Egyptian saint who lived secluded in the desert, battling the temptations of the Devil, and who fascinated Foucault. (Foucault, describing how St. Anthony had turned to the Bible to ward off the Devil, only to encounter a bloody description of Jews slaughtering their enemies, writes that "evil is not embodied in individuals" but "incorporated in words" and that even a book of salvation can open "the gates to Hell.")

Finally, Chris, repudiating what is considered the ultimate moral truth, kills his girlfriend Mary. "I tightened the noose around her neck, holding her down with one hand," he says. "With my other hand, I stabbed the knife below her left breast. . . . Everything was covered in blood." He then ejaculates on her. In a perverse echo of Wittgenstein's notion that some actions defy language, Chris says of the killing, "There was no noise, no words, no movement. Complete silence."

In "Crime and Punishment," Raskolnikov confesses his sins and is punished for them, while being redeemed by the love of a woman named Sonya, who helps to guide him back toward a premodern Christian order. But Chris never removes what he calls his "white gloves of silence," and he is never punished. ("Murder leaves no stain," he declares.) And his wife—who, not coincidentally, is also named Sonya—never returns to him.

The style and structure of "Amok," which is derivative of many postmodern novels, reinforces the idea that truth is illusory—what is a novel, anyway, but a lie, a mytho-creation? Bala's narrator often addresses the reader, reminding him that he is being seduced by a work of fiction. "I am starting my story," Chris says. "I must avoid boring you." In another typical flourish, Chris reveals that he is reading a book about the violent rebellion of a young author with a "guilty conscience"—in other words, the same story as "Amok."

Throughout the book, Bala plays with words in order to emphasize their slipperiness. The title of one chapter, "Screwdriver," refers simultaneously to the tool, the cocktail, and Chris's sexual behavior. Even when Chris slaughters Mary, it feels like a language game. "I pulled the knife and rope from underneath the bed, as if I were about to begin a children's fairy tale," Chris says. "Then I started unwinding this fable of rope, and to make it more interesting I started to make a noose. It took me two million years."

Bala finished the book toward the end of 2002. He had given

Chris a biography similar to his own, blurring the boundary between author and narrator. He even posted sections of the book on a blog called Amok, and during discussions with readers he wrote comments under the name Chris, as if he were the character. After the book came out, in 2003, an interviewer asked him, "Some authors write only to release their . . . Mr. Hyde, the dark side of their psyche—do you agree?" Bala joked in response, "I know what you are driving at, but I won't comment. It might turn out that Krystian Bala is the creation of Chris . . . not the other way around."

Few bookstores in Poland carried "Amok," in part because of the novel's shocking content, and those which did placed it on the highest shelves, out of the reach of children. (The book has not been translated into English.) On the Internet, a couple of reviewers praised "Amok." "We haven't had this kind of book in Polish literature," one wrote, adding that it was "paralyzingly realistic, totally vulgar, full of paranoid and delirious images." Another called it a "masterpiece of illusion." Yet most readers considered the book, as one major Polish newspaper put it, to be "without literary merit." Even one of Bala's friends dismissed it as "rubbish." When Sierocka, the philosophy professor, opened it, she was stunned by its crude language, which was the antithesis of the straightforward, intelligent style of the papers that Bala had written at the university. "Frankly, I found the book hard to read," she says. An ex-girlfriend of Bala's later said, "I was shocked by the book, because he never used those words. He never acted obscenely or vulgar toward me. Our sex life was normal."

Many of Bala's friends believed that he wanted to do in his fiction what he never did in life: shatter every taboo. In the interview that Bala gave after "Amok" was published, he said, "I wrote the book not caring about any convention. . . . A simple reader will find interesting only a few violent scenes with a graphic description of people having sex. But if someone really looks, he will see that these scenes are intended to awaken the reader and . . . show how fucked up and impoverished and hypocritical this world is."

By Bala's own estimate, "Amok" sold only a couple of thousand copies. But he was confident that it would eventually find its place among the great works of literature. "I'm truly convinced that one day my book will be appreciated," he said. "History teaches that some works of art have to wait ages before they are recognized."

In at least one respect, the book succeeded. Chris was so authentically creepy that it was hard not to believe that he was the product of a genuinely disturbed mind, and that he and the author were indeed indistinguishable. On Bala's Web site, readers described him and his work as "grotesque," "sexist," and "psychopathic." During an Internet conversation, in June of 2003, a friend told Bala that his book did not give the reader a good impression of him. When Bala assured her that the book was fiction, she insisted that Chris's musings had to be "your thoughts." Bala became irritated. Only a fool, he said, would believe that.

DETECTIVE WROBLEWSKI UNDERLINED various passages as he studied "Amok." At first glance, few details of Mary's murder resembled the killing of Janiszewski. Most conspicuously, the victim in the novel is a woman, and the killer's longtime friend. Moreover, although Mary has a noose around her neck, she gets stabbed, with a Japanese knife, and Janiszewski wasn't. One detail in the book, however, chilled Wroblewski: after the murder, Chris says, "I sell the Japanese knife on an Internet auction." The similarity to the selling of Janiszewski's cell phone on the Internet—a detail that the police had never released to the public—seemed too extraordinary to be a coincidence.

At one point in "Amok," Chris intimates that he has also killed a man. When one of his girlfriends doubts his endless mytho-creations, he says, "Which story didn't you believe—that my radio station went bankrupt or that I killed a man who behaved inappropriately toward me ten years ago?" He adds of the murder, "Everyone considers it a fable. Maybe it's better that way. Fuck. Sometimes I don't believe it myself."

Wroblewski had never read about postmodernism or language games. For him, facts were as indissoluble as bullets. You either killed someone or you didn't. His job was to piece together a logical chain of evidence that revealed the irrefutable truth. But Wroblewski also believed that, in order to catch a killer, you had to understand the social and psychological forces that had formed him. And so, if Bala had murdered Janiszewski or participated in the crime—as Wroblewski now fully suspected—then Wroblewski, the empiricist, would have to become a postmodernist.

To the surprise of members of his detective squad, Wroblewski made copies of the novel and handed them out. Everyone was assigned a chapter to "interpret": to try to find any clues, any coded messages, any parallels with reality. Because Bala was living outside the country, Wroblewski warned his colleagues not to do anything that might alarm the author. Wroblewski knew that if Bala did not voluntarily return home to see his family, as he periodically did, it would be virtually impossible for the Polish police to apprehend him. At least for the moment, the police had to refrain from questioning Bala's family and friends. Instead, Wroblewski and his team combed public records and interrogated Bala's more distant associates, constructing a profile of the suspect, which they then compared with the profile of Chris in the novel. Wroblewski kept an unofficial scorecard: both Bala and his literary creation were consumed by philosophy, had been abandoned by their wives, had a company go bankrupt, travelled around the world, and drank too much. Wroblewski discovered that Bala had once been detained by the police, and when he obtained the official report it was as if he had already read it. As Bala's friend Pawel, who was detained with him, later testified in court, "Krystian came to me in the evening and had a bottle with

him. We started drinking. Actually, we drank till dawn." Pawel
went on, "The alcohol ran out, so we went to a store to buy another bottle. As we were returning from the shop we passed by a
church, and this is when we had a very stupid idea."   '

"What idea did you have?" the judge asked him.

"We went into the church and we saw St. Anthony's figure,
and we took it."

"What for?" the judge inquired.

"Well, we wanted a third person to drink with. Krystian said
afterward that we were crazy."

In the novel, when the police catch Chris and his friend drinking beside the statue of St. Anthony, Chris says, "We were threatened by prison! I was speechless. . . . I do not feel like a criminal,
but I became one. I had done much worse things in my life, and
never suffered any consequences."

Wroblewski began to describe "Amok" as a "road map" to a
crime, but some authorities objected that he was pushing the investigation in a highly suspect direction. The police asked a criminal psychologist to analyze the character of Chris, in order to gain
insight into Bala. The psychologist wrote in her report, "The
character of Chris is an egocentric man with great intellectual
ambitions. He perceives himself as an intellectual with his own
philosophy, based on his education and high I.Q. His way of
functioning shows features of psychopathic behavior. He is testing
the limits to see if he can actually carry out his . . . sadistic fantasies. He treats people with disrespect, considers them to be intel-
lectually inferior to himself, uses manipulation to fulfill his own
needs, and is determined to satiate his sexual desires in a hedonis-
tic way. If such a character were real—a true living person—his
personality could have been shaped by a highly unrealistic sense
of his own worth. It could also be . . . a result of psychological
wounds and his insecurities as a man . . . pathological relationships with his parents or unacceptable homosexual tendencies."
The psychologist acknowledged the links between Bala and Chris,

such as divorce and philosophical interests, but cautioned that such overlaps were "common with novelists." And she warned, "Basing an analysis of the author on his fictional character would be a gross violation."

Wroblewski knew that details in the novel did not qualify as evidence—they had to be corroborated independently. So far, though, he had only one piece of concrete evidence linking Bala to the victim: the cell phone. In February, 2002, the Polish television program "997," which, like "America's Most Wanted," solicits the public's help in solving crimes (997 is the emergency telephone number in Poland), aired a segment devoted to Janiszewski's murder. Afterward, the show posted on its Web site the latest news about the progress of the investigation, and asked for tips. Wroblewski and his men carefully analyzed the responses. Over the years, hundreds of people had visited the Web site, from places as far away as Japan, South Korea, and the United States. Yet the police didn't turn up a single fruitful lead.

When Wroblewski and the telecommunications expert checked to see if Bala had purchased or sold any other items on the Internet while logged on as ChrisB[7], they made a curious discovery. On October 17, 2000, a month before Janiszewski was kidnapped, Bala had clicked on the Allegro auction site for a police manual called "Accidental, Suicidal, or Criminal Hanging." "Hanging a mature, conscious, healthy, and physically fit person is very difficult even for several people," the manual stated, and described various ways that a noose might be tied. Bala did not purchase the book on Allegro, and it was unclear if he obtained it elsewhere, but that he was seeking such information was, at least to Wroblewski, a sign of premeditation. Still, Wroblewski knew that if he wanted to convict Bala of murder he would need more than the circumstantial evidence he had gathered: he would need a confession.

Bala remained abroad, supporting himself by publishing articles in travel magazines, and by teaching English and scuba diving. In

January of 2005, while visiting Micronesia, he sent an e-mail to a friend, saying, "I'm writing this letter from paradise."

Finally, that fall, Wroblewski learned that Bala was coming home.

"AT APPROXIMATELY 2:30 P.M., after leaving a drugstore at Legnicka Street, in Chojnow, I was attacked by three men," Bala later wrote in a statement, describing what happened to him on September 5, 2005, shortly after he returned to his home town. "One of them twisted my arms behind my back; another squeezed my throat so that I could not speak, and could barely breathe. Meanwhile, the third one handcuffed me."

Bala said that his attackers were tall and muscular, with close-cropped hair, like skinheads. Without telling Bala who they were or what they wanted, they forced him into a dark-green vehicle and slipped a black plastic bag over his head. "I couldn't see anything," Bala said. "They ordered me to lie face down on the floor."

Bala said that his assailants continued to beat him, shouting, "You fucking prick! You motherfucker!" He pleaded with them to leave him alone and not hurt him. Then he heard one of the men say on a cell phone, "Hi, boss! We got the shithead! Yes, he's still alive. So now what? At the meeting point?" The man continued, "And what about the money? Will we get it today?"

Bala said he thought that, because he lived abroad and was known to be a writer, the men assumed that he was wealthy and were seeking a ransom. "I tried to explain to them that I didn't have money," Bala stated. The more he spoke, though, the more brutally they attacked him.

Eventually, the car came to a stop, apparently in a wooded area. "We can dig a hole for this shit here and bury him," one of the men said. Bala struggled to breathe through the plastic bag. "I thought that this was going to be the last moment of my life, but suddenly they got back into the car and began driving again," he said.

After a long time, the car came to another stop, and the men shoved him out of the car and into a building. "I didn't hear a door, but because there was no wind or sun I assumed that we had entered," Bala said. The men threatened to kill him if he didn't coöperate, then led him upstairs into a small room, where they stripped him, deprived him of food, beat him, and began to interrogate him. Only then, Bala said, did he realize that he was in police custody and had been brought in for questioning by a man called Jack Sparrow.

"NONE OF IT HAPPENED," Wroblewski later told me. "We used standard procedures and followed the letter of the law."

According to Wroblewski and other officers, they apprehended Bala by the drugstore without violence and drove him to police headquarters in Wroclaw. Wroblewski and Bala sat facing each other in the detective's cramped office; a light bulb overhead cast a faint glow, and Bala could see on the wall the goat horns that eerily resembled the image on the cover of his book. Bala appeared gentle and scholarly, yet Wroblewski recalled how, in "Amok," Chris says, "It's easier for people to imagine that Christ can turn urine into beer than that someone like me can send to Hell some asshole smashed into a lump of ground meat."

Wroblewski initially circled around the subject of the murder, trying to elicit offhand information about Bala's business and his relationships, and concealing what the police already knew about the crime—an interrogator's chief advantage. When Wroblewski did confront him about the killing, Bala looked dumbfounded. "I didn't know Dariusz Janiszewski," he said. "I know nothing about the murder."

Wroblewski pressed him about the curious details in "Amok." Bala later told me, "It was insane. He treated the book as if it were my literal autobiography. He must have read the book a hundred times. He knew it by heart." When Wroblewski mentioned several "facts" in the novel, such as the theft of the statue of St. Anthony, Bala acknowledged that he had drawn certain elements from his life. As Bala put it to me, "Sure, I'm guilty of that. Show me an author who *doesn't* do that."

Wroblewski then played his trump card: the cell phone. How did Bala get hold of it? Bala said that he couldn't remember—it was five years ago. Then he said that he must have bought the phone at a pawnshop, as he had done several times in the past. He agreed to take a polygraph test.

Wroblewski helped to prepare the questions for the examiner, who asked:

> *Just before Dariusz Janiszewski lost his life, did you know this would happen?*
> *Were you the one who killed him?*
> *Do you know who actually murdered him?*
> *Did you know Janiszewski?*
> *Were you in the place where Janiszewski was held hostage?*

Bala replied no to each question. Periodically, he seemed to slow his breathing, in the manner of a scuba diver. The examiner wondered if he was trying to manipulate the test. On some questions, the examiner suspected Bala of lying, but, over all, the results were inconclusive.

In Poland, after a suspect is detained for forty-eight hours, the prosecutor in the case is required to present his evidence before a judge and charge the suspect; otherwise, the police must release him. The case against Bala remained weak. All Wroblewski and the police had was the cell phone, which Bala could have obtained, as he claimed, from a pawnshop; the sketchy results of a polygraph, a notoriously unreliable test; a book on hanging that Bala might not even have purchased; and clues possibly embedded in a novel. Wroblewski had no motive or confession. As a result, the authorities charged Bala only with selling stolen property—

Janiszewski's phone—and with paying a bribe in an unrelated
business matter, which Wroblewski had uncovered during the
course of his investigation. Wroblewski knew that neither charge
would likely carry any jail time, and although Bala had to remain
in the country and relinquish his passport, he was otherwise a free
man. "I had spent two years trying to build a case, and I was
watching it all collapse," Wroblewski recalled.

Later, as he was flipping through Bala's passport, Wroblewski
noticed stamps from Japan, South Korea, and the United States.
He remembered that the Web site of the television show "997"
had recorded page views from all of those countries—a fact that
had baffled investigators. Why would anyone so far away be interested in a local Polish murder? Wroblewski compared the periods
when Bala was in each country with the timing of the page views.
The dates matched.

BALA, meanwhile, was becoming a cause célèbre. As Wroblewski
continued to investigate him for murder, Bala filed a formal grievance with the authorities, claiming that he had been kidnapped and
tortured. When Bala told his friend Rasinski that he was being
persecuted for his art, Rasinski was incredulous. "I figured that he
was testing out some crazy idea for his next novel," he recalls. Soon
after, Wroblewski questioned Rasinski about his friend. "That's
when I realized that Krystian was telling the truth," Rasinski says.

Rasinski was shocked when Wroblewski began to grill him
about "Amok." "I told him that I recognized some details from
real life, but that, to me, the book was a work of fiction," Rasinski
says. "This was crazy. You cannot prosecute a man based on the
novel he wrote." Beata Sierocka, Bala's former professor, who was
also called in for questioning, says that she felt as if she were being
interrogated by "literary theorists."

As outrage over the investigation mounted, one of Bala's girlfriends, Denise Rinehart, set up a defense committee on his

behalf. Rinehart, an American theatre director, met Bala while she was studying in Poland, in 2001, and they had subsequently travelled together to the United States and South Korea. Rinehart solicited support over the Internet, writing, "Krystian is the author of a fictional philosophical book called 'Amok.' A lot of the language and content is strong and there are several metaphors that might be considered against the Catholic Church and Polish tradition. During his brutal interrogation they referenced his book numerous times, citing it as proof of his guilt."

Dubbing the case the Sprawa Absurd—the Absurd Matter— the committee contacted human-rights organizations and International PEN. Before long, the Polish Justice Ministry was deluged with letters on Bala's behalf from around the world. One said, "Mr. Bala deserves his rights in accordance with Article 19 of the U.N. Declaration of Human Rights that guarantees the right to freedom of expression. . . . We urge you to insure there is an immediate and thorough investigation into his kidnapping and imprisonment and that all of those found responsible are brought to justice."

Bala, writing in imperfect English, sent out frantic bulletins to the defense committee, which published them in a newsletter. In a bulletin on September 13, 2005, Bala warned that he was being "spied" on and said, "I want you to know that I will fight until the end." The next day, he said of Wroblewski and the police, "They have ruined my family life. We will never talk loud at home again. We will never use Internet freely again. We will never make any phone calls not thinking about who is listening. My mother takes some pills to stay calm. Otherwise she would get insane, because of this absurd accusation. My old father smokes 50 cigs a day and I smoke three packs. We all sleep 3–4 hours daily and we are afraid of leaving a house. Every single bark of our little dog alerts us and we don't know what or who to expect. It's a terror! Quiet Terror!"

The Polish authorities, meanwhile, had launched an internal investigation into Bala's allegations of mistreatment. In early

2006, after months of probing, the investigators declared that they had found no corroborating evidence. In this instance, they insisted, Bala's tale was indeed a mytho-creation.

"I HAVE INFECTED YOU," Chris warns the reader at the beginning of "Amok." "You will not be able to get free of me." Wroblewski remained haunted by one riddle in the novel, which, he believed, was crucial to solving the case. A character asks Chris, "Who was the one-eyed man among the blind?" The phrase derives from Erasmus (1469–1536), the Dutch theologian and classical scholar, who said, "In the kingdom of the blind, the one-eyed man is king." Who in "Amok," Wroblewski wondered, was the one-eyed man? And who were the blind men? In the novel's last line, Chris suddenly claims that he has solved the riddle, explaining, "This was the one killed by blind jealousy." But the sentence, with its strange lack of context, made little sense.

One hypothesis based on "Amok" was that Bala had murdered Janiszewski after beginning a homosexual affair with him. In the novel, after Chris's closest friend confesses that he is gay, Chris says that part of him wanted to "strangle him with a rope" and "chop a hole in a frozen river and dump him there." Still, the theory seemed dubious. Wroblewski had thoroughly investigated Janiszewski's background and there was no indication that he was gay.

Another theory was that the murder was the culmination of Bala's twisted philosophy—that he was a postmodern version of Nathan Leopold and Richard Loeb, the two brilliant Chicago students who, in the nineteen-twenties, were so entranced by Nietzsche's ideas that they killed a fourteen-year-old boy to see if they could execute the perfect murder and become supermen. At their trial, in which they received life sentences, Clarence Darrow, the legendary defense attorney who represented them, said of Leopold, "Here is a boy at sixteen or seventeen becoming obsessed with these doctrines. It was not a casual bit of philosophy with him; it was his life." Darrow, trying to save the boys from the death penalty, concluded, "Is there any blame attached because somebody took Nietzsche's philosophy seriously and fashioned his life upon it? . . . It is hardly fair to hang a nineteen-year-old boy for the philosophy that was taught him at the university."

In "Amok," Chris clearly aspires to be a postmodern *Übermensch*, speaking of his "will to power" and insisting that anyone who is "unable to kill should not stay alive." Yet these sentiments did not fully explain the murder of the unknown man in the novel, who, Chris says, had "behaved inappropriately" toward him. Chris, alluding to what happened between them, says teasingly, "Maybe he didn't do anything significant, but the most vicious Devil is in the details." If Bala's philosophy had justified, in his mind, a break from moral constraints, including the prohibition on murder, these passages suggested that there was still another motive, a deep personal connection to the victim—something that the brutality of the crime also indicated. With Bala unable to leave Poland, Wroblewski and his team began to question the suspect's closest friends and family.

Many of those interrogated saw Bala positively—"a bright, interesting man," one of his former girlfriends said of him. Bala had recently received a reference from a past employer at an English-instruction school in Poland, which described him as "intelligent," "inquisitive," and "easy to get along with," and praised his "keen sense of humor." The reference concluded, "With no reservation, I highly recommend Krystian Bala for any teaching position with children."

Yet, as Wroblewski and his men deepened their search for the "Devil in the details," a darker picture of Bala's life began to emerge. The years 1999 and 2000, during which time his business and his marriage collapsed—and Janiszewski was murdered—had been especially troubled. A friend recalled that Bala once "started to behave vulgarly and wanted to take his clothes off and show his manliness." The family babysitter described him as increasingly drunk and out of control. She said he constantly berated his wife, Stasia, shouting at her that "she slept around and cheated on him."

According to several people, after Bala and his wife separated, in 2000, he remained possessive of her. A friend, who called Bala an "authoritarian type," said of him, "He continuously controlled Stasia, and checked her phones." At a New Year's Eve party in 2000, just weeks after Janiszewski's body was found, Bala thought a bartender was making advances toward his wife and, as one witness put it, "went crazy." Bala screamed that he would take care of the bartender and that he had "already dealt with such a guy." At the time, Stasia and her friends had dismissed his drunken outburst. Even so, it took five people to restrain Bala; as one of them told police, "He was running amok."

As Wroblewski and his men were trying to fix on a motive, other members of the squad stepped up their efforts to trace the two suspicious telephone calls that had been made to Janiszewski's office and to his cell phone on the day he disappeared. The public telephone from which both calls were made was operated with a card. Each card was embedded with a unique number that registered with the phone company whenever it was used. Not long after Bala was released, the telecommunications expert on the Janiszewski case was able to determine the number on the caller's card. Once the police had that information, officials could trace all the telephone numbers dialled with that same card. Over a three-month period, thirty-two calls had been made. They included calls to Bala's parents, his girlfriend, his friends, and a business associate. "The truth was becoming clearer and clearer," Wroblewski said.

Wroblewski and his team soon uncovered another connection between the victim and the suspect. Malgorzata Drozdzal, a friend of Stasia's, told the police that in the summer of 2000 she had gone with Stasia to a night club called Crazy Horse, in Wroclaw. While Drozdzal was dancing, she saw Stasia talking to a man with long hair and bright-blue eyes. She recognized him from around town. His name was Dariusz Janiszewski.

Wroblewski had one last person to question: Stasia. But she had steadfastly refused to coöperate. Perhaps she was afraid of her ex-husband. Perhaps she believed Bala's claim that he was being persecuted by the police. Or perhaps she dreaded the idea of one day telling her son that she had betrayed his father.

Wroblewski and his men approached Stasia again, this time showing her sections of "Amok," which was published after she and Bala had split up, and which she had never looked at closely. According to Polish authorities, Stasia examined passages involving Chris's wife, Sonya, and was so disturbed by the character's similarities to her that she finally agreed to talk.

She confirmed that she had met Janiszewski at Crazy Horse. "I had ordered French fries, and I asked a man next to the bar whether the French fries were ready," Stasia recalled. "That man was Dariusz." They spent the entire night talking, she said, and Janiszewski gave her his phone number. Later, they went on a date and checked into a motel. But before anything happened, she said, Janiszewski admitted that he was married, and she left. "Since I know what it's like to be a wife whose husband betrays her, I didn't want to do that to another woman," Stasia said. The difficulties in Janiszewski's marriage soon ended, and he and Stasia never went out together again.

Several weeks after her date with Janiszewski, Stasia said, Bala showed up at her place in a drunken fury, demanding that she admit to having an affair with Janiszewski. He broke down the front door and struck her. He shouted that he had hired a private detective and knew everything. "He also mentioned that he had visited Dariusz's office, and described it to me," Stasia recalled. "Then he said he knew which hotel we went to and what room we were in."

Later, when she learned that Janiszewski had disappeared, Stasia said, she asked Bala if he had anything to do with it, and he said no. She did not pursue the matter, believing that Bala, for all his tumultuous behavior, was incapable of murder.

For the first time, Wroblewski thought he understood the last line of "Amok": "This was the one killed by blind jealousy."

Spectators flooded into the courtroom in Wroclaw on February 22, 2007, the first day of Bala's trial. There were philosophers, who argued with each other over the consequences of postmodernism; young lawyers, who wanted to learn about the police department's new investigative techniques; and reporters, who chronicled every tantalizing detail. "Killing doesn't make much of an impression in the twenty-first century, but allegedly killing and then writing about it in a novel is front-page news," a front-page article in *Angora,* a weekly based in Lodz, declared.

The judge, Lydia Hojenska, sat at the head of the courtroom, beneath an emblem of the white Polish eagle. In accordance with Polish law, the presiding judge, along with another judge and three citizens, acted as the jury. The defense and the prosecution sat at two unadorned wooden tables; next to the prosecutors were Janiszewski's widow and his parents, his mother holding a picture of her son. The public congregated in the back of the room, and in the last row was a stout, nervous woman with short red hair, who looked as if her own life were at stake. It was Bala's mother, Teresa; his father was too distraught to attend.

Everyone's attention, it seemed, was directed toward a zoolike cage near the center of the courtroom. It was almost nine feet high and twenty feet long, and had thick metal bars. Standing in the middle of it, wearing a suit and peering out calmly through his spectacles, was Krystian Bala. He faced up to twenty-five years in prison.

A trial is predicated on the idea that truth is obtainable. Yet it is also, as the writer Janet Malcolm has noted, a struggle between "two competing narratives," and "the story that can best withstand the attrition of the rules of evidence is the story that wins." In this case, the prosecution's narrative resembled that of "Amok": Bala, like his alter ego Chris, was a depraved hedonist, who, unbound by any sense of moral compunction, had murdered someone in a fit of jealous rage. The prosecution introduced files from Bala's computer, which Wroblewski and the police had seized during a raid of his parents' house. In one file, which had to be accessed with the password "amok," Bala catalogued, in graphic detail, sexual encounters with more than seventy women. The list included his wife, Stasia; a divorced cousin, who was "older" and "plump"; the mother of a friend, described as "old ass, hard-core action"; and a Russian "whore in an old car." The prosecution also presented e-mails in which Bala sounded unmistakably like Chris, using the same vulgar or arcane words, such as "joy juices" and "Madame Melancholy." In an angry e-mail to Stasia, Bala wrote, "Life is not only screwing, darling"—which echoed Chris's exclamation "Fucking is not the end of the world, Mary." A psychologist testified that "every author puts some part of his personality into his artistic creation," and that Chris and the defendant shared "sadistic" qualities.

During all this, Bala sat in the cage, taking notes on the proceedings or looking curiously out at the crowd. At times, he seemed to call into question the premise that the truth can be discerned. Under Polish law, the defendant can ask questions directly of the witnesses, and Bala eagerly did so, his professorial inquiries often phrased to reveal the Derridean instability of their testimony. When a former girlfriend testified that Bala once went out on her balcony drunk and acted as if he were on the verge of committing suicide, he asked her if her words might have multiple interpretations. "Could we just say that this is a matter of semantics—a misuse of the word 'suicide'?" he said.

But, as the trial wore on and the evidence mounted against

him, the postmodernist sounded increasingly like an empiricist, a man desperately looking to show gaps in the prosecution's chain of evidence. Bala noted that no one had seen him kidnap Janiszewski, or kill him, or dump his body. "I'd like to say that I never met Dariusz, and there is not a single witness who would confirm that I did so," Bala said. He complained that the prosecution was taking random incidents in his personal life and weaving them into a story that no longer resembled reality. The prosecutors were constructing a mytho-creation—or, as Bala's defense attorney put it to me, "the plot of a novel." According to the defense, the police and the media had been seduced by the most alluring story rather than by the truth. (Stories about the case had appeared under headlines such as "TRUTH STRANGER THAN FICTION" and "MURDER, HE WROTE.")

Bala had long subscribed to the postmodernist notion of "the death of the author"—that an author has no more access to the meaning of his literary work than anyone else. Yet, as the prosecution presented to the jury potentially incriminating details from "Amok," Bala complained that his novel was being misinterpreted. He insisted that the murder of Mary was simply a symbol of the "destruction of philosophy," and he made one last attempt to assert authorial control. As he later put it to me, "I'm the fucking author! I know what I meant."

In early September, the case went to the jury. Bala never took the stand, but in a statement he said, "I do believe the court will make the right decision and absolve me of all the charges." Wroblewski, who had been promoted to inspector, showed up in court, hoping to hear the verdict. "Even when you're sure of the facts, you wonder if someone else will see them the same way you do," he told me.

At last, the judges and jurors filed back into the courtroom. Bala's mother waited anxiously. She had never read "Amok," which contains a scene of Chris fantasizing about raping his mother. "I started to read the book, but it was too hard," she told me. "If someone else had written the book, maybe I would have read it, but I'm his mother." Bala's father appeared in the courtroom for the first time. He had read the novel, and though he had trouble understanding parts of it, he thought it was an important work of literature. "You can read it ten, twenty times, and each time discover something new in it," he said. On his copy, Bala had written an inscription to both his parents. It said, "Thank you for your . . . forgiveness of all my sins."

As Judge Hojenska read the verdict, Bala stood perfectly straight and still. Then came the one unmistakable word: "Guilty."

THE GRAY CINDER-BLOCK PRISON in Wroclaw looks like a relic of the Soviet era. After I slipped my visitor's pass through a tiny hole in the wall, a disembodied voice ordered me to the front of the building, where a solid gate swung open and a guard emerged, blinking in the sunlight. The guard waved me inside as the gate slammed shut behind us. After being searched, I was led through several dank interlocking chambers and into a small visitors' room with dingy wooden tables and chairs. Conditions in Polish prisons are notorious. Because of overcrowding, as many as seven people are often kept in a single cell. In 2004, prison inmates in Wroclaw staged a three-day hunger strike to protest overcrowding, poor food, and insufficient medical care. Violence is also a problem: only a few days before I arrived, I was told, a visitor had been stabbed to death by an inmate.

In the corner of the visitors' room was a slender, handsome man with wire-rimmed glasses and a navy-blue artist's smock over a T-shirt that said "University of Wisconsin." He was holding a book and looked like an American student abroad, and it took me a moment to realize that I was staring at Krystian Bala. "I'm glad you could come," he said as he shook my hand, leading me to one of the tables. "This whole thing is farce, like something out of

Kafka." He spoke clear English but with a heavy accent, so that his "s"es sounded like "z"s.

Sitting down, he leaned across the table, and I could see that his cheeks were drawn, he had dark circles around his eyes, and his curly hair was standing up in front, as if he had been anxiously running his fingers through it. "I am being sentenced to prison for twenty-five years for writing a book—a book!" he said. "It is ridiculous. It is bullshit. Excuse my language, but that is what it is. Look, I wrote a novel, a crazy novel. Is the book vulgar? Yes. Is it obscene? Yes. Is it bawdy? Yes. Is it offensive? Yes. I intended it to be. This was a work of provocation." He paused, searching for an example, then added, "I wrote, for instance, that it would be easier for Christ to come out of a woman's womb than for me—" He stopped, catching himself. "I mean, for the narrator to fuck her. You see, this is *supposed* to offend." He went on, "What is happening to me is like what happened to Salman Rushdie."

As he spoke, he placed the book that he was carrying on the table. It was a worn, battered copy of "Amok." When I asked Bala about the evidence against him, such as the cell phone and the calling card, he sounded evasive and, at times, conspiratorial. "The calling card is not mine," he said. "Someone is trying to set me up. I don't know who yet, but someone is out to destroy me." His hand touched mine. "Don't you see what they are doing? They are constructing this reality and forcing me to live inside it."

He said that he had filed an appeal, which cited logical and factual inconsistencies in the trial. For instance, one medical examiner said that Janiszewski had drowned, whereas another insisted that he had died of strangulation. The Judge herself had admitted that she was not sure if Bala had carried out the crime alone or with an accomplice.

When I asked him about "Amok," Bala became animated and gave direct and detailed answers. "The thesis of the book is not my personal thesis," he said. "I'm not an anti-feminist. I'm not a chauvinist. I'm not heartless. Chris, in many places, is my antihero."

Several times, he pointed to my pad and said, "Put this down" or "This is important." As he watched me taking notes, he said, with a hint of awe, "You see how crazy this is? You are here writing a story about a story I made up about a murder that never happened." On virtually every page of his copy of "Amok," he had underlined passages and scribbled notations in the margins. Later, he showed me several scraps of paper on which he had drawn elaborate diagrams revealing his literary influences. It was clear that, in prison, he had become even more consumed by the book. "I sometimes read pages aloud to my cellmates," he said.

One question that was never answered at the trial still hovered over the case: Why would someone commit a murder and then write about it in a novel that would help to get him caught? In "Crime and Punishment," Raskolnikov speculates that even the smartest criminal makes mistakes, because he "experiences at the moment of the crime a sort of failure of will and reason, which . . . are replaced by a phenomenal, childish thoughtlessness, just at the moment when reason and prudence are most necessary." "Amok," however, had been published three years after the murder. If Bala was guilty of murder, the cause was not a "failure of will and reason" but, rather, an excess of both.

Some observers wondered if Bala had wanted to get caught, or, at least, to unburden himself. In "Amok," Chris speaks of having a "guilty conscience" and of his desire to remove his "white gloves of silence." Though Bala maintained his innocence, it was possible to read the novel as a kind of confession. Wroblewski and the authorities, who believed that Bala's greatest desire was to attain literary immortality, saw his crime and his writing as indivisible. At the trial, Janiszewski's widow pleaded with the press to stop making Bala out to be an artist rather than a murderer. Since his arrest, "Amok" had become a sensation in Poland, selling out at virtually every bookstore.

"There's going to be a new edition coming out with an afterword about the trial and all the events that have happened," Bala told me excitedly. "Other countries are interested in publishing it as well." Flipping through the pages of his own copy, he added, "There's never been a book quite like this."

As we spoke, he seemed far less interested in the idea of the "perfect crime" than he was in the "perfect story," which, in his definition, pushed past the boundaries of aesthetics and reality and morality charted by his literary forebears. "You know, I'm working on a sequel to 'Amok,'" he said, his eyes lighting up. "It's called 'De Liryk.'" He repeated the words several times. "It's a pun. It means 'lyrics,' as in a story, or 'delirium.'"

He explained that he had started the new book before he was arrested, but that the police had seized his computer, which contained his only copy. (He was trying to get the files back.) The authorities told me that they had found in the computer evidence that Bala was collecting information on Stasia's new boyfriend, Harry. "Single, 34 years old, his mom died when he was 8," Bala had written. "Apparently works at the railway company, probably as a train driver but I'm not sure." Wroblewski and the authorities suspected that Harry might be Bala's next target. After Bala had learned that Harry visited an Internet chat room, he had posted a message at the site, under an assumed name, saying, "Sorry to bother you but I'm looking for Harry. Does anyone know him from Chojnow?"

Bala told me that he hoped to complete his second novel after the appeals court made its ruling. In fact, several weeks after we spoke, the court, to the disbelief of many, annulled the original verdict. Although the appeals panel found an "undoubted connection" between Bala and the murder, it concluded that there were still gaps in the "logical chain of evidence," such as the medical examiners' conflicting testimony, which needed to be resolved. The panel refused to release Bala from prison, but ordered a new trial, which is scheduled to begin this spring.

Bala insisted that, no matter what happened, he would finish "De Liryk." He glanced at the guards, as if afraid they might hear him, then leaned forward and whispered, "This book is going to be even more shocking."

David Grann *is the author of the* New York Times *bestseller* The Lost City of Z: A Tale of Deadly Obsession in the Amazon. *He has been a staff writer at* The New Yorker *since 2003. His stories have appeared in several anthologies, including* What We Saw: The Events of September 11, 2001; The Best American Crime Writing, *of both 2004 and 2005; and* The Best American Sports Writing, *of 2003 and 2006. His work has also appeared in the* New York Times Magazine, The Atlantic, *the* Washington Post, *the* Wall Street Journal, *and* The New Republic. *A collection of his stories will be published by Doubleday in 2010.*

Coda

In December of 2008, after several delays, Bala finally received a new trial. This time the verdict came even quicker: Bala was found guilty of orchestrating the murder. He is currently serving his twenty-five-year sentence.

Michael J. Mooney

The Day Kennedy Died

FROM *D Magazine*

In crumpled white coats filled with folded papers and stethoscopes and the various tools of the third-year medical student, they file into a cramped office. The walls are lined with books. Andrew Jennings and Jeff Konnert sit at opposite ends of the leather couch while Scott Paulson takes the leather chair. They face a 79-year-old man in a crisp, bright white jacket. Dr. Robert Nelson McClelland, not a large man, has thick glasses and tufts of white hair that match his coat.

This is the students' second meeting with the old doctor. He offers them soda and coffee. They are scheduled to talk about pancreatic surgery. Instead they will receive a lesson in living history. When they leave, one student will refer to this hour as the most fascinating conversation of his life.

As they get settled, ready to hear about surgical manipulation of the biliary tract, Jennings notices a magazine on the coffee table. From the cover, it appears the entire magazine is dedicated to conspiracy theories revolving around the John F. Kennedy assassination. Six floors and 44 years separate the place where they are sitting from that moment in November 1963 when the president of the United States was carted into the emergency room in a condition witnesses would later describe as "moribund."

Andrew points to the magazine. "Were you here when they brought him in?"

"Yeah, I helped put in the trache," McClelland says matter-of-factly. The students gasp, as if the old East Texas doctor had put an ice-cold stethoscope to their chests. With no hesitation, McClelland continues, "So you're here to talk about the pancreas—"

"Whoa! Whoa!" one of the three students interrupts.

"Is there any way you could tell us what happened?" asks another.

"We can read a book about pancreatic surgery, but this—"

"Well, I feel like a broken record," McClelland says. "I've probably told this story 8,000 times."

They plead with him.

He leans back in his chair, behind a desk covered with stacks of paper. He nods slowly. His eyes close for a moment as he transports himself back to that fall afternoon, just two days after his 34th birthday. The day that JFK died.

It was a little after "noontime," he tells them. Everyone knew the president was in town that day. McClelland was in a second-floor conference room at Parkland Memorial Hospital, showing a film of an operation for a hiatal hernia to some of the residents and students.

He begins the narrative he's told so many times. "I heard a little knock on the door," McClelland says. At the door was Dr. Charles Crenshaw. He asked McClelland to step into the hall for a moment. When he returned, McClelland turned off the projector and left the students. The two doctors moved immediately to the elevator.

In the elevator, McClelland tried to reassure Crenshaw. He mentioned there had been a lot of alarming stories from the emergency room recently, and most cases turned out not to be too bad.

When the elevator doors opened, they turned right and saw a wall of dark suits and hats. ("Everyone wore hats in those days," he tells the students. Their conceptions of that time come mostly from a film made in 1991.)

The open area at the center of the emergency room was called "the pit." Neither doctor had ever seen the pit so jammed with people: Secret Service men, nurses, medical students, residents, reporters, photographers, and curious bystanders.

In the shuffle, the dark suits parted. About 50 feet away, McClelland could see Jackie Kennedy seated outside Trauma Room One. Her pink dress was covered in blood.

"This is really what they said it was," he said quietly to Crenshaw.

McClelland thought for a moment that he might be the most senior faculty member on site. His boss, Dr. Tom Shires, chair of the department of surgery, was in Galveston at a meeting of the Western Surgical Association. Because it was near lunch, he worried the other doctors might be off the premises. ("The food was so bad at the hospital," he tells the students, "we often went out to the hamburger place across the street.")

His instincts were to move the other direction, but he forced himself to keep walking toward Trauma Room One, fighting through the crowd. A large woman named Doris Nelson stood in front of the doors, directing traffic, her voice bellowing above the bedlam. She was the nurse director of the emergency room. She told the Secret Service men who was allowed in and whom to keep out. When McClelland and Crenshaw arrived, she waved them in.

THE FIRST THING HE SAW was the president's face, cyanotic— bluish-black, swollen, suffused with blood. The body was on a cart in the middle of the room, draped and surrounded by doctors and residents. Kennedy was completely motionless, a contrast to the commotion around him. McClelland was relieved there were so many other faculty members there.

Dr. James Carrico, a resident at the time, had inserted an endotracheal tube into the president's trachea and secured an airway when the president first entered the emergency room. Many years later, Carrico would become the chief of surgery at Parkland. Dr. Malcolm Perry and Dr. Charles Baxter had arrived just before McClelland and had begun a tracheotomy, cutting into a quarter-size wound in the center of Kennedy's throat. Dr. M. T. Jenkins, an anesthesiologist, was near the head of the cart, administering oxygen.

McClelland put on surgical gloves. None of the men in the room had changed clothes. At their wrists, the surgical gloves met business suits and pressed white shirt cuffs.

Jenkins had his hands full, but nodded down to Kennedy's head. He said, "Bob, there's a wound there." The head was covered in blood and blood clots, tiny collections of dark red mass. McClelland thought he meant there was a wound at the president's left temple. Later that gesture would cause some confusion.

McClelland moved to the head of the cart. "Bob, would you hold this retractor?" Perry asked. He handed McClelland an army-navy retractor, a straight metal bar with curves on each end to hold back tissue and allow visibility and access. McClelland leaned over the president's blue face, over the gape in the back of his head, and took the tool.

For nearly 15 minutes, McClelland held the retractor as blood ran over its edges. As the other doctors labored on Kennedy's throat and chest or milled around the room, McClelland stood staring at the leader of the free world. His face was 18 inches from the president's head wound. Kennedy's eyes bulged slightly from their sockets—the medical term is "protuberant"—common with massive head injuries and increased intracranial pressure. Blood oozed down his cheeks. Some of the hair at the front of his head was still combed.

McClelland looked into the head wound. Stray hairs at the back of the head covered parts of the hole, as did bits of bone, blood, and more blood clots. He watched as a piece of cerebellum slowly slipped from the back of the hole and dropped onto the cart.

(In the room with his students, Dr. McClelland softly touches the rear-right part of his own head. "Right back here," he tells them. "About like this." He puts his hands together to signify the size of the wound, about the size of a golf ball. "Clearer in my mind's eye than maybe you are sitting in front of me right now.")

Jenkins and McClelland would both testify later that the slimy chunk of tissue they saw plop on the cart was cerebellum. Jenkins, however, changed his mind and decided what he saw must have been cerebrum. It might seem like a minor nuance to casual observers, but no details of the biggest mystery in American history are minor. The difference between cerebellum and cerebrum could mean a difference in the location of the fatal head wound. It could mean a different bullet trajectory, which could indicate where the fatal shot originated.

For years the two would argue.

"You don't remember, Bob," Jenkins would say.

"Yes I do. You don't remember. You were fiddling with the anesthesia machine. I was just standing there looking at it."

As their fingers moved in and out of the president's body, and through that afternoon, the doctors debated where the bullet came in and went out. Perry said he assumed the smaller hole in Kennedy's neck was an entrance wound. They knew nothing of the events downtown, where some witnesses claimed a gunman by the infamous grassy knoll fired a shot from in front of the moving president. Lee Harvey Oswald fired from behind Kennedy as the limousine moved away from the book depository. At the time, the doctors hypothesized that perhaps a bullet entered at the front of the throat, ricocheted off the bony spinal column, and moved upward out the back of Kennedy's head. At that point, the doctors were unaware of the wound in Kennedy's back.

McClelland stared at the hole in the back of the president's head. He looked at where the skull crumpled slightly around the edges. Knowing nothing else of the assassination at the time, he, too, assumed a bullet had come out of that opening.

He wouldn't feel confident in his initial assessment until 11 and a half years later, when he and his wife watched an episode of *The Tonight Show with Johnny Carson*. As the couple got ready for bed, Carson introduced his guest, a young, ambitious television host named Geraldo Rivera. Rivera had with him footage of the assassination previously unseen by the public, footage known simply as "the Zapruder film." Shot by Abraham Zapruder, an immigrant from the Ukraine, the 8-millimeter Kodachrome movie shows the motorcade through the duration of the assassination. As McClelland watched it for the first time, he saw the back of the president's head blasted out. He saw the president swayed "back and to the left," a phrase later repeated ad nauseum in Oliver Stone's JFK. McClelland was convinced he had been standing over an exit wound.

At approximately 1 p.m., Dr. Kemp Clark pronounced John Fitzgerald Kennedy, the 35th president of the United States, dead. Everyone seemed to agree the cause was the massive brain injury, and Clark was the neurosurgeon, so Clark called the death. A blanket was put over the body, and the body was put into a wooden coffin and taken to the airport, a violation of Texas state law at the time.

The doctors were taken upstairs to fill out brief reports for the Secret Service. Each was instructed to write about a page describing what had happened. McClelland was the only doctor to mention a wound in the temple, the place he believed Jenkins was nodding at earlier. He would later clarify for the Warren Commission that he did not see such a wound. He would give his testimony to the assistant counsel of the President's Commission,

Arlen Specter, four months after the assassination. Before Mc-Clelland finished his report, Lyndon B. Johnson had been sworn in as president aboard Air Force One.

Years later, when Senator Arlen Specter ran for president himself, he stopped by Parkland for a photo-op with the doctors he questioned in March of 1964.

The rest of the day, doctors discussed the day's events by the coffee pot. Surgeons drink coffee like cars drink gas. They looked at each other with solemn glances, many still wearing blood-splattered suits. "Did that just happen?" they asked one another. "Did the president just die in our hands?"

McClelland got home about 6 p.m. His mother was visiting from East Texas. She met him at the door and hugged him.

AFTER TELLING HIS TALE, more than half the scheduled hour has passed. "Wow," one of the students says. That's all they can muster. Wow. And again, perhaps not noticing the amazement of the students, perhaps so used to it from telling the story over the years, McClelland drops a second bombshell.

"I worked on Oswald, too," he says.

"You're kidding."

That Sunday, with McClelland's mother still in town, the family decided to go out to lunch. As his wife was upstairs getting ready with their 2-year-old and infant, McClelland decided to watch television. As he switched on his Admiral, before the picture flickered to life, he heard an announcer: "He's been shot. He's been shot."

When the picture came in, Lee Harvey Oswald was on the floor, a sheriff's deputy leaning over him. The crowd had the gunman, Jack Ruby. McClelland called upstairs to his wife.

"They've shot Oswald!"

"Who's that?" she called back.

"Don't you remember? That's the guy they said shot—"

"Oh."

"Well, I've gotta go."

He headed for the hospital. Coming down Beverly Drive, just before Preston Road, McClelland began flashing his headlights. He saw the car of Shires, his boss, on his way home from Parkland after seeing his patient, Governor Connally.

Shires stopped and stuck his head out the window. "Did you hear what I just—"

"I just saw it on television," McClelland said.

"I just heard it on the radio."

McClelland followed Shires to Parkland. When they arrived and changed clothes—something they didn't take the time for with Kennedy—Oswald was just being wheeled in. When Kennedy arrived, every faculty member on site was called into the emergency room. With Oswald, there were only a few doctors working on him. Twenty-eight minutes after Jack Ruby's shot, they were inside Oswald's abdomen.

("He was as white as this piece of paper," McClelland tells the med students. "He had lost so much blood. If he hadn't turned when he saw Ruby coming, he might have been all right.")

When Oswald saw the gun in Ruby's hand, he had cringed slightly, flinching. Because of this, the bullets went through his aorta and inferior vena cava, the two main blood vessels in the back of the abdominal cavity. There was enormous loss of blood. The medical team pumped pint after pint of untyped blood, 16 in all, through his body. Shires and Perry eventually got a vascular clamp to stop the bleeding, and the two set about clearing away intestines to get enough room to repair the damage.

They worked on Oswald for an hour when his heart arrested. The blood loss was just too much, and the brief but severe shock too damaging. Perry opened Oswald's chest, and he and McClelland, who was also assisting, took turns administering an open heart massage.

("You pumped Oswald's heart in your hands?" a student asks.

THE DAY KENNEDY DIED   137

"We took turns, each going until we got tired. We went for, oh, about 40 minutes.")

The heart got flabbier and flabbier. They squeezed and pumped. The blood around his heart collected on their gloves. Then, no more. Almost two hours after being shot, Lee Harvey Oswald was pronounced dead. The first live homicide on public television was witnessed by 20 million viewers.

The entire emergency room was in a daze. First the president. Two days later, in the room next door, the president's assassin. It was as if the community had tumbled into one of Rod Serling's *Twilight Zone* episodes.

For McClelland, it got stranger. One of the sheriff's deputies who had been escorting Oswald during his public transfer—the taller deputy America saw in the Stetson hat—was waiting outside the trauma room to see how Oswald was doing. He told the doctors something odd had happened, even more odd than the public murder.

After the shot, the deputy explained to McClelland, when Oswald was on the ground, he got on his hands and knees and put his face right over Oswald's.

"I said, 'Son, you're hurt real bad. Do you wanna say anything?'" the deputy said. "He looked at me for a second. He waited, like he was thinking. Then he shook his head back and forth just as wide as he could. Then he closed his eyes."

They would never open again. Looking back, McClelland would wonder if Oswald was tempted to say something. If maybe he was worried he would regret it. He didn't know he was going to die, McClelland thought.

THE STUDENTS BEGIN TO REALIZE McClelland is not just a living portal to the history in their textbooks. He might also be the most credible conspiracy theorist alive. He explains that too many things don't add up. Doctors at Parkland reported seeing the president's body put into a coffin with a blanket over it. But that it somehow got into a body bag by the time it got to Washington. He says he's from East Texas and has seen enough deer hunting to know a body moves in the direction of the bullet. That the president moved backward because he was shot from the front.

He mentions an odd phone call the operator at the emergency room got when Oswald was in surgery. Someone claiming to be from the White House inquired about Oswald's condition. He talks about a British documentarian's theory that three hitmen flew from Corsica to Marseille to Mexico City and drove across the border and up to Dallas to murder the president.

"Were you ever scared?" a student asks.

"No. Maybe I should have been. Maybe I was just too dumb to be scared." His voice is soft, and he smiles.

There are other coincidences, he says. One extraordinary one, in fact.

"I'd actually met Kennedy before that," he says.

"You what?"

Almost two years exactly before the assassination, McClelland was a resident at Parkland. His new wife was a nurse at Baylor hospital, across Dallas from Parkland. She asked him one day if he could pick up her paycheck. He took off work a little early and ventured to Baylor, where he hardly ever went.

He parked across the street from the hospital, got out and looked to his left, where a group of school children were running from an elementary school. As they ran in his direction, a pack of motorcycle police rounded the corner from Washington Avenue onto Gaston Avenue. Behind them was a limousine. He crossed the street toward the hospital's side entrance. The children and the motorcade arrived at the same time he did.

Surrounded by children, a motorcycle cop got off his bike and gently nudged McClelland back and opened the car door. "How 'bout that," McClelland thought to himself. "Hey, I know him. That's the president of the United States."

Speaker of the House Sam Rayburn had just been hospitalized with cancer at Baylor. A fellow Democrat, President Kennedy had come to pay Mr. Sam a final visit. That night, when he got home, McClelland told his wife, "You'll never believe who I saw today." News of the presidential visit made the front pages the next morning.

Two years later, as McClelland stared into the pale, swollen face of the same man, he thought back to that brief encounter.

Another coincidence: years after the Warren Commission's report. After Jim Garrison, the New Orleans district attorney, tried to have the only trial related to the assassination, bringing conspiracy charges against Claw Shaw. After interest in the mystery had waxed and waned several times. A surgeon friend of McClelland's called and told him about a stomach cancer patient he had operated on earlier that day. The doctor explained the patient wasn't doing well, and he thought he might have leaked one of his suture lines. He asked if McClelland might be at Presbyterian that day, and if he could scrub-in on the surgery. McClelland had patients to see there anyway, so he agreed.

He arrived at Presbyterian and found the surgery schedule: the patient's name in black marker on a white board was A. Zapruder.

Zapruder recovered eventually, and the two talked periodically. For some reason, though, they never discussed their mutual involvement in the events of November 22, 1963. Neither ever brought it up.

This happens every so often, he tells the students. He goes for years without talking about that week. He goes weeks without thinking about the blood clots. The face. The hole in the head. Sometimes it seems to come up over and over. The event is woven into his life, wrapped around his white hair, tied to his surgeon fingers. He's been married 50 years. His children have children. He is one of the most renowned surgery scholars in the country. He knows the history of virtually every operation, from how doctors performed it in the Civil War to new experimental processes. He pores over medical journals (as past editor of *Selected Readings in General Surgery*, which he originated).

But new debates begin, like a recent one when two books about the assassination were released at the same time. One has 1,600 pages worth of evidence declaring the Warren Commission's conclusion spot on, the other claiming to have irrefutable evidence that there were multiple shooters. He can list the documentaries, the biographies, the first-hand accounts like a catalogue.

As the students walk out, they thank him profusely. They have unshaven faces and disheveled hair. Surgery rotation is notoriously difficult because of the lack of sleep. But they walk past McClelland's secretary, stirred by the story. Once, everyone in America could remember where they were when they heard the news of JFK's death. For a younger generation, the event was 30 years in the past when they learned about the book depository and the Texas Theatre. For some, it might as well be Ford's Theatre and John Wilkes Booth.

Andrew Jennings pulls out his cell phone. "I'm going to tell my grandkids about this," the 24-year-old says. "People will say, 'I know a guy who knows the guy who worked on Kennedy and Oswald.'"

ONCE IN A WHILE, at home, McClelland pulls a box from his shelves. He passes the Lincoln bust he purchased at the Petersen House in Washington, D.C., where Abraham Lincoln died, and the epic volumes he has of all Lincoln's writings, and the history books he's amassed over the years.

His hands glide over the wooden box, painted blue. He opens it. Inside is a transparent zip-lock bag with what once was a white shirt pressing against the sides.

He thinks about a trip to Washington, where he visited the Armed Forces Pathology Museum. There, hanging in a display, was the shirt Lincoln was wearing when he was shot in 1865. Blood had poured from the left side of his head, down his arm, collecting at the cuff of the shirt.

McClelland opens the bag and pulls out the folded shirt.

The day after he worked on Kennedy, he took his suit to the cleaners. When he explained the blood-drenched clothing, they told him they didn't want to clean it. It was part of history, they told him. "I only have two suits," the young doctor said. "You have to clean it."

But he folded the shirt he had been wearing and put it in a bag. He eventually got a nice box to keep it in. As he unfolds the shirt and holds it up, there, on the left sleeve, mostly around the cuff, is a brown stain. Because he had a suit on, much of the shirt is clean. But as with the Lincoln shirt, a pool of blood had collected on the left side. Like the event itself, the blood started at his hands and worked its way up, onto him.

He thinks about the tragic event. Things that seem disparate, but somehow come together. "Jungian synchronicity" he calls it. Meaningful coincidences.

Rarely, he takes the shirt out for someone. For his daughter, a school teacher in nearby Plano, and her class. For a cousin's kid's show and tell. The class didn't believe it was really Kennedy's blood, of course. He begins his story of one of the most important days in American history. He says the same things. The same way. With the same inflections and the same dialogue.

He starts with "I feel like a broken record."

Then: "There was a little knock on the door."

MICHAEL J. MOONEY *is a staff writer at* New Times, *a Village Voice Media alt-weekly in Fort Lauderdale, where he writes about crime, sports, and the eccentric characters of South Florida. Before moving to Florida, he was a feature writer at the* Dallas Morning News. *His writing has also appeared in* D Magazine, Condé Nast Portfolio, *and other newspapers, magazines, and literary journals. His story "Royal Flushed" was selected for* The Best American Sports Writing 2009.

Coda

I first heard about Dr. McClelland from my good friend, Andrew Jennings. I was at the other end of the call he made as he was leaving Dr. McClelland's office. By the time Andrew was done recounting his conversation, I was already composing a letter to the doctor. Writing this piece was a challenge because so many of the key participants were dead or had long ago stopped talking about the assassination. Dr. McClelland was very generous with his time though. We went over his experiences several times and his remarkable memory for details personalized events that seemed distant and unimaginable. Most people who grew up around Dallas have been to the Sixth Floor Museum at least once, usually on a class field trip or to entertain out-of-towners. Everyone's seen the window where Oswald perched and the grassy hill across the street. But hearing Dr. McClelland's story reminded me that history is comprised of real human beings, with bones that shatter, blood that stains, and hearts that get cold and flabby when they stop beating.

After "The Day Kennedy Died" was published, I received a number of e-mails from people around the world who wanted help either proving or disproving one theory or another. I also heard from plenty of people wanting to know why it is that the media can't just "move on" or "get over it." When it comes to the events of November 1963, Dallas is still torn. While some people can't seem to get enough of the Kennedy assassination, others can't get far enough away from it. Some still feel shame, a collective guilt. It was years before any of the doctors involved would speak about what happened. Even for generations who weren't born at the time, the city struggles with how to deal with this part of history.

Dr. McClelland is now retired from teaching. He hasn't decided what—if anything—he will eventually do with the bloody shirt.

Mark Arax

THE ZANKOU CHICKEN MURDERS

FROM *Los Angeles* magazine

IN A MANSION IN THE HILLS above Glendale, a man named Mardiros Iskenderian rose from his bed one morning and put on a white silk suit he hadn't worn in 20 years. He stuffed a 9 mm handgun into his waistband and a .38-caliber revolver into his coat pocket and walked step by small step down the stairs. His wife, Rita, who had fallen in love with him when she was 12, couldn't believe the sight. For a man who was so near death, cancer everywhere, he looked beautiful. It had been months since he had ventured outside by himself, months since he had driven one of his fancy cars, and she fretted that he was too weak to go anywhere. He told her not to worry. He was feeling much better now, and besides, he was only going to Zankou Chicken to see an old friend.

He had lived his life like one of those princes of Armenian fable, maybe Ara the Beautiful or Tigran the Great. His story began in a tiny storefront in Beirut, where his mother in her apron hand spooned the fluffy white garlic paste that would become the family fortune. From Hollywood to Anaheim, he had opened a chain of fast-food rotisserie chicken restaurants that dazzled the food critics and turned customers into a cult. Poets wrote about his Zankou chicken. Musicians sang about his Zankou chicken. Now that he was dying, his dream of building an empire, 100 Zankous across the land, a Zankou in every major city, would be his four sons' to pursue. In the days before, he had pulled them aside one by one—Dikran, Steve, Ara, Vartkes—and told them he had no regrets. He was 56 years old, that was true, but life had not cheated him. He did not tell them he had just one more piece of business left to do.

There was one son, the second son, Steve, who always seemed to know what was on his father's mind. He was the son most like Mardiros. His smile, his temper, his heart. Had Steve been home that day, he might have sensed trouble or at least insisted that his father not go alone. But Mardiros had sent Steve off to the mall to fetch him one of those slushy lemonades, the only thing he still had a taste for. By the time Steve got home, the lemonade still icy, his father was gone. The boy would forever be tormented by the question of whether design or chance had prevailed that day. Was this errand a ruse, part of his father's plan, or had he simply failed to hurry home fast enough?

"Steve, something bad has happened," his mother cried at the door. "There's been a shooting. At your Aunt Dzovig's."

"Where's Dad?"

"He's gone."

"What do you mean, he's gone?"

"He took the car. He said he was going to Zankou. But I don't believe him now. They heard shots at Dzovig's."

Dzovig was Mardiros's younger sister, as pretty as he was handsome. She lived in a big house on the other side of the Verdugo Hills with her husband and two sons. She managed a pair of Zankous for Mardiros and had taken on the chore of caring for their mother. Of course, everyone knew this was no chore at all, because the mother, Margrit lskenderian, the creator of the garlic paste and most every dish worth tasting at Zankou, was a woman who pulled her load and the load of three others.

The drive to Aunt Dzovig's house was a winding seven miles. Steve ran every stop sign, racing down one side of the canyon and up the other. As he rounded the bend and the Oakmont Country Club came into view, he could see TV news helicopters circling like vultures.

"No, Dad," he shouted. "Please, Dad, no."

Up the hill, where the canyon oaks gave way to palm trees, neighbors had spilled out of their million-dollar estates. Police were everywhere, and he could see that his aunt's house had been cordoned off. He jumped out of the car and made a dash for it. He ran with the lean of a man who had every right to whatever reality existed on the other side of the yellow tape. A detective halted him short.

"Who are you?"

"I am Steve Iskenderian."

"Who are you looking for?"

"Mardiros Iskenderian. I am his son. Is he inside?"

"Yes."

"Is he dead?"

"Yes. He's dead."

For a moment he felt a strange relief that only later would he attribute to gratitude that his cancer-ridden father had finally found release from his suffering. Then, almost in the same instant, it occurred to him to ask the question that he already knew the answer to.

"My grandmother and aunt. Are they dead, too?"

The cop stared into his eyes and nodded. "Yes, they're dead, too."

The police had questions, and he tried his best to answer them. On the drive home, he had to forgive himself for allowing his mind, at such a moment, to consider the family business. Who would take it over now that his father and grandmother, the heart and soul of Zankou Chicken, were gone? His mother, Rita, by design, had never worked a single day at Zankou. His older brother, Dikran, was a born-again evangelist whose fire took him to street corners, and a younger brother, Ara, was addled by drugs. No one was more lost than Steve himself. Just three years earlier, he had been charged with shooting at a prostitute and her pimp and had faced a life sentence. The case ended in a mistrial. He did have two cousins, Aunt Dzovig's sons, who were capable enough. But how could they be expected to work beside the sons of the man who had murdered their mother and grandmother?

"My God, Dad," he said, climbing the hillside to give his mother the news. "What have you done?"

IN THE WEEKS and months and years to follow, five years to be exact, the Armenians of Glendale, Hollywood, Montebello, and Van Nuys, and their kin up and over the mountains in Fresno, told and retold the story. "Let's sit crooked and talk straight," the old Armenian ladies clucked. There was no bigger shame, no bigger *ahmote*, than an Armenian son taking the life of his own mother. And who could explain such a shame from a man like Mardiros Iskenderian? He was the same son who had honored his mother on Mother's Day with lavish ceremonies at the church, celebrations in which Margrit Iskenderian, short and plump, salt-and-pepper hair cut in a bob, was invariably crowned queen. Wherever they went as a family, he made his wife take a seat in the back so his mother could sit beside him. For 25 years, she had lived with Mardiros and Rita and their children, her bedroom the master bedroom, where a single photo, that of her and her son back in 1950s Lebanon, graced her dresser. Each day at 6 p.m., when Margrit returned home from her long shift cooking at Zankou, Rita was there to greet her at the door. So why, after all those years of devotion, did Margrit Iskenderian leave the house of her son and move in with her daughter Dzovig?

The old ladies gave answers, some less cruel than others: The cancer that filled Mardiros's body had gone to his brain. He was thinking like a crazy man. No, it wasn't cancer, it was the scars of growing up in Lebanon with a father who was the drunkard of Bourj Hamoud. No, haven't you heard the talk about the Pepsi company offering the family $30 million for the Zankou chain and trademark? Greed split the family house in two.

Others insisted there was no sense to be made of it because life made no sense, death made no sense. Yes, we Armenians were the first people to accept Christianity as a nation, way back in 301 A.D., before the Romans, before the Greeks. But to answer this question of why Mardiros Iskenderian killed his mother and his sister and then himself, Armenians had to reach back to their pagan past, to a way of seeing older than the Bible itself: *Pakht*, they called it. Fate. *Jagadakeer*, it was muttered. Your destiny is etched into your forehead at birth. What is written no one can change.

Thus, from Turkey to Beirut to Hollywood to Glendale, from the genocide to the garlic paste to the mansion to the murders, it was all foretold.

RITA WAS AN ARMENIAN CATHOLIC SCHOOLGIRL growing up in the suburbs of Beirut in the late 1960s when she first set eyes on Mardiros Iskenderian, the bad boy gunning his banana yellow 442 Oldsmobile up and down the lane. When he blew the engine, he turned up the next week with a brand-new 442 Olds, this one burgundy. The pampered son of Zankou Chicken hardly noticed Rita Hovakimian, who was seven years younger. He kept a rooftop apartment across the alley from where she lived with her family. From balcony to balcony, she spied on him. She got her money's worth.

"There was no missing him. He always came and went with

big noise," Rita would say years later. "His reputation as a playboy was very bad. Arab girls, Maronite Christian girls, Armenian girls, single girls, married girls. For me, he was the most beautiful guy in the world. Nobody was like him. His smile was gorgeous. His hair was gorgeous. He wore the most beautiful perfume. He was always dressed in Pierre Cardin or something. And when he would open his mouth, out came the charm. What more did a young girl want?"

Her parents had forbidden her from seeing any boy, much less such a man. A few years earlier, Mardiros had been implicated in a notorious jewelry store heist and murder, an inside job by three Armenians who had killed the handsome scion of one of Beirut's wealthiest Arab families. Not knowing that a friend was one of the three robbers, Mardiros let him use his apartment. Only later did he discover the stash of jewels in the attic. His testimony ended up sending the trio to prison, and from that day on, alert to revenge, he carried two pistols wherever he went.

The gap in their ages seemed to narrow as Rita blossomed into a tall beauty with big round eyes. They began meeting on the sly, Mardiros tossing her messages in an empty cologne bottle from the roof. For three months, they kept their relationship hidden, until a nosy Armenian neighbor saw her riding in his car and told her mother. It became a big family scandal, with lots of threats back and forth. In the end, her parents knew they were deeply in love. She was 19; he was 26. Their wedding came amid the fierce fighting of Lebanon's civil war. She wore a full white gown, but he wanted no part of a tuxedo. His Angels Flight pants touched so low to the ground you couldn't tell if he was wearing shoes or not.

They shared a two-bedroom walk-up in the crowded Armenian quarter of Bourj Hamoud with his parents, his two sisters, and his mother's mother, a survivor of the Armenian genocide. Right below was Zankou Chicken, the takeout they had named after a river in Armenia. There was no cash register, no table, no chairs. They used every square foot to clean and salt the chickens, roast them inside a pair of rotisserie ovens, and keep the golden brown wholes and halves warm. Customers parked on the one-way street, ran in, handed the cash to Mardiros's father, and ran out with their steaming birds and dollops of pungent garlic paste.

"It was a drive-thru before there were drive-thrus," recalled Garo Dekirmendjian, a Beiruti Armenian who befriended the family. "The mother would be standing in the mezzanine in her apron, cleaning the garlic cloves and whipping up her paste. And the father was a cash machine. All day long the same movement, his right hand stuffing wads of money into his left shirt pocket and pulling out the change. Mardiros was helping turn the chickens when he wasn't having fun."

Rita understood that Mardiro's position in the family—first child, only son—gave him a kind of exalted status. *The prince. The pasha.* In time, it would shoulder him with great burden. But she was confounded by the degree of devotion between mother and son. "Before we married, he told me, 'I am going to live with my parents my whole life. I will never leave my mother.' I figured this was my pakht. But it was too much. 'My mother. My mother.' She was the queen of the house, not me. Next to God, it was his mother."

Unraveling the family dynamic was not easy. Her father-in-law, a smart and generous man, disappeared on long binges of alcohol. Day and night, from bottom floor to top floor, her mother-in-law worked. Even if she was compensating for her husband, her capacity for labor bordered on the maniacal. Rita wondered if Mardiros simply felt sorry for his mother and sought to honor her service. Or maybe deep down he understood that no one who worked as hard as she worked did it for free. He watched her punish his father with the guilt of indebtedness. Maybe Mardiros feared that his own debt would be turned against him if he didn't pay her back with absolute allegiance. Whatever it was, Rita felt swallowed up by their world.

Stuck inside the apartment with baby Dikran, she could smell the flavors of Zankou floating through the cracks. This was as close as she would come to the business. Her job, set down by custom, was to raise her children and tend to her mother-in-law's mother. So each day, without complaint, Rita finished rocking the baby and listened as the old lady told her story of survival, of the Turks rounding up all the Armenians in her village of Hajin in the spring of 1915 and herding them on a death march to the Syrian Desert. Was it jagadakeer? "She said she came upon the skull of one dead Armenian and picked it up. She looked at the forehead to see if any words had been written there, but there weren't any. She said she learned that day that there were no words to read. For her, the only words were God's words."

The survivors had streamed into Beirut by the thousands and formed a new Armenia in the "Paris of the Middle East." They built 60 Armenian schools and published ten Armenian-language newspapers and held sway far beyond their number. Without them, the Muslim Arabs would have ruled the country. With them, the Christian Arabs kept a narrow edge. It stayed that way until 1975, when the civil war upended everything. The Iskenderians, like so many other Armenian merchants, didn't want to leave. Zankou was a gold mine. They poured its profits into rental properties throughout the city.

Then one evening in 1979, the war struck home. Mardiros was sitting outside one of their empty storefronts, not a block from Zankou, when two men on motorcycles sped by. He had no reason to suspect that a dispute over rent with an Armenian tenant, a man connected to a political party, would turn violent. But the motorcycle drivers, wearing masks and clutching AK-47s, circled back around. They fired dozens of rounds, hitting Mardiros with bullet after bullet, 16 shots in all. They say it was a miracle he didn't die right there.

MARDIROS HAD ALWAYS BEEN a student of maps, but what he found when he came to America was something else. "Rita," he shouted from a backroom. "These Thomas brothers. What geniuses!" They had taken a city that made no sense to itself and given it a structure, a syntax, that even foreigners like him could fathom. Here was a whole bound guide of maps that divided up the sprawl of Southern California into perfect little squares with numbers that corresponded to pages inside. Turn to any page, and you had the landscape of L.A. in bird's-eye: parks in green, malls in yellow, cemeteries in olive, and freeways, the lifeblood, in red. He pored over the maps at night, reviewed them again in the morning, and then took off to find his new city. By car and foot, he logged hundreds of miles that first week, close to a thousand the next. He was looking for the right business in the right location and wasn't in any particular hurry. They had come with plenty of cash.

One thing was certain. His parents, looking for something easier, wanted no part of the food business. There would be no Zankous in America. They settled instead on a dry cleaning shop, only to find out that the chemicals made Mardiros sick. Father and son traveled to Hong Kong to explore the trade of men's suits, then decided the business wasn't practical. The deeper Mardiros journeyed into Los Angeles, the more he bumped up against growing pockets of immigrants fresh from the Middle East. No restaurant, though, seemed to be dedicated to their cuisine, at least none that served it fast and delicious and at a price that would bring customers back. So in 1983, he went to his parents and pitched the idea. His father resisted. His mother cried. They threatened to return to Beirut. In the end, sensing their son's resolve, they consented.

d a tiny place next to a Laundromat on the corner of
Normandie—could there have been an uglier mini-
of Hollywood?—and erected a sign with block letters
in blue and red. ᴢᴀɴᴋᴏᴜ ᴄʜɪᴄᴋᴇɴ. Before long, the Arabs and
Persian Jews and Armenians found it. So did Mexican gang-
bangers and nurses from Kaiser Permanente and the flock from L.
Ron Hubbard's church, who methodically polished off their plates
of chicken *shawarma,* hummus, and pickled turnips and returned
to their e-meters with a clearness that only Margrit's paste could
bring.

This wasn't Beirut. Mardiros put in long hours. He tweaked
the menu; his mother tinkered with the spices. It took a full year
to find a groove. The first crowd of regulars brought in a second
crowd, and a buzz began to grow among the network of foodies.
How did they make the chicken so tender and juicy? The answer
was a simple rub of salt and not trusting the rotisserie to do all the
work but raising and lowering the heat and shifting each bird as it
cooked. What made the garlic paste so fluffy and white and piercing? This was a secret the family intended to keep. Some customers swore it was potatoes, others mayonnaise. At least one fanatic
stuck his container in the freezer and examined each part as it
congealed. He pronounced the secret ingredient a special kind
of olive oil. None guessed right. The ingredients were simple and
fresh, Mardiros pledged, no shortcuts. The magic was in his
mother's right hand.

Word of a new kind of fare, fast and tasty and light, spread to
the critics. The *L.A. Times* would call it "the best roast chicken in
town at any price." Zagat would anoint Zankou one of "America's
best meal deals." No one, though, was more breathless in his
praise than the guerrilla warrior of city chowhounds. Jonathan
Gold called the chicken "superb," and nothing in heaven or on
earth compared with the garlic paste.

The hole-in-the-wall was raking in $2 million a year, half of
it pure profit. In Mardiros's mind, the family was growing and

the business needed to grow with it. This is America, he told his parents. We've got something good. Let's duplicate our success. His parents fought expansion, but he kept pushing, and in 1991 the family agreed to a split. Mardiros would take the Zankou concept and build a chain across the region. Any new restaurants he opened, success or failure, would belong to him. In return, he would sign over his stake in Hollywood to his parents and two sisters. The split was hardly a parting. The garlic paste still would be prepared by his mother and used by all the Zankous. As a favor to his sister Dzovig, he would pay her to manage some of his new stores. Nothing, he assured them, would change at home.

After so many years playing the pampered son, Mardiros now saw himself as the patriarch, a role that became official after his father's death. Over and over, he preached: Success means nothing if we don't stay as one. Greed must never rear its head. There is plenty for all of us. He loved Dzovig's two boys as he loved his own, and he knew she felt the same way about his sons. The boys were more like brothers than cousins. They lived only a few minutes apart in Glendale and attended the same private Armenian school. Dzovig would take them each morning, and Rita would pick them up. A gang of six, they climbed the hills, rode bikes, played video games. They had the coolest toys, the latest gadgets. If they were spoiled, and they were, it came with the turf. As the grandchildren of Margrit, each one was something of a food snob. No one's cooking could measure up to hers. She made the best lentil soups, the best raw-meat-and-bulgur *chekufta*. She wasn't big on hugs or kisses; she could be downright stern, but she wanted her grandchildren to know what good food tasted like. When they turned up their noses at her sheep's brain soup, she bribed them with $20 bills just to get them to take one sip.

Mardiros didn't need to travel far to find his next spot. Glendale was a city made new by three successive waves of Armenian refugees, first from Iran, then from Beirut, and now from Armenia itself. He picked a less grimy minimall squeezed behind a gas station for Zankou no. 2. As soon as it began turning a profit, he found a spot in Van Nuys for Zankou no. 3. Then came Zankou no. 4 in Anaheim and Zankou no. 5 in Pasadena. His white house, way up in the Verdugo Hills, was now known as the home of the rotisserie chicken mogul. It sat higher than the mansions of doctors, lawyers, and investment bankers. Only a porn king looked down on him. He and Rita drove a Jaguar and a black Mercedes-Benz. They had live-in servants. Yet it wasn't the kind of wealth that let them lounge around playing golf or tennis. When Rita wasn't tending the boys, she was feeding and bathing Mardiros's 97-year-old grandmother. His mother, Margrit, had her own seamstress, and she dressed in the finest silks and wools. But more often than not, her clothes were covered by the apron she put on each morning at 7:30 sharp. When she finished preparing dishes for the customers, she began cooking delicacies for the employees.

As for Mardiros, he spent his days driving from Zankou to Zankou. He did the payroll, made sure the food tasted right, and timed the customers from the second they walked in to the second they were served. When he wasn't working, he was catting around with his own gang of rich buddies. He went to Vegas with them, to Cabo with them. Every so often, he'd pile Rita and the kids into the Mercedes and take them to his favorite Chinese restaurant. This was what passed for family time. If he felt bad about neglecting his wife and children, he tried to make up for it by giving to the Armenian community. He gave to schools, dance troupes, and starving artists. He gave to orphans and widows and soup kitchens back in Armenia. He gave so often that a cartoon in one Armenian American newspaper showed two doors leading into Zankou. One was for food, the other for philanthropy. All in all, he had done what he had set out to do. At night, out on the balcony, he sat in his chair and could see all the way to Catalina Island. He'd take his telescope and look up at the stars and then look back down at the twinkling lights of Los Angeles. He belonged here. This was his place now. He and his Zankous had become part of the map.

HE COULD FEEL THE PAIN down below growing worse. Something terrible, he knew, afflicted him. Next week, he told himself. Next week. By the time he got to the doctor, it was too late. The cancer in his bladder had spread to his rectum. Chemotherapy would buy only a little time. He broke the news to Rita and the boys, and then he gathered his mother and sisters in the living room to tell them. He was going to fight it, he said, but if he died, he wanted them to know this: His sons—Dikran, 25, Steve, 23, Ara, 18, and Vartkes, 17—would be taking over his Zankous. The room fell silent. His sisters, Dzovig and Haygan, seemed tongue-tied. His mother sat stone-faced. She didn't ask what kind of cancer he had or what kind of prognosis the doctors had given him. Instead, as she put down her demitasse of Turkish coffee, she blurted out in Armenian: "Your sons. The shadow they cast is not yours." Then she rose, walked up the stairs to her bedroom, and shut the door.

Each one of his boys, it was true, was struggling to find his place. Vartkes, the youngest and perhaps the brightest, was using his allowance to buy marijuana. Ara, pent up and quirky, was addicted to painkillers. Dikran, the oldest, had found the Lord and was preaching salvation during the day and telling his brothers at night, in bed, that they were all headed to hell. He had become a born-again after a scandal in 1977 that had cost him his dream of being a lawyer. A top student at Woodbury University, Dikran had been caught in an elaborate scheme to cheat on the law school entrance exam. He paid a fine and served probation, but no credentialed law school would ever accept him.

For Steve, it was a different weakness. He had gone to the 777

Motel in Sherman Oaks on a winter night in 2000 to meet a call girl. He didn't know she had a listening device broadcasting to a pimp, who stole his money. Steve gave chase down a freeway, and shots were fired at the pimp and the prostitute, hitting their car. Steve was charged with two counts of attempted murder, and bail was set at $1.4 million. If the verdict didn't go his way, he faced life in prison. As it turned out, the prosecutor made a small blunder during the trial; telling the jury about a prior crime that Steve did not commit. His attorney, Mark Geragos, objected, and the judge declared a mistrial. Steve pleaded guilty to a lesser crime, did a year of work furlough, and was let go.

In the days that followed the news of his cancer, Mardiros couldn't help but notice that his mother's behavior toward him had changed. She would come home from work, Rita would greet her as usual at the front door, and she would walk right past him and into the kitchen without a word. No "How do you feel today?" No "Are your treatments working?" She would pour a glass of water from the refrigerator, turn around, and walk upstairs to her room. He wouldn't see her again until the next day, when she would repeat her silence. His hair fell out, he lost 60 pounds, but not once did she seem to notice. It didn't occur to Rita that her mother-in-law might be miffed about Mardiros's desire for his sons to take over the business. After all, Margrit had opposed the expansion from day one, and Mardiros alone owned Zankous nos. 2, 3, 4, and 5.

This went on for more than a year, not a word spoken between mother and son. Mardiros might have taken it upon himself to ask what crime he had committed to deserve such treatment. But all he had left was his pride. Then one day, while his mother was away at work, he walked into her bedroom and reached atop the dresser and grabbed the photo of him and her when he was a child in Lebanon. He could see that she had the faintest smile on her lips as she was leaning over to hug him. *Her prince. Her pasha.* He took the photo out of its frame, tore off the side depicting his mother, lit a match, and watched it burn. Then he folded up his side of the photo and threw it away. A day or so later, as it happened, the house caught fire. Flames shot up from the maid's bedroom downstairs. He and Rita were stuck on the balcony, choking on smoke, when firefighters finally rescued them. They packed what they could and went to live at a hotel in Glendale while the house was refurbished. It was the next to last time he would see his mother. She had taken all her possessions and moved in with Dzovig.

Over the following year, as he lay dying, his mother never once called him. Neither did his sisters or his nephews. His treatments had caused a buildup of fluid on his brain, and he was thinking all kinds of crazy thoughts. He told Steve about setting the image of his mother to flames, and how that image had come back to light the fire that had burned the house. In more rational moments, he thought that a mother capable of disowning her son at the hour of his greatest need, a son who had dedicated his life to her, was capable of engineering great mischief when he was gone. Yes, the Zankous he had built belonged to him alone, and he believed the trademark was his, too. But how could he be certain that his mother and sisters wouldn't challenge the inheritance of his wife and sons?

His head began to throb, the pain so severe that his sons had to take turns rubbing his skull with their knuckles. He told Steve he was certain that his mother and sisters were plotting against him. He could barely stand up, but each week he made Steve drive him to the two Zankous that Dzovig managed and open the safe so he could count the receipts. Steve, tugged by his love for his grandmother, asked his father if he could ever find it in his heart to forgive her. "God will forgive the devil before I can forgive my mother," he said, "because this is a mother, not the devil."

HE ROSE FROM HIS BED on the morning of January 14, 2003, took a shower, and got dressed. His wife would recall his putting on the white silk suit that hadn't fit him in years. Only now, after losing so much weight, could he wear it again. He reached into the closet for his .38-caliber revolver and stuck it into his coat pocket. Then he jammed his 9mm semiautomatic Browning into his waistband, next to his diaper. The gun held 11 rounds, and he scooped up nine extra bullets. As he walked down the stairs and said good-bye to Rita, he had no intention of going to Zankou Chicken to see an old friend. He had called his sister at work and arranged a meeting with her and his mother to discuss family affairs.

He maneuvered his black BMW down the steep canyon, looped along La Crescenta Avenue, and climbed the backside of the mountain until he reached the split-level brick and stucco house on Ayars Canyon Way. He parked out front, walked up to the tall entrance past two sago palms, and knocked on the door. He was now wearing a dark brown jacket with gray pants. Perhaps he had changed clothes on the way over. Or maybe his wife's memory had played a trick, dressing him for the last time in white. A housekeeper led him into the dining room, where his 45-year-old sister, Dzovig Marjik, was standing. She was dressed in blue jeans and a long-sleeved brown sweater. Her hair was curly like his, as if she had just gotten out of the shower herself, and it was tinted an odd red. She asked him to take a seat at the dining table and poured him a glass of lemonade.

He chatted pleasantly with her for a half hour as he waited for their 76-year-old mother to come home from work. When Margrit Iskenderian walked in a little after 2 p.m., she was carrying a big box of food. She set it down on the kitchen table, put on her white slippers, and greeted his sister and then him. The housekeeper poured his mother a glass of lemonade and topped off his glass and the glass of his sister. Then she walked downstairs to her bedroom to let the three of them—mother, son, and daughter—talk.

His sister sat across from him, and his mother to his right. His voice was calm. Their voices were calm. He waited about five minutes, for the conversation to go from nothing to something, and then he reached for the gun in his waistband. He grabbed the handle, put his finger on the trigger, and extended his arm across the table and over the pitcher of lemonade. He fired once into his sister's brain. The bullet knocked her off the chair, and she fell facedown on the granite floor. He turned to his mother. She was screaming and running toward the door. He chased her down about 15 feet short of it and stood in front of her. He raised the gun and waited long enough to hear her plead for her life. "Don't shoot. Please," she said in Armenian. "Please don't shoot." He fired once into her chest, and she staggered backward, falling flat and faceup on the floor. He stood over her, straddling her body. She looked up at him and raised her right hand. He fired a second bullet, a third bullet, a fourth, fifth, sixth, seventh, and eighth. Each one he aimed straight into her heart. She was wearing a beautiful silk top, the color of eggplant, but he couldn't tell. She had died with her apron on.

As he looked around the room, he could see his 23-year-old nephew, Hagop, trembling halfway up the stairs. He didn't say a word to the young man he had once regarded as his fifth son. He turned away and walked a dozen paces to the leather couch in the living room. Then he sat down, pointed the gun at his right temple, and fired one time.

ON AN EARLY WINTER AFTERNOON not long ago, five years after that day, the widow of Zankou Chicken sat in her little office in the back of the Pasadena restaurant and stared into her computer screen. Live images from each Zankou, the four her husband had built and the two she had opened since, popped up with a mouse click. Every car in the parking lot, every customer standing in line, every worker taking an order or turning a spit of meat, from Burbank to Anaheim, came under her gaze.

She studied the movements the way she imagined her husband had scrutinized them from his perch inside each store, looking for signs that the service wasn't fast enough, or the food good enough, or that an employee, God forbid, might be stealing. She had her cell phone at the ready in case her sons needed to reach her—to discuss business or some difficulty in their lives. This had become Rita Iskenderian's vigil, watching her stores and bird-dogging her sons for any sign of trouble. A life-size photo of Mardiros, mustache drooping, middle-aged body thick in a suit, handsome still, kept watch on her. She looked up and shook her head.

"I didn't have time to cry. I had to get out of bed. I buried him, and 15 days later I was running this business. I was not a working woman. I had no position. No ground. But I know how impor-tant this business is. That is what my husband built. I have to be on top of it. I am doing for him. Everything for him." Her En-glish was broken by the backward phrasing and accent of a woman who carried Syria and Lebanon in her past. Two packs of ciga-rettes a day had turned her voice husky, and her whole manner had the weight of weariness. When a smile did come, she caught herself and put it away before anyone noticed. And yet she kept a sense of humor, a kind of gallows giggle, that life, luck, had turned out the way it had. Only when you got to know her well did she betray a hint of the anger she felt toward Mardiros. Her disquiet was not only for what he had done to her and her children and the rest of the family but also for what he had done to himself, the stain across his name.

"It's a shame that a man of this value has left behind this thing. Because he was a man who gave all his soul. He never said no to anybody. What his mother did to him, I cannot explain. What his sister did to him, I cannot explain. Can jealousy explain this? Can foolish pride? Five years later, it is still a mystery to me."

She regretted not putting aside her own pride back then and

visiting his mother and sister Dzovig. Maybe she could have helped broker a peace and kept the whole thing from happening. What had taken place since was its own crime. She and Mardiros's surviving sister, Haygan, had been best friends since childhood. After the deaths, they had met and consoled each other, and Rita continued to make gestures of reconciliation. But then the lawyers marched in, and a war between the two sides broke out.

If Mardiros's intentions had been to erase family entanglements and leave the business and its future to the next generation, he had left behind an even bigger mess.

His registration of the Zankou trademark had lapsed in 2000. Rita believed the chain's good name belonged to her as part of the 1991 split. But during probate, she received a letter from lawyers representing Dzovig's two sons. They intended to challenge her claim. She filed suit, and the matter went to trial. In late 2006, to the displeasure of everyone involved, the appellate court ruled that the trademark belonged to both sides. Rita's in-laws and one of her nephews then countered with a lawsuit of their own, alleging wrongful death and seeking tens of millions of dollars from Mardiros's estate. But their lawyers had failed to file within the statute of limitations, and the suit was dismissed.

Rita didn't discourage her sons when they talked about the love they still felt for their cousins and the desire to be one family again. But she was sure the other side was thinking up ways to take the Zankous from them. Indeed, her two nephews and sister-in-law, who would not speak publicly about the matter, were preparing a new lawsuit to not only take full control of the trademark but wrest away one of the two houses that Rita and her sons owned. "It never ends," she said. "It never ends."

She opened her office door and walked down a long hall to the front of the restaurant. A giant map of Los Angeles, lifted from the pages of a Thomas Guide, shouted a welcome to customers. Two Armenian cashiers, smiles from the old Soviet Union, took orders. Rita poured herself a soda, parted the black plastic curtain, and entered the main kitchen for all six of her Zankous.

Mexican men in yellow T-shirts with ZANKOU written in red were cleaning chickens, slicing chickens, marinating chickens, skewering chickens. They sent to the ovens 48,000 pounds of Foster Farms roasters and fryers each week, 2.5 million pounds a year. Blood dripped off their knives, down a gutter, and into a drain. On a big black stove, 20 stainless steel pots filled with garbanzo beans—next week's hummus—bubbled on the fire. Bins brimmed with tahini, the sesame seed paste, and *mutabbal*, the smooth, creamy roasted eggplant dip, and *tourshe*, the long, thin slices of pickled purple turnips. The skewers, both horizontal and vertical, were piled thick with beef and chicken. From the inside out, fat sizzled, dripped down, and coated the meat, turning the exterior into a delicate caramel. This was the dish that Mardiros had invented, the best-seller they called *tarna*.

Against the far wall, a Formica table and chairs had been set up gin rummy style. Four ladies, two from Mexico and two from Armenia, sat all day performing a kind of circumcision. They took every clove of garlic that came whole and peeled from Gilroy and excised the tiny stem at the tip. Bud by bud, they cleaned 1,500 pounds of garlic each week. "You would think they stink of garlic," Rita said, gesturing toward the women. "But get close and all you smell is soap."

Of all the possibilities, no one had thought that the widow who had never worked a day at Zankou would be the one to step into her husband's shadow. Her sons didn't think she could do it. She wasn't sure herself. Together, they had grown the chain by adding a store in West L.A. and one in Burbank, the fanciest of the bunch. For the most part, though, it was still a mom-and-pop. She took her workers into her extended family, for better and for worse. She paid them more than the minimum wage and provided free food for lunch. Many had stuck around for years; only a handful had left disgruntled.

She didn't apologize for being a hard driver, a stickler for quality. Indeed, her insistence on using the best and freshest ingredients and cooking everything from scratch was cutting into profits. The cost of tahini alone had doubled in the past year. Back in Mardiros's time, profits from one store had opened the next. In the case of Burbank and West L.A., Rita had to take out large loans on her house. She had no choice but to raise prices, so that a plate of chicken tarna now ran close to $10—the danger zone for fast food.

"Everybody thinks we are making millions," she said. "Would you believe it if I told you that the one Zankou in Beirut was making more money back then than all of the Zankous put together today?"

At age 24, Zankou was a survivor. Fending off challengers, some shameless in their imitation, was nothing new. The Internet droned with foodies debating the chain's "overrated" chicken or lamenting how the garlic paste had somehow lost its zest. "Zankou Chicken, I don't get the hype," one wrote. Another declared, "Arax is the best falafel stand in Hollywood. The only reason I go to Zankou now is when Arax is closed." Zankou defenders shouted back: "What do you mean overrated? It's better than ever."

Rita tamped down talk by sons Dikran and Steve about bringing in outside investors to triple the chain, or about selling Zankou nationwide as a franchise. Look around, she told them. Koo Koo Roo, Boston Market, Kenny Rogers—the street was littered with small chains that grew into bigger chains and imploded because they forgot what good food tasted like.

Dikran, the marketer who handled everything from menus to charity, seemed to understand. Steve took it personally. He was 28 now and knew more about the food operations than any of them. He had Mardiros's instinct for the business, Rita agreed, and his taste buds, too. He could take one bite of food and know immediately which spice was too much or too little. But he also had the curse of his father's temper. Rita worried that he might get into trouble again. And when it came to managing people, she did not trust his judgment.

Five months earlier, Steve had insisted on hiring a supervisor for Pasadena, a woman who had a long career managing fast-food franchises such as McDonald's. After much discussion, Rita gave in. The new manager wasted no time making small changes (name tags) and big ones (hour-by-hour tracking of sales). Steve saw an operation evolving from unprofessional to professional. Rita saw it going from friendly to sterile. It was a classic battle, pitting the virtues of smallness against the efficiencies of bigness. It turned ugly. The manager was fired.

Steve became furious with his aunt, Rita's sister, who worked at the Pasadena Zankou and had complained bitterly about the manager. He confronted her. She was ten years older than his mother and blind in one eye. His mother wouldn't speak of the details, but it was clear that Steve had gotten physical with his aunt. Rita felt she had no choice but to fire him and kick him out of the house.

"What Steve did to his aunt, I am too ashamed to talk about," she said. "He is a good boy, and he's got a big heart. But he has given me no choice. He has to learn how to control his temper. His anger, we will not accept."

STEVE KNEW THE BACK STREETS of Los Angeles every bit as well as his father. Tooling from Glendale to Hollywood, cranking the wheel from freeway to road, he could tell his Global Positioning System a thing or two about the best way to get there. He had been blaring Bob Marley for two days, ever since his mother had given him the boot. Now it was time to continue his education of *The 48 Laws of Power.* He slipped the CD into his player, and a voice, eerily disembodied, began to intone:

"Power is more God-like than anything in the natural world. . . . Power's crucial foundation is the ability to master your emotions. . . . If you are trying to destroy an enemy who has hurt you, far better to keep him off guard by feigning friendliness than showing anger. . . . Make your face as malleable as an actor's. Practice luring people into traps. Mastering arts of deception are among the aesthetic pleasures of lying. They are also key components in the acquisition of power."

Law 1 seemed easy enough: "Never Outshine the Master." He was having more difficulty with Law 15: "Crush Your Enemy Totally." It didn't occur to him that the tape, like his favorite movie, *Scarface*, was so over-the-top that another listener might find it comical. He wanted to believe in the message. Whether that message came from Sun Tzu or Donald Trump or Tony Montana, he was willing to hand over his whole being to it. He saw himself as putty going in, a rich and beloved American tycoon coming out.

"My goal in life," he said, "is to have as many people at my funeral, to have affected as many lives in a good way, as I can. I want to live a great life. I want to be a great person. I really enjoy hanging out with different people, intellectual people, important people. I know I really can't do that unless I have power."

He seemed, in a fundamental way, far too sweet a kid to become truly adept in the art of ruthlessness. Among Armenians and beyond, people were awed by his generosity in the same way they had admired his father's. Zankou didn't deliver, but there was Steve, bags of spit-roasted goodies loaded in his Lexus, heading to a school or a charity that needed free food for its function. He paid the monthly rent on a building in Ontario that a black preacher, a friend, had converted into his first church. Steve was the one whom friends called when they were nearing bottom and needed a push into rehab. He drove them there, nursed them through the cold turkey, and monitored their recoveries like a hawk.

As for his own life, it was a mess. He had dark circles under his eyes and was 30 pounds overweight. His younger brother Ara, whose addiction to Vicodin had morphed into an addiction to exercise, thanks in part to Steve, tried to work him back into shape. He kept skipping the gym to gorge on lobster and crab at

Mariscos Colima in North Hollywood. After one monumental meal, he caressed his belly. "Bro," he said, eyes twinkling. "You wouldn't know it, but underneath these pounds I used to catch a lot of ladies."

He was sure he was paying a price for all that softness. People saw him as an easy mark. No wonder his mother discounted his vision. "She thought the manager I hired was pulling the wool over my eyes. But she doesn't know what it takes to move this business forward. Don't get me wrong. My mother's been awesome. She surprised all of us with her work ethic. But she doesn't understand this business the way I understand it."

He had been at his father's side, watching and learning, since he was a kid. If only he were calling the shots now, the next move would be big. "I believe we can open a Zankou in every major city in America. But she doesn't want to hear it, bro. I have to sugarcoat everything. I have to walk on eggshells."

Walk on eggshells? Had he been walking on eggshells a few days earlier with his aunt?

"My aunt was totally provoking me the whole way," he said. "They are making it like I beat her up, but I didn't. They are insisting that I hurt her. And I didn't hurt her. I lost—I lost my control, bro. I was mad. You know?"

So he hit her?

"I slapped her on the hand. It didn't hurt, though, bro. I know it didn't hurt."

Now Steve wasn't sure what to do. Should he stay with friends? Get a place of his own? Leave town? He packed his bags and headed north, past Santa Clarita and Bakersfield, straight up Highway 99. The grape fields all around him were in winter slumber, and he felt his mind begin to race. One image after the other, his life over the past ten years, came back to him. He saw Dikran, the older brother he so admired, walk into the bedroom they shared and whisper at night: "Steve, you're going to hell if you don't change your ways." He saw the 777 Motel and the call girl and her pimp. He saw the courtroom in Van Nuys and the prosecutor making the tiniest of blunders. He saw his father lying on the couch, a hat covering his bald head, and his grandmother home from work, walking past him as if he were already dead. He saw his father burning the photo and telling him he would never forgive her. "God will forgive the devil before I can forgive my mother. Because this is a mother, not the devil." He saw his father asking him for a slushy lemonade from the Muscle Beach shop at the Glendale Galleria. He saw himself coming back home, the lemonade still icy, his father gone.

He kept driving through the California farm fields until he reached Fresno. That night, sitting in a friend's backyard, he heard the story about the Armenian kid who had stolen a crate of raisins in the 1920s. Fifty years later, at the church picnic, the old ladies sitting in their lawn chairs pointed to a boy standing in the shish kebab line. "See that young man," one old lady said. "That's the raisin stealer's grandson." No one needed to tell him the moral. He was the son of the Zankou Chicken mogul who had murdered his mother and sister and then had the decency to kill himself. What struck him wasn't the story's lesson—that you can never escape the past—but what the storyteller had left out. Did those whispers reach the ears of the raisin stealer's grandson? Or was he lucky enough to be just outside their reach? Did he manage to live his life never knowing the peculiar bent of his patrimony? Steve wasn't so lucky. He had heard the whispers, and it made him think about the son he might have one day. Would the whispers follow him? Or would his son know the story because Steve had chosen to tell it from his own mouth?

For three days, he ate white bean and lamb stew, drank whiskey, and imagined living in a place such as Fresno, the land of Saroyan, far from Zankou, far from family. On the fourth day, he climbed back into his car and headed home.

This time, as the highway opened up, his mind fixed on a different image from the past. It was 2005, two years after the murders, and the grieving was finished. The family had decided it was time to honor Mardiros and open a new store in West L.A. Because he was the son most like his father, the job was given to him. You find the location, his mother told him. You find the contractor. One day, the store half done, he found himself unable to get out of bed. For 90 days, he lingered in a state of deep depression. Doctors prescribed pills, but he wouldn't take them. Nothing could reach him. Not food or drink or sex. His mother didn't know what to do. She was paying $15,000 a month in rent for a restaurant with no opening in sight. She finally persuaded him to see a psychiatrist, a Greek doctor who heard the story and could see where the problem was buried.

All his life, he had been told he was Mardiros's son. And all his life, good and bad, he had done his best to make that true. The girls, the outbursts, the devotion to business, the loyalty to family, it became his way of honoring the father. But what it meant to be Mardiros Iskenderian's son had changed irrevocably that day. It was one thing to be the second coming of a patriarch beloved by family and community. It was another to know that all this legacy had been washed over by one act. Who was the father? Who was the son? How could Steve ever be expected to build a new Zankou in his father's name, without ever owning up to what his father had done?

Usually he did not plan his visits to Forest Lawn. He went only when the impulse seized him, and that was rare. Truth be known, he wasn't sure if he was strong enough. But that December day in 2007, as he barreled into Los Angeles, he decided he would do something different. Inside the cemetery gates, he visited the grave of his father, and then he headed to the opposite end to locate the graves of his grandmother and aunt. He hadn't gone to their funerals. He had never said a proper good-bye. "I know it sounds stupid, but it wasn't until I was standing there, staring into their headstones, that it hit me for the first time. That my father had killed them. I never really looked at it like that before. He took two lives. He was going to die anyway, so I don't count his life. But he took two lives with him. And those lives belonged to my grandmother and my aunt. There was no turning away from it. This is what my father chose to do as his final deed."

He wanted to believe that none of it was truly planned, that his father, racked by rage and cancer, was not of sound mind. He wanted to believe that in the living room of his aunt's house, his father awoke to his crime and felt immense sadness. He could only hope that his father had asked for forgiveness as he sat down on the couch and raised the gun to his head. What he didn't know was that the coroner had checked for traces of salt beneath his father's eyes and found none. Mardiros Iskenderian had shed no tears.

The son left the cemetery that day with the same questions he had been lugging around for five years. They were questions, he now knew, that had no answers. How could a woman who cooked with such love disown her son on his deathbed? How could a man so intent on passing to his sons the good name of his life's work hand them this name, this act?

He drove up the canyon to the mansion that sat on a ledge in the Verdugo Hills. He parked his car and walked up the driveway past the koi pond in the entrance and knocked on the door. His mother and three brothers were waiting for him. There was Ara, who struck an impressive bodybuilder's pose, and Vartkes, the university student who was still trying to finish a condolence letter he had been writing to Dzovig's sons for five years. And there was Dikran, the uneasy patriarch, who felt the need to speak for them all.

"Dad wanted us brothers to love each other and always support each other no matter what. We are different, each of us, but we are one. We love each other, and we will die for each other. As his sons, we can never let money or outsiders tear us apart. To do less would be to dishonor Dad's memory."

Steve sat down on the couch next to his mother, leaned back, and closed his eyes. Rita took a puff of her cigarette and smiled. *Her prince. Her pasha.* Then she opened the family scrapbook to a page from Beirut, the year 1975, and she began to narrate. "To this day, I never see anybody as beautiful as my husband was. I met him when I was 12. Roof to roof, we passed each other notes. It was forbidden, but we fell in love."

MARK ARAX *is the author of three books, including* In My Father's Name, *about his twenty-year search to find the men who murdered his father, and the upcoming* West of the West: Dreamers, Believers, Builders, and Killers in the Golden State. *During his twenty-year career at the* Los Angeles Times, *Mark won many national awards for both his investigative reporting and feature writing. He now teaches literary nonfiction at Claremont McKenna College.*

Coda

The story ends where it ends. No epilogue, other than Rita and her four sons still trying to come to terms with Mardiros's final act. If the piece feels as if the writer had something extra invested in the telling, something deep down but never expressed, it may be because I saw so much of my own story in their story. My father was murdered when I was fifteen, and the mystery of that crime bent my entire life, for good and bad. I saw my mother in Rita, a woman who knew nothing about her husband's business yet had no choice but to take it over. I saw myself in Steve, a son trying to honor his father and yet so confused about the choices his father had made at the end of his life. I wanted to use my Armenian heritage to inform the story, to get close to the family and give the reader the most intimate portrait I could. But I had to be careful not to rely on my heritage so much that I was conning the family or pulling punches with the reader. It was not an easy balancing act and I think now that I may have failed. Rita, for one, will no longer speak to me. Not because of some factual error or even a contextual one but because, her friends tell me, the story was too personal, too intimate.

Charles Bowden

MEXICO'S RED DAYS

FROM GQ magazine

THERE WAS A TIME when death made sense in Juárez. You died because you had a drug load or because you lost a drug load. You died because you tried to do a deal or because you were a snitch, or because you were a poor woman and it was dark and someone thought it might be fun to rape and kill you. There was a pleasant order to death, a ritual of cartel thugs or corrupt police or the army taking you, then tying your hands and feet with duct tape, torturing you, and finally killing you and tossing your body into a hole with a dose of "milk"—the friendly term for lime. Your death would be called carne asada, a barbecue. Life made sense then, even in death. But those were, of course, the good old days, when murders averaged two or three hundred per year.

Now the world has changed. Since January, El Paso, the sister city of Juárez, just across the remnants of the Rio Grande, has had just five murders. In the first 160-odd days of 2008, Juárez has had nearly 500—no one knows the exact number, except that it just goes up and up and up. The killings have the cold feeling of butchery in a slaughterhouse, and they are everywhere: done in broad daylight, on streets, in markets, at homes,

and even in Wal-Mart parking lots. Women, children, guilty, innocent—
no one is safe.

These are red, endless days.

SHE CAME TO JUÁREZ FROM SINALOA, the state on the Pacific that is the mother of almost all the major players in the Mexican drug industry, probably to visit her sister who works in the city. She was very beautiful—her hair hung down to her ass and her skin was oh so white. They called her Miss Sinaloa. I know this because when Elvira, who works at an asylum on the outskirts of Juárez, starts talking about her, she includes this *Miss* part. Yes, Miss Sinaloa, a beauty queen who came to Juárez. "Once," Elvira says with pride, "we had a very beautiful woman— Miss Sinaloa. The police brought her here; she was 24 years old."

The city cops claimed they had found her wandering on the street one morning, but Miss Sinaloa had actually been at a party. No one knows how she left the party—in Juárez there are many versions of every event—but everyone agrees on what happened after: The police took her and then raped her for three days. Eight policemen, in turn, over and over. In the mid-1990s, when girls from Juárez first began vanishing and then reappearing in the desert as corpses, the cops referred to them as *morenitas*, the little dark ones, because they came from the darker-skinned barrios where the women who slave in American-owned factories live. But Miss Sinaloa hailed from a different world: She was fair-skinned, middle-class, a beauty queen. And a fair-skinned woman is a special treat for street cops. By the time she got to the asylum, Miss Sinaloa's buttocks bore the handprints of many men. There were bite marks all over her breasts.

I have been coming to Juárez for thirteen years, and like everyone here, I have an investment in the dead. And the living. Miss Sinaloa is a story, and like all stories, for a moment it tantalizes. Then it vanishes—swept up into one of the many theories that attempt to account for all the violence happening in Juárez. Some blame the massive migration of the poor to the city to work in the factories; another favorite theory has it that the violence is because of the drug world. Those who focus on the murder of the girls sense a serial killer prowling the lonely dark lanes. Others simply see the state waning in border towns like Juárez, the violence a new order replacing the fading state with criminal organizations.

But I am a tiny minority on this matter. I see no new order emerging but a new way of life, one beyond our imagination and beyond the code words we use to protect ourselves from the horror of violence. In this new way of life, no one is really in charge—and no one is safe. The violence has crossed class lines. The violence is everywhere. It has no apparent and simple source. It is like the dust in the air, part of life itself.

So I sit on the sand outside the asylum and think of Miss Sinaloa. She understands what is happening in Juárez. And soon I think I will, too, if I am given enough time on the killing ground.

Victor Alejandro Gomez Marquez, 28
D. March 16, 2008

In January a list appears on a Juárez monument to fallen police officers. Under the heading THOSE WHO DID NOT BELIEVE *are the names of five recently murdered cops. And under the heading* FOR THOSE WHO CONTINUE NOT BELIEVING *are seventeen names, including one belonging to Victor Alejandro Gomez Marquez. No one knows who is responsible for the list, but a few days later, four cops on it are killed.*

In March, Marquez tells his mother he has fifteen days to live. A week later, he comes over to his mother's house again and sits with a friend as they drink a liter of whiskey. That time he tells his mother he has eight days to live, at best. "Be positive," she tells him. "Christ's blood is covering you and protecting you."

On the morning of Palm Sunday, the beginning of Holy Week,

Victor Marquez rides in a police convoy through the quiet of Juárez when his car is pinned at a light by a car in front. Another car pulls alongside and machine-guns his vehicle. He is now done with living.

By the end of April, ninety Juárez cops have left the force, and those who remain have announced they will no longer be leaving their station houses. In late May, another list goes up. Beneath the names of marked men and women, it reads: THANK YOU FOR WAITING

IN DECEMBER 2006, Felipe Calderón, the incoming president of Mexico, unleashed the nation's army to attack the multibillion-dollar drug industry, which had flourished during the later years of Vicente Fox's administration and was beginning to rival the government in scale and influence. Organized crime was close to gaining complete control of certain Mexican states, Calderón said; it had to be stopped, And besides, after having barely won his seat as president, it seemed like a smart idea to do something popular—such as hunt the cartels—so Calderón gave the army a pay raise and sent 30,000 soldiers out among the people.

At first, Calderón's gambit was sold as a resounding success. In just four months of the operation, the government claimed to have apprehended the leader of a major drug gang and to have captured more than 1,102 drug dealers and 630 cars, fifteen boats, and two airplanes used to transport drugs. "We have managed . . . to calm people's fears and let them know that government is here for them," the president said.

For most of 2007, things remained quiet, or at least relatively so—a few murders, some disappearances, nothing unusual.

But when I arrive in Juárez in January, something is stirring. That month, the violence explodes—one, two, sometimes more people die per day, and many more go missing. Forty are killed in Juárez and hundreds across Mexico, and the numbers only go up from there. (By the time I sit down to write, in June, roughly

2,500 have died in Mexico this year.) In early May, the director of Calderón's national drug-enforcement agency is gunned down in his own home—he dies asking, "Who sent you?"—and later the government determines the hit was done by the Sinaloa cartel, with the killers reportedly led by a former agent of the director's own force.

Suddenly, it seems Calderón's war may be hurting the Mexican people more than it hampers the drug trade.

When it comes to explaining the causes of all this carnage, the DEA, the U.S. Border Patrol, and America's media and government leaders claim that it stems from a battle between various drug cartels, made increasingly desperate as Calderón's army puts on the squeeze. This is a perfectly plausible explanation, except for the fact that the violence is failing to kill cartel members. After several months, there is hardly a body in Juárez that can be connected to the cartels. Nor can the Mexican Army seem to locate any of the leaders of the cartels—men who have lived in the city for years. A rumor is everywhere in Juárez about what happened at Aroma, a café on a plush avenue next to an area of mansions and a country club. The rumor is that on May 17, fifty heavily armed men arrived here, took the cell phones of the customers, and told people they could not leave. Then Joaquín "El Chapo" Guzmán, the head of the Sinaloa cartel, swept in, dined, and left around 2 A.M. while out in the street Calderón's army guarded the serenity of the establishment. Guzmán paid everyone's tab. He is a man with a $5 million bounty on his head who is said to be at war with the Juárez cartel, yet everyone in the city seems to know of his visit to Aroma and to believe it.

That weekend at least ten people are murdered as El Chapo dines in peace.

The other problem with the cartel theory is that Calderón's army has seized tons of marijuana in Juárez but only a few kilos of cocaine—the main stream of cartel revenue. The Mexican government itself has estimated that 60 percent of the killings are gang violence over street drug sales, and less than 10 percent are assigned to organized crime, meaning the cartels.

And yet it is the cartel-war story that appears on the pages of newspapers such as *The Washington Post* and *The New York Times* and tumbles from the tight smile of Lou Dobbs. It is apparently easiest on the nerves when the main victims of the slaughter in Mexico are drug lords—bad men who get what they deserve.

Juan Carlos Rocha, 38
D. March 10, 2008

He stands on a freeway island peddling P.M., a tabloid that features murders and sells to working-class people. Two men approach and shoot him in the head. The killers walk away from the killing. No one sees anything except that they are armed, wear masks, and move like commandos.

A crowd gathers to watch the police clean up. Rocha, the people say, sold more than P.M. He also offered cocaine at $4 to $6 a packet and allegedly earned about $300 a week as his cut—about four times what the neighboring factory workers, his customers, make. He'd been warned twice by mysterious strangers to cease this activity.

He did not listen.

As he lies in a pool of blood in the bright sunlight, his brown jacket is neatly folded on the traffic island, his cap on the pavement where it tumbled from his shattered skull. The next day, the vendor is the cover story of P.M. His street name was El Cala. This man who sold newspapers and little packets of cocaine: the Skull.

PALOMAS FEELS EMPTY even though its church is full of flowers from a big expensive wedding. Padre José Abel Retana stands with his vestments as the bride and groom beam on the church steps, a mariachi band strumming them into their new lives. The padre is a short, solid man. He looks a lot like El Chapo Guzmán, who is credited with many of the murders going on in this small community about a hundred miles west of Juárez, on the border just below Columbus, New Mexico.

"Yes," he softly smiles when I point out the likeness, "people tell me that. Let me change into my jeans so I look handsome."

Padre Abel's flock is now a bloody mess. So far this year, his town of 8,000 has witnessed more than forty murders. Seventeen more have vanished. During one week this spring, Padre Abel held funeral Masses for nine people. Two of the slain were a father and son slaughtered on a Friday; five more were men killed leaving the father and son's wake on Sunday. Calderón's army stood by at the burial ceremonies, since follow-up murders at the cemetery are a real possibility in the current climate of Mexico.

For decades an old system kept Palomas in order. The town fed off tourists and the drug trade—when Padre Abel arrived five years ago, he remembers, each week a shipment of three to five tons of marijuana would roll through and pass, without a problem, right into the United States. In the late '90s, human smuggling boomed: The town exploded with motels, big units thrown up for storing people for shipment. But as the border tightened in recent years, the drug and people smuggling moved away. The motels emptied out; there was no way to make money, and so Palomas starved. The old order disappeared. And then the killing started.

In a town this small, killers and slain know each other, and Padre Abel tends to them all. I've come to visit the padre because he recently gave a sermon against the killings—naming names in the drug industry—saying, This must stop. A newspaper account of his sermon noted everything he said but did not print the names that he announced in the pulpit; such disclosures are generally fatal for reporters. But Padre Abel is not worried. He says that no one will kill a priest and insists the naming thing was overblown—that he mentioned only a few, and everyone already knew who they were.

"It started last April," the padre says, "and then it got calm. Until this January. We are not just talking about dead people but the disappeared—a lot of people. They just take them away."

He seems to sink into himself as he rolls through the history and nature of the drug business, how each town or city or state has a man in charge, how that man controls all the smuggling and killing, how it has always been that way—and yet this tidal wave of blood is without any precedent, so something must have changed.

"I think the government is causing more insecurity—because the army does nothing," he says. "There is a shoot-out, and the army does not come because they say they don't have orders to get close. I don't know if the army is doing the killing or the hit men—but whoever it is, we think the government is behind it."

Since the army began patrolling down the road in Juárez, dozens of city cops have been busted by soldiers—many claim to have been beaten—and two female police officers are found blindfolded and stripped to their underwear. They are rumored to have been raped. The cops fear the army, and the army is ill-equipped to police the streets, so law and order breaks down. There have always been little gangs besides the major cartels, and these little gangs now flourish because drugs are everywhere and drug use has exploded as people seek ways to endure the strife of normal life. Without the cops or the cartels to keep them in line, the gangs fight for the corner, scrambling for a cut of the small-scale action. And after a while, the killing takes on a life of its own—a final contact high for those with no future. The padre sees this chaos even in tiny Palomas.

"The plaza," he offers, "belongs to the Juárez cartel, and it seems like Chapo Guzmán wants this area. The army drives around, but the soldiers don't do anything. There are a few cops here, but when the hit men come, it is like 1,000 against ten. . . ."

He suddenly becomes animated and imitates the burst of an AK-47. He is fumbling now, reaching out for conventional explanations—a cartel war, the army, hit men—theories that worked in the past.

He is okay, for the moment: He is convinced that no one will kill a priest.

But what if the old rules that allow him to believe this no longer apply?

A week after our conversation, a man from Palomas crawls into the U.S. port of entry at Columbus. His body is covered in burns. Someone has spent a week pouring acid on his skin and applying hot irons.

This was apparently happening as the padre and I spoke softly of the slaughter.

Alexia Moreno, 12
D. June 9, 2008

She is 12 years old and scared of the killings. She wants to go live with her mother in El Paso, but she does not get out in time. She is sitting in a park with two girlfriends when some guys in a nice new Chevy Tahoe snatch them—the guys are being trailed by killers and want the girls as human shields. The girls make a break for it; two get away. Alexia doesn't. She is shot in the head. The killers take the guys in the Tahoe and disappear. No one has seen them since.

ONE MURAL DEPICTS A CONQUISTADOR; another wall is a collage of snapshots of the asylum's work; a sign by the gate says GOD IS GREATER THAN MY PROBLEMS. This is the office of El Pastor, José Antonio Galvan: the man who took in the battered remains of Miss Sinaloa and gave her sanctuary. He is sitting in front of me—a mop of graying hair, a fleshy body, a ready smile—showing me a movie about his asylum: men beaten by police and dumped on the streets, addled addicts with seeping wounds, women who will never remember what happened to them and never want to remember.

El Pastor has seen a lot of violence in his city, and he tells me what is going on.

"Young people come to Juárez to have the American dream—it is so close," he says. "They come from the south; they are hard-working, and they don't know anything about the streets. But now the border is harder to cross, and soon they are selling their bodies and using drugs. After a year, they have gang tattoos. The capos now make enough money selling drugs here; they don't have to transport them into the United States.

"You can't do anything to be safe here," he continues. "Cocaine is everywhere and cheaper than marijuana. They smoke cocaine with marijuana. We're talking about people 18 to 25—the people who get executed. They are ghosts, human trash walking naked in the city."

I ask El Pastor if he remembers a patient called Miss Sinaloa.

"Oh yes," he says. "She was at an orgy. At the Casablanca."

The Casablanca is a hotel where men bring women for sex and love and joy and whatever other terms they prefer. There are many such places in Juárez, a city where few can afford privacy in their homes and so must rent it at the moment of desire. In front of the hotel stands a large nightclub with red-tiled domes, a playground for cops and narcos alike—anyone who wants booze, dope, and women. This, El Pastor says, was where the cops took hold of Miss Sinaloa.

When the city police brought her out and dumped her with El Pastor, she had lost her mind. The asylum was her home for at least two months, but no one could reach her. She raved; she was very angry. And she was bald. The staff had to cut off her long beautiful hair because it was an occupational risk here: Some patients have shown a tendency to take another patient's long hair and strangle her with it. In part she was locked up to protect her from the other patients, who crave her fair skin and beauty.

And in part she was locked up because otherwise she would go berserk.

El Pastor shows me her cell. It is maybe nine feet by five feet, and it is in here that, after two months, Miss Sinaloa seems to recover some of her mind. El Pastor locates her relatives, and they drive up from Sinaloa. They must be surprised that she is alive. I certainly am. After such a frolic, death would not be unusual, and Miss Sinaloa would be just one more mysterious body in Juárez. But something saved her. Perhaps it was her madness—the way she raged against the cops—that set her apart.

When the family comes to retrieve their daughter, the father concludes that El Pastor and his patients have been having their way with her. El Pastor is horrified, and there is a terrible argument, and then Miss Sinaloa leaves with her family for home. But as we stand in the dust and wind outside the asylum walls, and El Pastor recounts his reaction to that moment ("I am a family man!"), we both understand the father's reaction. They are middle-class people, El Pastor notes, unaccustomed to having a daughter go missing on Juárez's streets. They had a nice car, and they paid for all the medical bills Miss Sinaloa had run up.

And in a country where the weak are always prey, where the favorite verb is *chingar*, to fuck over, the desire to place blame is irrepressible.

Armando Alvarado López
D. January, 2008

Ten or twenty men with automatic rifles and black masks descend on a poor barrio of shacks cut in the hills outside town, where one man, an ex-municipal cop in his early thirties, runs a little store that sells beans, bread, and milk to men and women who work in the American-owned factories known as maquiladoras. The men torture him until he reveals who supplied him with the drugs he also sold out of his little store. He cannot really be surprised by the visit: After all, he'd been warned in two phone calls to stop selling drugs. The armed men take him to his supplier and then carry the two captives off a short distance and execute them. Everyone in the barrio hears the shots. The action is hard to miss; it happens around noon on a sunny day.

Now I am here at the kill site. A woman stares at me and shouts, "Who are you looking for?" From her tone, I don't think she is trying to be helpful. As I rolled in, I could feel the eyes of loitering cholos burn into my hide.

So I leave.

BUT HERE IS A QUESTION: Why is it that we must believe that these murders happening all over the city—like this one of a small-time grocer who sold a little coke to neighbors in his poverty-stricken neighborhood—are simply the result of a battle between big cartels and the Mexican government over who will control this crossing into the United States?

Every day in Juárez, at least 200,000 people get out of bed to pull a shift in the maquiladoras. The exact number varies: Right now roughly 20,000 jobs have vanished as a chill sweeps through world markets; just after the millennium, about 100,000 jobs left the city for mainland China, because as *Forbes* magazine pointed out, the Mexicans wanted four times the wages of the Chinese. (Those greedy Mexicans were taking home $60, maybe $70 a week in a city where the cost of living is essentially 90 percent that of the United States.) The barrios where these maquiladora workers live are drab, dirty, and largely unvisited by anyone but their inhabitants. Turnover in the grinding maquiladoras runs from 100 to 200 percent a year. The factory managers say this is because of the abundant economic opportunities of the city. And in a sense, they are right: A drug peddler, for example, makes a maquiladora worker's monthly wage each week. And there's even more money to be made in other trades: A few years ago, the going rate for professional murders in Juárez was $250 apiece.

But in America, we know nothing of such matters. Officially, Juárez has healthy wages and almost no unemployment. It is a beacon of the global economy that was poised to become a modern city in a Mexico that was to become a modern nation. But when Mexico instead lingered in the shadow of tyranny and poverty, this was ignored by successive American administrations, since a quiet neighbor was and is the best kind of neighbor for a global economic empire. When Mexico persisted in being a trampoline for drugs to bounce from the cocaine belt of South America into the United States, it was the fault of American habit and addiction. Finally, when these habits could not be contained, the North American Free Trade Agreement was ballyhooed as the answer that would bring prosperity and end the violence.

What America got from NAFTA was cheap prices at Wal-Mart, lower wages at home, and an explosion of illegal immigration from the barrios of places like Juárez into the United States. What Juárez got was more drugs and more violence.

The main reason a U.S. company moves to Juárez is to pay lower wages. The only reason poor people in Juárez sell drugs and die is to earn higher wages. The only reason they go north is to survive.

I HAVE A VISION in which all the dead in Juárez since January will gather in the plaza before the cathedral downtown. They will sit in rows of chairs just as in Thornton Wilder's *Our Town*. There will be 500 separate tales of how they loved things and enjoyed life and how they were murdered and who murdered them. It is a play, of course, that will never end.

I will sit with Miss Sinaloa, and I know I will be mesmerized by the accounts but she will be bored. Her perfect face will be blank, her beautiful eyes, cocooned in makeup, will wander to the hills outside town where she stayed in the asylum. By now her hair will have grown out and the handprints on her buttocks will have vanished. She will retain nothing but barbed memories of her time at the Casablanca.

But of course, nothing she knows will matter to most people— just as the dead of Juárez will vanish and this killing season will be forgotten. You can believe in the war on drugs, in battles between the cartels, in secure borders, in free trade, in official states and statesmen. You don't have handprints on your ass and bite scars on your breasts and fragments of your mind that tell you of places that presidents never mention. I prefer the company of Miss Sinaloa, her skin so fair, her bruised thoughts more knowing than the governments that pretend to rule the chaos that now rules Juárez.

And as I watch this new *Our Town* in the plaza before the cathedral, one image sticks in my head—a fragment whispering of a murder. There is a barrio near here where people scavenge old televisions and bits of metal from both Juárez and El Paso and sell them. A man peddles cocaine on the street and is warned to stop, but he is in his thirties and has no other livelihood. So he persists, and then armed men come with masks and blow his brains out. He falls dead on the street near his mother's house.

But his body is not what I imagine.

What I see is his mother. It is night now. The body has been taken away and there is a light on, the screen door is pushed open and an old woman with a blank face stares down at the street. She is there alone, and her son is not coming home. Her face is a portrait of Juárez: silent, enduring, doomed.

CHARLES BOWDEN *is the author of twenty-two books, including* A Shadow in the City: Confessions of an Undercover Drug Warrior; Down by the River: Drugs, Money, Murder, and Family; Juárez: The Laboratory of Our Future, *and* Blood Orchid: An Unnatural History of America. Inferno, *with photographer Michael Berman, was a finalist for the Orion Book of the Year for 2007. His most recent book is*

Exodus, *with photographer Julian Cardona.* Trinity *and* Some of the Dead Are Still Breathing *will both he published in 2009.*

Bowden is a correspondent for GQ *magazine, and his work has appeared in* Harper's, Mother Jones, National Geographic, *and* Esquire. *A Pulitzer Prize nominee and winner of the Lannan Literary Award for Nonfiction and the Sidney Hillman Foundation Award, he lives in Tucson, Arizona, with a standard poodle, a desert tortoise, and a witch.*

Coda

I have been going to Ciudad Juárez for fifteen years because I could sense the future was unfolding there—violence, poverty, American-owned factories with low wages, and a vast drug business. Starting around January 2008, Juárez probed further into its destiny. In 2007, there were 301 murders, in the following year 1,607, including dozens of police. The pace has continued into 2009. All this will be in a forthcoming book, *Miss Sinaloa*.

R. Scott Moxley

Hate and Death

FROM *OC Weekly*

If Thien Minh Ly had looked up as he Rollerbladed in slow circles on the Tustin High School tennis courts, he would have seen a few stars flickering in the partly cloudy night sky over the nearby Santa Ana Mountains. The 5-foot-6, 117-pound immigrant with a gentle demeanor and a curiosity for discovery had been back in Orange County for a year after returning from graduate school at Georgetown University, and he was still mulling his next career move. Doctor? Lawyer? He'd even voiced a hope to one day serve as the first Vietnamese American ambassador to his birthplace.

The 24-year-old's boyish looks belied his tenaciousness. With his family, Ly—born in Tuy Hoa, a coastal village in Central Vietnam—fled brutal conditions in communist Vietnam via boat in 1983 after his father, an officer in the South Vietnamese military, was released from a concentration camp. After a stint living in an Indonesian refugee camp, the family arrived in California. Only 12 years old at the time, Ly led his non-English-speaking parents and two younger siblings through the early difficulties of life in an alien country. The family eventually opened a video rental shop in Santa Ana. A few months before he went Rollerblading on that cool January 1996 night, he had used a blue-ink pen and a yellow Post-It note to memorialize a thought he'd stick to a page in his diary.

"I live in today and not very far into tomorrow," he wrote. "I do my best every minute of the day, and when it's over, I know there is more to come."

But hazel-eyed death—dressed all in black, with Jack in the Box on his breath and carrying a butcher's knife—appeared suddenly from the darkness, taunted Ly on the tennis courts, mocked his fear, showed him no mercy and robbed him of his dreams.

Time has a habit of letting us forget tragedies, even ones that spark outrage, like this one did in Little Saigon and in Asian communities across the nation. It's been 12 years, but a key question about the murder is now the subject of a debate at the California Supreme Court. In coming weeks, the justices will finally announce if Ly really was the victim of a hate crime. For the killer, that decision is a matter of life or death.

"I guess if your [sic] not white your [sic] not right."
——Ly's murderer in a letter to a friend

Less than a quarter-mile from Ly's home, on an apartment wall over a futon, was taped a big-toothed caricature of Dr. Martin Luther King Jr. with a gaping bullet hole between his eyebrows. The image came with a message: "If we could have killed four more, we would have had the rest of the week off."

But that wasn't enough for Gunner Jay Lindberg. The 21-year-old Orange County native had used a yellow crayon to add the word "DEATH" to the upper-left corner of the poster on his bedroom wall. A second, mass-produced poster on the same wall showed two young white girls playing joyously.

The room had a dirty white bedsheet for a curtain. On top of a small, cheap television and a cheaper VCR sat a plastic skull wearing a helmet with a swastika, two cross-country running trophies and miniature models of 1950s cars. A nightstand contained three bottles of Jack Daniels; books on violence; videos depicting gruesome real-life deaths; correspondence with the Aryan Nation, KKK groups, White Aryan Resistance, the New Order (a successor to the American Nazi Party) and National Association for the Advancement of White People; a folder with a list of people he wanted dead (mostly ex-friends and co-workers); a black notebook with thoughts on a coming intergalactic battle; an obnoxious spoof of an application to the National Association for the Advancement of Colored People (NAACP); and a red-letter edition of the King James Bible, in which he had scrawled personal addresses for white supremacists in various states and this ominous note: "It's not God's will that everyone be healed in this life."

A quick-tempered box stocker at a Tustin Kmart with a penchant for picking fights with Asians, African-Americans and Latinos—anyone, really—Lindberg didn't graduate from high school and possessed few social skills but was artistically gifted. He'd converted both a white 2.5-pound Gourmet's Choice fruit container and a cardboard San Francisco 49ers checkers box into storage for his marijuana stash after redecorating them with swirling, hand-drawn psychedelic images of anger, death and Hitler. If pot soothed other people's minds, it only fueled Lindberg's fantasies of becoming, he wrote, "the king of all evil and distruction [sic]."

Lindberg, who also took methamphetamines, never lived up to his narcissistic imagination. During an eight-year crime spree beginning at age 12, he proved himself to be little more than a thug who preyed on the defenseless. His victims included a cop's 11-year-old son, whom he chased and shot in the throat with a BB gun; a day laborer, whom he attacked with a tree limb for the money in his pocket; a skateboarder, whom he repeatedly kicked in the stomach as he stole the board; the peers he angrily chased, firing a shotgun, over a perceived slight; an on-duty prison guard, whom he brutally ambushed; and an elderly woman, whom he pummeled during a home-invasion robbery for drug money.

But he committed his most heinous act on Ly. At 8 p.m. on Jan. 28, 1996, Lindberg took Domenic Michael Christopher, a Kmart co-worker, to his apartment after they finished a shift that consisted largely of watching the Super Bowl on television in the store's break room. According to his own writings, Lindberg hoped to mold the impressionable 17-year-old, who liked karate and hadn't been in trouble before, into his protégé. They smoked pot, talked about "robbery and shit like that" and left on foot—Lindberg carrying a butcher knife he'd stolen from his grandmother's kitchen, according to police files. They stopped for dinner at Jack in the Box, and then walked the streets searching for a victim. At one point, they encountered a group of teenagers standing in a front yard, attempted to start a fight, failed and moved on.

Minutes later, they found and trapped the unsuspecting Ly, whose last seven minutes of life were the stuff of horror flicks. Lindberg called him a "Jap," demanded his car keys, cursed him, punched him, stomped on his head, kicked his face, slashed his throat and stabbed him 22 times—in part, to celebrate a victory earlier that evening by what Lindberg hailed as "America's team," the Dallas Cowboys.

Among Ly's final words were "What the fuck?"

> *"I thought [Lindberg] was a cool guy, you know, cool. He's funny. He is . . . He's cool, you know what I mean? . . . If I'd known he was psycho, I wouldn't have hung with him."*
>
> CHRISTOPHER TO POLICE
A MONTH AFTER THE MURDER

LAW-ENFORCEMENT OFFICIALS SAY Lindberg was the first person Orange County sent to San Quentin State Prison's death row under California's hate-crime statute. Christopher, his now-remorseful accomplice, is serving a sentence of 25 years to life and is eligible to request parole in 2023.

Lindberg's days are filled with exercising, writing pen pals, creating art, playing chess, day-dreaming about Nordic lore and writing satanic poems that mock Ly's death. Thanks to an automatic appeal of every death-penalty case, he's also waiting for word from California's highest court on the pending hate-crime question. The answer could remove him from death row.

During supreme court oral arguments in June, deputy state public defender Ronald F. Turner pleaded Lindberg's case. He told Chief Justice Ronald George and six associate justices that his client's death-penalty punishment must be overturned. Turner argued that two special circumstances the jury found to be true—that the murder was committed during the commission of an attempted robbery and that Ly's race was a key factor in the crime—were, in fact, false.

"We're not dealing with a rational individual here," said Turner. "This was just a thrill kill, a bravado murder . . . motivated by male testosterone and nothing else."

In a February 2005 letter to the *Weekly*, Lindberg echoed Turner's assertion. "[The Orange County district attorney's office] blew up the white-supremacist issue," he wrote. "I'm not like that. I did have some things [reading materials] but it was something I had in prison in Missouri and I only viewed it with passing interest long ago."

Oh, I killed a Jap a while ago. I stabbed him to death at Tustin High School. I walked up to him. Domenic was with me and I seen this guy Rollerblading and I had a knife. We walked in the tennis court where he was. I walked up to him. Domenic was right there. I walked right up to him and he was scared. I looked at him and said, "Oh, I thought I knew you," and he got all happy that he wasn't gonna get jumped. Then I hit him with one of my motherfuckers and he fell to the ground and he said in a very low voice, "What the fuck?" and "You can have whatever I got. I have nothing—only a key. You can have it." Then I said, "You got a car." Oh, I pulled the knife out—a butcher's knife and he said, "No!" Then I put the knife to his throat and asked him, "Do you have a car?" And he grabbed my hand that I had the knife and looked at me, trying to get a description of me, so I stomped on his head three times and each times said, "Stop looking at me." Then he was kinda knocked out. Dazzed. Then I stabbed him in the side about 7 or 8 times. He rolled over a little, so I stabbed his back about 18 or 19 times. Then he layed flat and I slit one side of his throat on his jugular vein. Oh, the sounds the guy was making were like "uhh-hhh." Then Domenic said, "Do it again," and I said, "I already did, dude," so I cut his other jugular vein and Domenic said, "Kill him . . . Do it again." I said, "He's already dead." Domenic said. "Stab him in the heart." So I stabbed him about 20 to 21 times in the heart . . . He was dying just then, taking in some bloody gasps of air so I nudged his face with my shoe a few times. Then I told Domenic to kick him, so he kicked the fuck out of his face and he still has blood on his shoes all over [smiley face]. Then I ditched the knife after whipping it clean on to the side of the 5 freeway [smiley face]. Here's the clippings from the newspaper and we were on all the news channels. [I'm] having a ball in Tustin. Wish you were here.

—LINDBERG IN A LETTER TO HIS COUSIN

IF LINDBERG HADN'T WRITTEN that letter describing the killing to a cousin in New Mexico and the cousin's wife hadn't contacted authorities, there's a good chance the case would remain unsolved to this day.

Of course, Lindberg's "Jap" was Thien Minh Ly.

At Tustin High, Ly wowed teachers by enrolling in advanced-placement classes in calculus, physics, Spanish, English, civics and economics—quite an achievement for an immigrant who'd known English fewer than six years. He earned an eighth-place ranking in a class of about 400. At UCLA, he served as president of the Vietnamese Student Association. In August 1995, he emerged from Georgetown University in Washington, D.C., with a master's degree in physiology.

The devout Buddhist returned to his parents' OC home to decide his next move. Friends saw that he carried a study guide to the law school admissions exam, but he also spoke about his interest in medicine. While he debated his decision, he volunteered at a legal clinic established to help poor Asian immigrants in Southern California.

"My brother was such a loving, kind person," Ly's sister Thu says. "I can't describe to you the pain his death caused my family. There were so many tears. How could this happen to him? It tore our hearts apart. . . . He inspired me to be the best person I can be."

Though it's been more than a decade since the crime, Thai—Thien's younger brother—still can't talk about it, according to Thu, who is married with several young children and living in San Diego. She dedicated her life to her slain brother, entered the military and served four years as a naval officer in places such as Kuwait and Iraq.

"He wanted me to be a strong and intelligent woman with the courage to find my own adventure," she told the *Weekly*. "I often wonder what he would think of how I turned out if he were here. Such a thought often brings both smiles and tears."

"All I want to do is hurt and kill. . . . I'm a pure fucking evil dog and that's no shit."

—LINDBERG IN A LETTER TO A RELATIVE
TWO YEARS BEFORE THE MURDER

IN ANTICIPATION OF THIS STORY, I initiated contact with the condemned Lindberg at San Quentin several years ago. In return, I received handwritten letters loaded with smiley faces. Lindberg also likes to tell people that he's insane, a word that's tattooed on his upper left arm.

When I told him that I was going to write about him and requested a face-to-face interview, he first told me that a key witness who'd pissed him off during the Ly trial had died. He wrote, "Sounds like foul play!" Then he explained the conditions of our meeting.

"You'll be locked into a small cage with me, and won't be allowed a recorder or anything," he wrote. "At first I was going to say NO. But if your [sic] wanting to do it then OK. Here's your visiting form. You just fill it out and send it with a letter to me. Always, Gunner."

The Department of Justice's death-row-visitation form is lengthy, containing detailed questions about addresses, phone numbers, financial information, work history, schooling and relatives. It's a treasure trove of personal data. And Lindberg wanted me to provide him with mine.

Suspicious, I called a high-ranking prison official, who laughed when I told him what Lindberg suggested.

"He knows damn well that he's not supposed to receive that," the official told me. "You have to be exceptionally careful with these people. Are you sure you want to be locked in the same room with him?"

I remembered that Senior Deputy District Attorney Debbie Lloyd, who prosecuted Lindberg, had told me that he is "a sick, sick dangerous man."

"Would he be chained to a chair or a table?" I asked.

"No," he said. "Like he told you, it'd just be you and him in a small room."

No, thanks.

"I thought [Ly] was a kid. Next thing I know, we're [on the tennis courts], trying to hassle the guy, you know? Have some fun, you know?

Screw around with the guy. We're just playing around. The next thing
I know, the dude's on the ground. . . . He was gone. Weird. Toast."
            —CHRISTOPHER EXPLAINING THE MURDER TO POLICE
                                    AFTER HIS ARREST

LINDBERG IS A MESS OF CONTRADICTIONS. He's a white
supremacist who has also described himself as "half Apache Indian." ("Stay White," he liked to write to friends.) He has claimed
to believe in Christianity, but simultaneously espoused a satanic
view of life. ("You must kill to learn on your way to learning infa-
nate [sic] wisdom knowledge from beyoned [sic] the grave," he
advised in a handwritten instruction manual.) He has declared his
hatred of Asians, but his best friend, a cousin, was half-Japanese.

"Gooks and Nips . . . sound like a bunch of mice talking, like a
fast-forward cassette," he told fellow inmates inside the Orange
County Jail, where he violently attacked two Vietnamese inmates
while awaiting trial for killing Ly.

Predictably, Lindberg's background was, according to a court-
ordered psychiatric analysis obtained by the *Weekly,* "tumultuous
and dysfunctional." His mother and grandmother, an expert concluded, "apparently gave Gunner too much love . . . and covered
for him when he got into trouble."

He never had a steady father figure, either. His biological father,
a marine stationed at the old El Toro Marine Corps Air Station,
abandoned the family in 1977 after the birth of Lindberg's younger
brother, Jerry. Gunner, born at St. Joseph's Hospital in Orange,
was just two years old. Their mother then dated a series of men,
prompting relocations to such places as Riverside, Oceanside, Las
Vegas, Missouri and Kansas.

The mother married a marine stationed at Camp Pendleton in
1988. After a reassignment, the family moved to the U.S. military base on Okinawa. The following year, Gunner and several
junior-high-school classmates stole a vehicle and sparked a wild,

high-speed chase that ended with a collision. Japanese authorities were not amused. They expelled Gunner from the island. Afterward, he told friends he hated Asians.

Back in the U.S., Lindberg—now living with his grandmother in Oceanside, near San Diego—continued to slide into drugs and crime. He began to get drunk and smoke marijuana at the age of 12. He was cited for an assault a year later.

But the month of October 1990 truly signaled the horrors to come, according to his rap sheet. Then just 15, he chased a day laborer in a strawberry field, called him a "wetback," and assaulted him with a tree limb for the money in his pocket. The man's face was so severely cut that it took 19 stitches to sew up, and his arm was broken, with the bone protruding through the skin.

Also that month, Lindberg beat another teenager for a perceived slight and led a knife-drawn home-invasion robbery of 82-year-old Helen Tillman. Not satisfied with just the $50 robbery, he turned around at the front door, returned to the kitchen and slugged his victim in the face. The month ended with an arrest for possession of a controlled substance (methamphetamine).

The Tillman attack won Lindberg a court-ordered trip to Vision Quest, a program in San Diego for juvenile offenders. Reports show he socialized well and excelled at sports, especially running. Was he on the verge of turning his life around?

"I have a good personality. I'm honest and enjoy laughing and having fun. I enjoy most every sport, reading books, working out. I like good movies, some TV, mostly heavy metal music and some older rock. I'm into drawing. I was a bit of a wild child. I am very adventurous and love challenges. I am a great listener and always respectful."
—LINDBERG'S CURRENT PEN-PAL REQUEST

LINDBERG ULTIMATELY FAILED at Vision Quest. Taking orders from adults and living in a structured environment annoyed him; he ran away. When he reappeared in Missouri, he continued his monstrous ways. He chased an 11-year-old on a bike in a park and shot him in the throat with a BB rifle after the kid said he was a cop's son. The pellet lodged in the kid's heart and required surgery. Lindberg attacked another boy, repeatedly kicking him in the ribs, to steal his skateboard. He chased two acquaintances down a highway, firing shotgun blasts at them. He interrupted a high-school beer party by shoving a shotgun under a teenager's throat and threatening to pull the trigger; he ended up merely walloping the guy in the face with his fist.

During this crime spree, he was in and out of a Missouri juvenile facility and eventually landed in a state prison, where he ran the White Aryan Resistance, plotted the murders of enemies and ambushed a guard. On Halloween 1994, Lindberg began writing Gordon Jack Mohr, a Korean War veteran and right-wing racist who advocated that the enemies of Christ are those "who have mixed blood—the Oriental and Negroid races." These people, Mohr (now deceased) claimed, are the "real enemies of freedom," and "they have been trying and will continue to try to destroy the pure bloodline by interbreeding."

Lindberg was hooked.

"Dear Mr. Mohr, I have received a copy of the *Christian Patriot Crusader*," he wrote. "And I would like to stress my many thanks for yours and the Lord's support while I've done my time in the Gulag! If it weren't for you and God's word I would have gave up a long time ago."

After his release, Lindberg violated parole, fled Missouri and became a fugitive, according to court records. He landed undetected in Tustin, moved into a two-bedroom apartment with an older man and took a job at Kmart using a fake identity: Jerry Scott Lindberg, the name of his younger brother, who had committed suicide two years earlier on Gunner's 18th birthday.

Three months later, he and Christopher left Ly's mutilated, dying body on the tennis courts. Dripping their victim's blood for several hundred feet, they walked away, excitedly analyzed their work, tossed the murder weapon down an embankment off Interstate 5, stopped at a Circle K for cigarettes, returned home, stored blood-soaked gloves, smoked more marijuana, played Super Nintendo, and then watched two videos: *The Shining*, a horror movie starring Jack Nicholson as a possessed, ax-wielding psychopath, and Kiefer Sutherland's *The Lost Boys*, about two young men who battle a group of teenage vampires.

At sunrise the following morning, a Tustin High School groundskeeper driving a golf cart found Ly's corpse. Police were both disgusted and perplexed. Lindberg, back in the safety of obscurity, felt rejuvenated. To celebrate, he wrote a song, a portion of which goes like this:

> *Spill the blood of the meek.*
> *The meek shall inharet shit.*
> *I reak Havek. Melt minds Drifting*
> *Threw the sands of time time time time*
>   *(echo to fade)*
> *To the insane the sound is*
> *Real. You inshure them a quick kill*
> *From your so called reality pill.*
> *The shuffle*
> *The shuffle*
> *The shuffle*
> *In the ruffle beneath your skin*
> *You fill my vibes, oh your so Alive.*
> *I hear, I smell, is that pain or*
> *Fear I hear. Can't you hear or see*
> *I just killed thee, see your shattered*
> *Body beyond the brushhhhhhh.*
> *Your soul is mine*
> *For the beginning and*

All Time. At the end of this
Rhyme
Satan

There are 669 killers—including "Night Stalker" Richard Ramirez and Scott Peterson—awaiting execution in California. Every person facing the ultimate punishment is afforded an automatic appeal at taxpayer expense. The goal is to ensure that the arrest, trial and conviction were righteous. Ronald F. Turner, the deputy state public defender for Lindberg, is arguing that Lindberg was denied a fair trial. His claims include:

- Evidence of two uncharged robberies Lindberg committed as a juvenile prejudiced the jury against him on the murder charges.

- Ronald Miller, a Huntington Beach cop, should not have been allowed to testify as an expert on the relationship between Lindberg and white-supremacist groups, in part because he'd never interviewed the defendant.

- Judge Robert Fitzgerald repeatedly shifted the burden of proof to the defense and gave defective jury instructions that allowed the panel majority to pressure several jurors who'd proclaimed "sympathy" for Lindberg and a desire to keep him off death row.

But at the June 3 supreme court session in Los Angeles, Turner spent the bulk of his time arguing against the two special circumstances—the commission of an attempted robbery and the commission of a hate crime—that transformed the case from a simple killing to a death-row matter. Both were defective findings, he says.

"The evidence presented at trial was insufficient to prove that

Lindberg attempted to rob Mr. Ly," he said. "Nothing was taken from the victim, even though Lindberg had the opportunity to take Mr. Ly's [baseball] cap, his [house] key or his Rollerblades," said Turner.

Supervising Deputy Attorney General Rhonda L. Cartwright-Ladendorf reminded the justices that Lindberg had asked Ly at knifepoint, "Do you have a car?"

But to Turner, Lindberg had been "merely posing the question."

"If Lindberg had any real intent to take a car, he would have stopped and questioned Mr. Ly further," he said. "Instead, Lindberg repeatedly kicked Mr. Ly in the head, and then stabbed him in the side, back and chest."

The public defender saved his most strenuous attack on the case for the hate-crime enhancement. He told the justices that the evidence presented at trial "did not establish that Lindberg possessed a racial bias," did not prove that he hated Asians or "murdered Ly because of his race."

Turner also said "it tainted the jury to equate Lindberg with Hitler" because his client was not educated and there is no way to know if he understood the meaning of the Nazi SS lightning bolts he drew on letters and displayed in his bedroom.

"When we see murder on a high-school campus, we get angry and we try to make sense of it," Turner told the court. "The killer was white and the victim was Vietnamese, therefore [people conclude] it must be a hate crime."

Turner provided an alternative rationale for the crime. It wasn't white supremacy that dominated Lindberg's mind but "his fascination with death and with the occult." His client's post-murder writings proved, he said, that the killing was the "very first level" in Lindberg's "dark journey to godhood."

Associate Justice Carol A. Corrigan interrupted Turner's presentation to ask, "Are we to ignore all of his [racist] literature?"

Yes, he replied. "We don't know if he believed it. . . . Lindberg was an extremely angry individual who was caught up in ideas of death and destruction, but neither indicated his anger was directed to nonwhites or Asians specifically."

To bolster his point, the public defender claimed that poor lighting conditions at the high-school tennis courts would have prevented Lindberg from determining the race of the person Rollerblading on the night of the murder. During the trial, the jury considered and dismissed this point. And it didn't seem to impress Corrigan, either.

She interrupted Turner's presentation again. This time, her words may have been more of a statement than a question:

"How about this," Corrigan said. "Was he close enough to tell [Ly was Asian] while he was stabbing him?"

Turner had no good answer.

The supreme court is expected to issue its ruling this summer.

R. SCOTT MOXLEY *is senior editor for news and investigations at* OC Weekly, *a* Village Voice Media *alt-weekly in Orange County, California. He's won national awards for exposing both a deceitful congressman and a powerful, crooked sheriff. In 2007, he was awarded a top prize by the Los Angeles Press Club for revealing how a convicted felon/ ex-drug addict used the Americans with Disabilities Act to enrich himself. In 2006—the year his coverage of the sensational Haidl Gang Rape case won national attention—his investigation into a carjacking/robbery case proved that police and prosecutors sent the wrong man to prison. In 2005, FBI agents relied on his articles to arrest a wealthy Newport Beach doctor who was charging HIV and AIDS patients as much as nine thousand dollars per shot but injecting them with common saline solution. In 2004, a grand jury used his exclusive work to indict an assistant sheriff on abuse of office charges. In 2001, he helped free a young woman facing the death penalty from jail after proving sheriff's investigators doctored key crime-scene evidence at a killing. In 2000, he proved that the newly elected district attorney's best friend was a longtime organized crime suspect. He lives in Southern California.*

Coda

After the article appeared, Gunner Jay Lindberg wrote me a letter from San Quentin State Prison's death row. He expressed sorrow, writing, "I've never denied that I took Mr. Thien Minh Ly's life—but not for the reasons I was convicted. It was not a robbery nor was it a hate crime. I do believe I should pay for my crimes as I took his life, so I see my punishment as justice. I know if it were someone in my family I'd want justice and no amount of 'sorry' would change that. I'm nowhere near perfect, but I'm not a monster. I've done a terrible wrong not only to Mr. Ly but his family and I can't take it back." So why did he stab Ly twenty-two times? He told me it was merely "reckless actions."

In August 2007, the California Supreme Court issued a sixty-nine-page ruling that rejected Lindberg's arguments against his "special circumstances" convictions. The justices wrote "there is substantial evidence" that Ly was murdered during the commission of a robbery and a hate crime.

Lindberg is one of 680 men awaiting lethal injection in San Quentin. He says he spends most of his days creating art and writing pen pals.

Members of Ly's family continue to live in Southern California but, even after twelve years, still have difficulty discussing events.

Stephen Rodrick

Dead Man's Float

FROM *New York magazine*

IT ENDED IN THE POOL. The whole tragic cartoon.

That morning, it was last Labor Day, Seth and Phyllis Tobias woke up together in the master bedroom of their not-quite-finished dream home. The $5 million, 6,700-square-foot mansion is located in the Bear's Club, a gated community built on a golf course in Jupiter, Florida, twenty minutes north of Palm Beach. Designed in the style of Addison Mizner, the house is very big and very *faux*—*faux* Spanish architectural themes, *faux* this and *faux* that. There's a Ritz-Carlton condo complex in the development, too. Phyllis liked to work out there, get massages, and have her hair blown out.

Seth had bought the house for Phyllis in late 2006 from an upscale Palm Beach broker named Linda Olsson. It was a gesture of reconciliation after the couple had almost divorced. There was a lot of that—reconciliation—but that's because there was also a lot of fighting. You get the picture. The home included a state-of-the-art office for Tobias, the founder and chief executive of Circle

T, a quarter-billion-dollar Manhattan-based hedge fund. The pool was in the backyard.

The day before, the couple had invited friends over for a barbecue. The party broke up with Seth and Phyllis at each other's throat. But by the next day, the couple had made up, and now they'd decided to have lunch at the Breakers, the tony Palm Beach resort. At about 5:30 P.M. Seth and Phyllis left the hotel. Over the course of the afternoon, they'd rung up a $323 bill. Phyllis went home to Jupiter. Seth met up with this guy he'd known since he was a kid, Brett Borgerson. The two of them drove to a bar called E.R. Bradley's.

Over the next two hours, Seth and Borgerson had a few more rounds. Seth called his wife nineteen times, but she didn't call him back. It was getting dark, and Seth drove home. He passed through the gates of the Bear's Club and pulled into their brick driveway.

At 8:08 P.M., Tobias texted Borgerson to let him know he'd gotten home safely. Seth and Phyllis had dinner together and then, according to Phyllis, tried to have sex in the pool. They eventually gave up, Phyllis says. Seth was too drunk.

Phyllis went inside and began her nighttime beauty regimen. After a shower, she walked downstairs and squinted through the gloaming. She thought she caught a glimpse of Seth swimming naked in the pool. Then she went back upstairs and got ready for bed. But shortly after midnight, Phyllis called Brett Borgerson's wife and left a voice-mail that said, "Please call me back, Seth is acting weird. I don't know if he's passed out."

About half an hour later, she called 911. "I don't know if my husband has passed out or what." Her accent was thick, New Jersey. The dispatcher asked if her husband was breathing. "I don't know, he's turned over!" Phyllis screamed. "Please just send me somebody. He's outside [in] the pool." She could then be heard shouting at her floating husband, "Seth, don't play with me."

About fifteen minutes later, a Jupiter Police Department squad car arrived, and two officers shone their flashlights into the pool. The lights eventually settled on Phyllis. She was holding Seth in the shallow end. Paramedics arrived and began CPR. Geysers of water shot out of Seth's lungs; rigor mortis had already set in. At 1:08 A.M., Seth Tobias was pronounced dead. He was 44.

BEFORE SETH TOBIAS WOUND UP DEAD in his pool; before the accusations surfaced that his wife was a thrice-divorced pill-popper and cocaine user who drugged Seth and killed him for his money; before the claims that Seth had led a secret life in which he drank too much, snorted a boatload of coke, and liked to pick up male hustlers and strippers, including one named Tiger; before Seth's brothers filed suit in Palm Beach to block Phyllis from getting her hands on Seth's estimated $25 million estate; and certainly before I found myself face-to-face with the main source of all the dirt—a 300-pound gay con man and Internet psychic with a long criminal history named Billy Ash who claims to have been the couple's personal assistant and may well have fabricated all or part of his claims regarding Seth and Phyllis because he's a proven liar and self-serving attention seeker . . . Before all of that, Seth Tobias was known to the world, to the extent he was known at all, as an upright cable-TV talking head and multimillionaire hedge-fund manager. But that's getting ahead of the story. Let's just start at the beginning.

SETH TOBIAS WAS RAISED in Plymouth Meeting, a well-to-do suburb of Philadelphia. His father was a doctor, his parents got divorced. It was a common story. After high school, Tobias went to Boston University, where he was an indifferent student majoring in finance.

In his early twenties, Tobias commuted from Philadelphia to New York on the 5:55 "Triple Nickel" train to a series of jobs on

Wall Street. Some of the jobs worked out, some didn't. At 24, he got his first break. That's when Tobias began processing trades for a then-unknown portfolio manager named Jim Cramer. Tobias impressed Cramer, but the job didn't last long. Tobias traded up to a position with the much larger JRO Associates hedge fund. Five years later, Tobias headed out on his own.

Tobias founded Circle T in 1996, at age 32. He named the company after the first letter of his last name, which he had tattooed on his left shoulder just after college. He started the firm with just one other employee, Steve Schwartz, a 25-year-old protégé of Tobias's from JRO. He'd sit there in the middle of the room, taking in all the data and chatter, and then bark a buy or sell order. He seemed to have a gift for making the right call. "Seth could just tell when to get in and get out of a stock," says Schwartz. "Seconds matter. He could see a movement in the cost of steel and figure out how that was going to impact companies that did business with GM and make a snap decision two, three moves ahead of other people."

Tobias lived for what he called "the game," and to him it *was* a game—who could analyze a company's quarterly report or process a bit of information fastest and make the first move. He had a pet ritual after the market's closing bell rang. He'd exhale, check his numbers, then call his friends at other hedge funds and ask them a simple question: "Are you up or are you down?" Simple.

In the early days of Circle T, Tobias was mostly up. By 2002, the firm was valued at almost $500 million, and Tobias was personally worth tens of millions of dollars. He bought homes—in suburban Philadelphia, on the Jersey shore, and in midtown Manhattan. He bought a luxury box at Veterans Stadium, where the Philadelphia Eagles played. A JRO colleague introduced Tobias to some pals at CNBC, and Tobias became a regular on the network's *Squawk Box* program.

Tobias also liked to party. His longtime friend Patrick Bransome said in a recent deposition that there were many nights when Tobias would get so loaded he had to drive him home. Bransome would drop his friend on his couch and leave once Tobias passed out.

"Look, Seth was a little crazy," a former colleague told me. "But we all are. You have to have a screw loose to be in this business and take the risks. You have to blow off steam, or you'll combust. He liked to blow off steam, too; we'd go to strip clubs and go out drinking. He just blew off steam a little harder than most."

IT'S SHORTLY AFTER NEW YEAR'S, and I'm in the West Palm Beach office of Jay Jacknin. Jacknin, Phyllis Tobias's third husband, is serving as counsel to his ex-wife in the death of Seth Tobias. He's a short, jolly man with hearing aids in both ears. At one point, he reaches into a file and brings out a picture of Seth and Phyllis on a beach. He starts to make a point about the case but then offers an aside. "She had a great body," he says. "Women love her. Men find her fascinating. I just couldn't afford her."

Phyllis Tobias was born Filomena Manente in 1966 and was raised in Union City, New Jersey. She was brought up by a strict Italian family, and went to Catholic schools. Now and then, she worked as a waitress. Her nickname, a nod to her personality, was Sunny. Just after she graduated from high school, in 1984, she married Vince Racanati. She was 18, he was 24. They had a daughter but got divorced after a year. Phyllis took a job as a secretary on Wall Street, where she met and married a twice-divorced stockbroker named Arthur Tolendini. That was 1987. They lasted just three years.

Phyllis moved to Palm Beach and was selling insurance when she met Jacknin, a divorce attorney. They got married in 1993 and had two children. But in October 2002 Jacknin filed for divorce, claiming Phyllis had gotten numerous credit cards without his consent and run the balance to the maximum. Jacknin didn't move out of the couple's home after they separated. He was worried about his two children. Phyllis was furious about that. The police were summoned three times in 2003, and each time, Jay Jacknin said his wife was the aggressor. He said she struck him, threw a phone, and pulled his hair.

In July 2003, Phyllis got a restraining order against Jacknin, accusing him of assault. Jacknin denied it and retaliated with his own statement. He said Phyllis's violent moods had reduced him to barricading himself in the nanny's room. He said that "she will kill" if he tries to gain custody of the kids.

Jacknin also said that Phyllis was on a cocktail of Xanax, Vicodin, and Ritalin and kept coke in the house. He finished by saying that Phyllis had abandoned the children one weekend in July so she could spend time with her boyfriend at the Breakers Hotel in Palm Beach.

The boyfriend was Seth Tobias.

SETH AND PHYLLIS MET while they were both in San Diego for the 2003 Super Bowl. The twist is, Jay Jacknin introduced them. Jacknin actually knew Seth first. The two men had met through a mutual friend, Daniel Borislow, an entrepreneur and racehorse owner from Philadelphia who spends part of the year in Palm Beach. At the time, Tobias was separated from his first wife, Tricia White, a South Jersey native. Phyllis was married to Jacknin, but they were fighting all the time and got divorced later that year.

Seth fell for Phyllis right away. Why not? She was blonde, fit, and sexy.

Sure enough, Tobias told his brothers and Circle T partners that he was moving down to West Palm in pursuit of Phyllis. "I can run Circle T from down there," he said. He and Phyllis could often be seen around town at the Breakers or black-tie charity events.

Seth and Phyllis's relationship was insane, even in the early days. Phyllis blasted Seth about his coke habit, but they both were heavy drinkers, especially of Champagne. A former Circle T employee says he personally saw Phyllis give Seth coke and use the drug herself on many occasions. (Jacknin denies those claims.) Seth questioned Phyllis's emotional stability. They each accused one another of infidelity. It went back and forth like that.

Seth and Phyllis split up for a while, with Seth returning to New York. The former Circle T employee says that Seth told him that Sam Tobias was concerned, warning his brother, "That woman is going to kill you or bankrupt you."

Tobias didn't listen. "He was addicted," says the former Circle T employee, "to Phyllis's ups and downs."

After another breakup, Seth was moping around New York and called Phyllis. By the time he hung up, the two were engaged. Knowing that Seth's friends and family disapproved, the couple eloped on March 4, 2005. "Seth just didn't show up for work, and we didn't know where the hell he was," says the former Circle T staffer. "That afternoon, he called in all sheepish and said, 'I'm in Belize. I just got married.'"

THAT SUMMER, Circle T took a big financial hit. Seth's Palm Beach pal Doug Kass had a son, Ethan, who was looking to break into the business, and Seth took him on. In July 2005, Google went public. The question at the time was whether the $85 initial offering price was a good deal. Ethan bet it wasn't. Circle T lost $12 million when he shorted the stock.

The trades weren't just wrong. Seth hadn't signed off on them. The firms' investments, almost half a billion dollars in 2003, sank to $220 million after the Google screwup. Many hedge funds booked monster years in 2005, but Circle T was down 5.3 percent. There were whispers that Seth was distracted by Phyllis.

Tobias's marriage was also tanking. Phyllis would often appear at the office and demand cash. "Give me 15,000 fucking dollars," she hissed on one visit, according to the former Circle T staffer. Tobias had promised Phyllis that he would stop using cocaine, but she didn't believe him. In the fall of 2005, the couple was having dinner at Bice, a Palm Beach restaurant, with six other people. Just after sitting down, Phyllis jumped from her seat and placed her lips over Tobias's nose and began sucking. She was searching for cocaine residue.

A few weeks later, the couple returned to their West Palm Beach home after a night of drinking, and Tobias ripped down a set of drapes that Phyllis had purchased without his knowledge. The police were called, and Phyllis claimed Tobias threw a jar at her. He was arrested for assault, a charge eventually expunged from his record when Phyllis declined to press charges.

There were more fights, more police visits. The following February, one night when she hadn't returned home from dinner by 2 A.M., Tobias drove to Cucina, a West Palm Beach restaurant, and confronted Phyllis, who was having drinks with a male friend.

"You're a whore!" Tobias screamed, according to police reports.

A passing officer witnessed the rest: "F. Tobias immediately responded by striking S. Tobias across the left side of his face with an open hand. The force of the slap turned S. Tobias' head and made a loud popping sound . . . it became clear she was intoxicated. I had to grab F. Tobias so she could not get close enough to strike S. Tobias again. I placed F. Tobias in handcuffs."

Phyllis spent a night in jail, but the charges were dropped.

On it went. The West Palm Beach police answered a number of calls to the couple's home in their first year of marriage. Just before the couple's first anniversary, Phyllis confronted her husband with evidence of an affair. Tobias responded by filing for divorce on March 10.

Three days later, the two engaged in an instant-message exchange:

Phyllis: YOU ARE NOT CAPABLE OF STOPPING TO DRINK, OR DOING YOUR COKE OR BEING HONEST . . .

Seth: I am sad about this.

Phyllis: I HOPE YOU GET AIDS WIT ALL THE WHORES YOU FUK TOO.

Seth: I am sorry . . . take a breather.

Phyllis: NOW IT'S WAR!!!

Phyllis cited her husband's infidelities, gambling losses, and unspecified "illicit activity" in her request for spousal support. She asked for nearly $47,000 a month, including $9,429 for vacations, $1,000 for makeup, $4,400 for clothing, and $3,000 for unreimbursed counseling fees. Her lawyer at the time argued that Tobias had promised a lifestyle grander than the one she could afford on Jay Jacknin's alimony. Tobias responded by accusing his wife of forging his signature on expensive purchases, including a $74,000 Porsche.

The couple was on the verge of finalizing their divorce. But within minutes of meeting with their lawyers Seth and Phyllis were apologizing, professing their love, and kissing at the conference table.

That's when Tobias promised to move Phyllis from their $1.75 million West Palm Beach home to the Bear's Club. Phyllis was unsure. The reason, she told Tobias, was that she was now running all her decisions past her online psychic.

THIS IS WHERE BILLY COMES IN. Billy Ash had a Website called askbilly.com, where he advertised himself as the winner of "many titles" including Best Psychic at the Las Vegas Psychic

Convention. Others had a less charitable view. One rival displayed a picture of the 300-pound Ash with the words "Worst. Psychic. Ever."

Phyllis started e-mailing Billy through keen.com, an online psychic service, paying the standard $3.99-a-minute rate. Then the two started e-mailing directly. According to Jay Jacknin, Ash told Phyllis that his clients included Sarah Jessica Parker and Nancy Reagan. Jacknin also says that Ash once mailed Phyllis a necklace that Ash claimed the former First Lady had given him. (Ash denies those claims.)

Phyllis began talking to Ash regularly, paying him as much as $2,500 a month, Jacknin says.

Not only did Phyllis consult Ash on all decisions. Now she urged Seth to make use of his powers, too. Tobias would roll his eyes, but on a few occasions he called Ash. (Ash says he spoke to Seth "all the time.") Maybe he could help him understand his wife.

One day in the summer of 2006, Seth Tobias was back in Circle T's New York office. According to a deposition Tobias's longtime secretary has given, she got a call from someone whose name she had never heard before. Billy Ash. Tobias said he would take the call. A few minutes later, he walked out of his office. He looked out of sorts.

"This man is totally crazy," Tobias said. "He says I owe him $156,000."

According to one of Tobias's lawyers deposed in the estate case, Ash told Tobias he was billing him for services rendered during their chats. Tobias called his lawyer, who sent Ash an e-mail urging him to cease contacting his client. Ash responded by suggesting that, if he wasn't paid, he would have no choice but to publicly announce what he'd learned about Seth from their conversations. Ash, Tobias's lawyer alleged, suggested that the disclosures would not sit well with Circle T's investors. (Ash denies pressuring Tobias.)

Phyllis continued to consult with Ash, and Tobias was furious about it. On November 18, 2006, Tobias wrote Phyllis an e-mail. He said he thought their marriage was permanently broken. He saved his harshest words for Ash and for Phyllis's relationship with him. "In the end, if I threatened your livelihood with lies and extortion; if I manufactured the craziness that he did to me you would have gone nuts. I still have some pride. You promised me you were finished with him. I believed you. I lost."

On April 2, 2007, the West Palm Beach police logged a report from the Tobias home at 4:19 P.M.: "Male is calling. States his wife is throwing bottle of wine and food at him. Female is in the background yelling."

Tobias was done. Then he wasn't. Phyllis continued consulting with Ash, who advised her not to give up on their marriage. She thanked Ash by FedExing him a $10,000 watch.

Over the last weeks of Tobias's life, the couple fought over home renovations, over Tobias's cocaine use, and, of course, over Ash. Seth again threatened to leave her. "This divorce is going to cost me a lot less than the last one," Tobias told his driver in August. "I've lost a lot of money since then."

The next month, Tobias was dead.

JUPITER POLICE OFFICERS EXAMINED Tobias's body shortly after he died. They noted scrapes on his nose and forehead. His glasses had floated to the bottom of the pool. Phyllis Tobias told Officer Elizabeth Juric that she believed her husband had been snorting cocaine at Bradley's that evening with Brett Borgerson. Juric then called Borgerson, who admitted it was possible Seth had been doing coke earlier in the day. Phyllis gathered up McGee, the couple's dog, and left the house a few minutes later. The police got a search warrant and found in the house two small plastic bags, one containing a white powder, the other a bluish substance.

Tobias was laid to rest in Bucks County, Pennsylvania, on September 7. All his Wall Street friends were there. Phyllis sat silent mostly, occasionally letting out a sob.

Phone records show that Phyllis spoke to Billy Ash eighteen times in the week following her husband's death, including for 81 minutes on the day after his drowning. After one of the talks, Ash made a call of his own. It was to Sam Tobias, the brother closest to Seth and Seth's heir apparent at Circle T. Ash told Sam that he had served as the couple's assistant, which Sam thought was odd since he never remembered meeting him. Ash then told him that Phyllis had crushed Ambien tablets into a pasta sauce that she'd served his brother the night he died.

The following day, Sam Tobias called Ash with his lawyer present. Ash repeated his story, and told Sam that he had been paid for his work for the Tobiases through both a PayPal account and with cash FedExed to his San Diego apartment. Sam passed the information to the Jupiter Police Department. About two weeks after Seth's death, the department sent two officers to San Diego, where they took Ash's statement and then flew back to Florida. The police won't say what Ash told them, but they were apparently not too impressed with his story. An investigation is still going on, but the cops have yet to classify Tobias's death as suspicious.

In late September, Tobias's will was read. The will, signed on May 12, 2004, divided Tobias's estimated $25 million fortune between his brothers, parents, and friends. Strangely, he had made no adjustment to the document after his 2005 marriage. Under Florida law, this nullified the will and left his wife as sole inheritor of her fourth husband's assets.

In a panic, and armed with Ash's claims, the Tobias brothers filed a motion in Palm Beach County probate court seeking to block Phyllis from inheriting the money, citing Florida's "slayer statute," a law that prevents a spouse from profiting from the murder of his or her partner. Phyllis hired four lawyers of her own, including Jay Jacknin.

Billy Ash, meanwhile, began carpet-bombing reporters with his claim that Phyllis had confessed to him that she had killed Seth. He also added this little tidbit. Seems Seth had led a secret gay life. A brief gossip item appeared in the Palm Beach *Post* on October 17 publicizing Ash's claims, but almost no one read it outside the area.

On December 4, however, the New York *Times* published a story on the front-page of the "Business" section about Tobias's death. The paper retailed Ash's more lurid allegations, including his claim that Phyllis had lured Seth into the pool with promises she would arrange a sexual liaison with a gay porn star-exotic dancer who went by the name Tiger because of the tiger stripes he had tattooed on his body. Ash alleged that Tobias met Tiger at Cupids, a West Palm Beach gay bar. The *Times* story included a confirmation of sorts from Adiel Hemmingway, the manager of Cupids, who said, "Seth used to come in here back when it was crazy." Everyone read that.

Seth's family was silent. Ash, meanwhile, hired Debra Opri, an attorney best known for repping Larry Birkhead in his successful quest to prove his paternity of Anna Nicole Smith's child. Opri had parlayed Birkhead's celebrity, through book deals and other projects, into more than $1 million.

BILLY ASH'S GROUND-LEVEL APARTMENT in the predominantly gay Hillcrest neighborhood of San Diego would just about fit in the foyer of Seth and Phyllis's Jupiter mansion. It's the morning after Christmas, and Ash, wearing a blue baseball cap and a red-striped Tommy Hilfiger polo shirt, is supervising two movers as they pack up an artificial tree and a fake wreath.

"I can't talk to you," Ash tells me. "You need to call my lawyer, Debra."

I was starting to leave when Ash said, "Well, I can give you just some basic information."

Ash told me that he met Seth Tobias in San Diego, about five and a half years earlier. "I was shopping in La Jolla, and he came up to me. I'm obviously gay, and he asked me, 'Do you know where the good gay clubs are?' We became fast friends, and I went to work for him after that, doing travel, making sure his television appearances happened on time, introducing him to guys."

When I asked Ash if he had slept with Seth, he took on a scolding tone. "That's way, way too personal," he said.

I said I was sorry and asked him when he first met Phyllis Tobias.

"Oh, I never met her," Ash said. "Our whole relationship was over the phone. But you really need to call Debra. I'm super-busy."

We said good-bye, but as I started to walk to my car, Ash's words hit me. He had never met Phyllis Tobias? The man driving a murder investigation that was the subject of a major New York *Times* story, the man who claims to have first-hand knowledge of the alleged killer's thoughts, had never met the woman?

I rang the doorbell again.

I asked Ash if I'd understood him correctly. "Yes," he said matter-of-factly. "We talked and texted ten times a day. We were really close. I knew everything about her."

Then Ash talked for another hour. He said that Seth and Phyllis had met at a suburban San Diego sex party in 2003, and that their 2005 marriage was one of mutual convenience. "He needed a trophy wife for his investors, and she needed someone with lots of cash. I think they had sex maybe twice."

According to Ash, he was bombarded with calls from Phyllis over Labor Day weekend. "That Sunday, they were having a housewarming barbecue for a few friends and she got pissed because Seth was checking out a cute guy who was there. She'd just had enough."

Then he told me how Phyllis killed Seth. His version, that is. "That Monday, they went to the bar at the Breakers and Seth was doing coke and drinking, but Phyllis wasn't. Seth called me [later], and I told him he needed to go home to his wife and make nice. He was pissed because she had spent $16,000 on drapes, and I told him, 'You can't take them back, they're custom made. But take them down and put them in the office so she knows no means no.' But she thought he'd taken them back, so she was extra-pissed. In their new bedroom they both have these big walk-in closets, and she had put a Baggie filled with crushed Ambien in the safe in her closet. Seth needed the Ambien to balance off the coke. So she tells him that she wants to start new, and she's going to cook him dinner and make him pasta à la vodka. She mashed the pills into the sauce, but the problem was it turned the sauce purple and Seth said, 'This tastes like shit, I'm not gonna eat it.'"

Ash paused, and glared at one of the movers. "Hey, the lights are part of the tree, it's the tree that comes apart.

"Now, where was I? Then Phyllis said, 'Eat it, you'll feel better, and then I'll call Tiger over, and I'll watch you two have sex in the pool.' But first she took these pictures of him looking all fucked up. Then Seth walked into the pool, and the Ambien started having its effect. She went back inside, did the dishes, took the dog for a walk, came back, and went out to the pool. The only problem was, he was still alive; he was passed out but floating on his back. She rolled him over, and that's how he died."

Um, how did he know all of this? "Phyllis told me," he said. "I was coming back from Penn State with a friend that day, and I had turned off my phone because I just could not deal with them anymore. When I turned my phone back on, I had a message from Phyllis saying, 'Seth's dead.'"

Ash says at that point he called the lawyer Gloria Allred, of Laci Peterson fame. "I knew her because of the Peterson case, and I lived around where Laci did. She told me I had to go to the police."

Ash stopped to direct the movers again, then delivered this doozy. This past September, he said, he was sitting at home speaking to the Jupiter detectives when he got a FedEx box from

Phyllis. "A while back, she had me track down two cases of Krug Champagne that went for $2,000 a bottle. So I get this box before Seth's funeral, and I was like, 'Oh my God. Is Seth's head in that box?' But it was a bottle of Krug with a note that said, 'The scumbag is dead.'"

At one point, Ash had said that Phyllis had explicitly fessed up and that he had her confession on tape. But now he retreated a bit. Now he told me she had only *implied* on the tape that she'd poisoned her husband. Still, he insisted that she had, in fact, confessed to him—just not when the tape was running.

I asked Ash if he could provide a snapshot or any other evidence to back up his claim that he and Seth Tobias had ever met. I asked him if I could see the photos of Tobias taken the day he died. He tugged at his cap and shifted his weight. "You really need to call Debra and make a proposal." He wanted money before speaking to me further. "I'm only telling you one percent of it. Make a good proposal, and I'll tell you more."

THE NEXT DAY, I started checking out Ash's story. Phone records confirm that he talked to Phyllis more than a dozen times in the days after Tobias's death. At one point, Ash had told me that he had been "deputized" by the San Diego Police Department to tape Phyllis, but the department says it didn't happen. The Jupiter detectives won't say if Ash received a FedEx package from Phyllis while they were interviewing him at his home, but really, how likely is that? Under oath, Lucille Schiavone, Tobias's secretary, maintained that she had heard of Ash only in relation to his attempted shakedown of Seth. And Schiavone said she was the one who handled Tobias's travel arrangements.

Most reporters covering Ash's stories have included a quick disclaimer saying Ash had been arrested multiple times for prostitution before quoting him extensively. None of them, however, have gone into any detail about Ash's criminal history.

When I Googled "William Ash," the search led me to a 2001 cover story in the Broward–Palm Beach *New Times*, a free weekly. The story documented more than a dozen cons that an overweight man by that name perpetrated on the South Florida gay community. There was a picture: It was the same guy.

The swindles listed in the *New Times* included stealing the client list of a company that sold goods manufactured by the disabled and setting up a rival company; a stint working at Fort Lauderdale's CenterOne, an AIDS-counseling center, that ended when Ash was fingered for lying to a tabloid and telling them Tina Turner was a patient; and chartering a boat for his 31st birthday and spending thousands of dollars on flowers and balloons by telling vendors he was throwing a party for Dolphins owner Wayne Huizenga and that the Miami businessman would be footing the bill. In 1997, Ash spent six months in jail on a combination of those charges and for running a prostitution ring. At the time, Ash was billing himself as Mr. Madam and boasted he had an offer to write a book about his days as a Heidi Fleiss–like pimp. The book never happened. Ash headed out for San Diego shortly after the *New Times* story appeared.

DAVID FOREST, a prominent agent in the gay-stripper business, gave me Tiger's phone number. I reached him at his parents' home outside of Spokane. Now married, Tiger has a baby daughter who could be heard screaming in the background. After the New York *Times* story broke, Tiger, a.k.a. Christopher Dauenhauer, at first offered a denial of sorts. He didn't recall meeting Tobias, he told reporters. "I meet a lot of people, I don't always remember names," he told me when I asked him to explain. But once Ash's story gained momentum, Tiger changed his mind. "When I thought about it more, I did remember Seth," he says.

Then he told me that he hooked up with Tobias six or seven times, including on more than one occasion in Las Vegas. "Seth was a nice guy," he said. "He was very good to me." As with Ash, I asked him if there was any tangible evidence that he knew Tobias. Tiger said there was none.

Next came a story that might have made Billy Ash blush. In fact, it's a story that seems flat-out loony. As Tiger tells it, he was living in Los Angeles a few years ago when he went to get his hair cut in West Hollywood. Out front were two attractive women. Tiger, who says he is bisexual, chatted them up. He said the girls were interested in rough sex, and the trio headed back to his RV in Orange County. "We were tying each other up," says Tiger. "When it was my turn, they handcuffed me and threw a blanket over my head. Then they let in a guy who starting beating the shit out of me and forced drugs in my mouth. I woke up in prison. Then when I heard about Seth, I listened to the 911 tapes and heard Phyllis's voice. She was one of the women. She must have heard about my affair with Seth." What Tiger was saying, in other words, is that a jealous Phyllis Tobias traveled all the way across the country, deliberately hunted him down, lured him into a lurid sexual tryst, and assaulted him. Jacknin emphatically denies it. "That story is such bullshit, I can't even believe I'm answering it."

I asked Tiger for the name of the hospital he was treated at, specific dates of the assault, or any other corroborating details. "I don't know," he told me. "My memory isn't so good."

On January 9, Billy Ash added yet another wild twist to the story. He told the New York *Daily News*'s "Rush & Molloy" that Phyllis had paid $100,000 to Madam Simbi M'Arue, a voodoo artist who sometimes goes by the name Mama, to place a hex on her husband while he was still alive. Two days later, he told the same column that Tobias liked to have his genitals sheared by another gay porn star named Angel. Ash claimed Phyllis had even FedExed him a lock of Tobias's public hair. No Mama or Angel ever came forward.

That same week, I received an e-mail from Ash asking me if I wanted to come to his deposition. January 31 and February 1, in Beverly Hills. For the estate case. Ash told me this was my formal invitation, and no RSVP was required. He signed the e-mail, "Hugs, Billy." I flew back to California.

AN HOUR BEFORE THE DEPOSITION was set to start, Debra Opri's conference room was being prepped for television. A crew of four vacuumed up debris and installed a stylish new tabletop. An ugly hole in the wall was covered with a blue-sky backdrop. A curtain was removed so that reporters could watch through a glass wall. Ash was dressed in a black suit and white shirt, with a yellow tie. His face was covered in pancake makeup.

Despite Ash's best efforts, the media turnout was disappointing, just a CNBC crew and me. Every now and then, Opri would get out of her seat for a cup of coffee and wink at me and the CNBC cameraman on the other side of the glass.

Ash worked the phones on his lunch break. "Call 'Page Six' and tell them what's going on," he told someone on the other end of his cell phone. He clicked off and then told me, "I'm glad to get this over with. This is a fight about money. I didn't want to have anything to do with it. I wish she had never told me she killed Seth. I've already cried twice today. I didn't know I'd feel this emotional."

Phyllis's lawyers spent much of the first day poking holes in Ash's story. By the end of the day, Ash looked exhausted as he headed toward a car and driver who would take him back to his Hollywood hotel. "Her lawyers are not nice people," Ash said. "How many ways can they tell me I'm a fat pimp?"

Once again, Ash's story continued to evolve. I asked him again when was the last time he had seen Seth. "In Las Vegas, over two years ago," he answered. When we first talked, he had told me San Diego. I mentioned in passing his role as Phyllis's online psychic, and he vigorously shook his head. "No, I was never her psychic, I was always their assistant." I then asked him if he had brought the Krug Champagne bottle as evidence. He just laughed. "Oh no, I re-gifted that and gave it to someone who was very nice to me."

If he had never met Phyllis in person, I asked him, if he had not seen Seth in the two years prior to his death, why would they confide the intimate details of their life to him? "They knew I had a dark past," Ash said. "They knew I didn't want that to come out, so I'd keep their secrets, too."

The next morning, Ash and Opri got their makeup done together. "God, my hair is so flat," said Opri. "How can I pouf it up?" Meanwhile, her client crowed over a new rumor. "Did you hear the toxicology report is back?" Ash said. "He had cocaine and Ambien in his system. It proves everything I've been saying has been the truth."

The second-day interrogation was even nastier than the first. Around noon, Ash could be heard shouting "You will respect me" at Gary Dunkel, one of Phyllis's attorneys. "I don't respect you," Dunkel responded. "You're a liar." Ash stormed out of the room and summoned me to Opri's office again. "I am not going to put up with this much longer," he said. "I've learned two important things: One, don't murder your husband and tell a fat fag with a big mouth. Two, the fat fag shouldn't talk to the press."

A WHOLE LOT ABOUT THE TOBIAS case remains unknown. Billy Ash was right about the toxicology report. It showed Tobias had cocaine and a lethal amount of Ambien in his bloodstream. But it reached no conclusions about how the drugs got there. Maybe Seth took the pills himself, in a drunken accidental overdose. Maybe Phyllis secretly fed the pills to him. Maybe

Seth took the pills himself, and Phyllis, finding him in the pool in his addled state, took the opportunity to let him drown. Without an eyewitness or some new smoking gun, and given Ash's—well, given Ash—it's hard to imagine the truth will ever really be known. Police won't comment on where their investigation stands or what they know.

Did Seth Tobias have a secret gay sex life? All I know is there are serious holes in Billy Ash's and Tiger's stories, close friends and colleagues insist they never saw any evidence of gay relationships or trysts, nor did they ever suspect Seth was gay, and no one else has come forward with other claims. Remember Adiel Hemmingway, the Cupids manager who told the New York *Times* that Tobias was a frequent visitor to his club? It turns out he had given a deposition in the Tobias-estate lawsuit a month earlier that flatly contradicts what he told the newspaper. In the deposition, he said that he had never met Seth or Phyllis Tobias, and, as far as he knew, Tiger had never performed at Cupids.

What about the fight over Tobias's estate? The Tobias brothers' lawyers filed a motion for summary judgment against Phyllis Tobias earlier in the month that lays out key parts of their case. The motion quotes Seth's personal secretary and driver saying that their boss was getting ready to divorce Phyllis in the weeks before his death. The Tobias brothers say that Phyllis knew the papers were imminent and that forced her hand. The motion also contains copies of a bill that shows that Phyllis had the couple's pool resurfaced nine days after her husband's death. Tobias's secretary told attorneys in the case that Seth told her that Phyllis "had fed him 'discolored eggs and he felt drugged' " shortly before his death. The Tobias brothers also say that the paramedics' ruling that rigor mortis had set in by the time they arrived suggests that Seth was dead long before Phyllis's 12:08 A.M. call to Brett Borgerson and the subsequent 12:45 A.M. 911 call.

Jay Jacknin, of course, sees things differently. "Their side tells a pretty story," he says. "But where's the proof? Where's the witness? They don't have any, because their case is all bullshit. This is a story based on the allegations of a convicted felon who's just not credible." And the Ambien in Tobias's system? Tobias, Phyllis's lawyers say, was a drug addict. He snorted everything, Ambien included.

The clincher, Phyllis's legal team says, is that a day or two before Ash contacted the Tobias brothers, Ash sent an e-mail to JoAnn Kotzen, Seth and Phyllis's family lawyer, saying, "The bottom line is Seth lived a lot longer by being with Phyllis." In the e-mail, Phyllis's lawyers say, Ash asked Kotzen for $35,000 in legal fees. She wrote back that as a witness, Ash shouldn't have legal fees, and no payment would be coming. It was only after that, Phyllis's lawyers say, that Ash called the Tobias brothers and claimed that Phyllis had told him that she killed Seth. (Ash denies asking for legal fees from Kotzen.)

Jacknin then floats a possible defense for Phyllis Tobias that won't win her wife of the year but might get her off the legal hook. "Look, the law isn't did she not call 911 quick enough or did she not pull him out of the water quick enough. The law asks whether she caused his death, and that is not provable." The request for summary judgment was recently continued by the judge. Who knows, in the end, who'll get what?

I never saw Phyllis Tobias. She wouldn't talk to me. She still hasn't been accused of any crimes. Seth Tobias's brothers wouldn't talk to me, either. Billy Ash? I e-mailed with him just the other day. He sent me a picture of himself. He said he was at Mardi Gras. He wore a mask, a string of baubles around his neck, and a fortune-teller's turban. He looked like he was having an excellent time.

STEPHEN RODRICK *is a contributing editor for* New York *magazine. He lives in Brooklyn and Los Angeles.*

Coda

Shortly after this story was published, Palm Beach County law enforcement announced no charges would be filed against Phyllis Tobias, citing insufficient evidence. Later in 2008 the Tobias brothers and Phyllis Tobias reached an out-of-court settlement regarding Seth Tobias's estate. The majority of his estate was granted to Phyllis.

Alec Wilkinson

Non-Lethal Force

FROM *The New Yorker*

A JUDGMENT SOMETIMES APPLIED by professionals to a non-lethal weapon is that if the weapon is any good—if it reliably protects someone from being attacked or subdues a person without causing harm —criminals will use it. Absent a small number of robberies committed with pepper spray, though, they haven't really taken to any. According to Charles Heal, an expert in non-lethal weapons, the problem is that the field is nascent, and "the options are primitive. The whole state of the art is only a shade over a decade old."

"Non-lethal" is an imperfect term. "Lethal weapons are defined by their capability," Heal says. "Non-lethal are defined by their intent." In the hands of the police, non-lethal weapons are meant to resolve a crisis (say, a Hells Angel in a bar who has broken a chair over someone's head and is overturning tables, and who, when asked to leave, draws a knife) without anyone getting badly hurt or being killed. They are also sometimes called less than le-thal, less lethal, controlled force, soft kill, mission kill, and minimal force. There is no established lexicon for non-lethal weapons, but there are accepted categories and concepts, including impact or kinetic weapons—things that strike, such as batons, billy clubs, saps, and projectiles fired from shotguns (including bean bags and stun bags, which usually have sand in them instead of lead pellets), and "vivi," meaning animals. "Dog is the only non-lethal weapon I can change my mind about after I deploy it," Heal says. "The suspect sees me and puts his hands up, I can call it back. If I launch a bean bag, it's downrange. Dog's also the only one with target-acquisition radar: suspect moves, dog does, too." In addition, there are irritants, such as tear gas, which was first used on a crowd in Paris, in 1912; malodorants (stink bombs); obscurants, which interfere with seeing, either by means of lasers or smoke or other substances; electrical, such as Tasers; physiological, which includes noises that are too loud and lights that are too bright, sometimes combined in devices called flashbangs; reactants, which include activities such as cloud seeding (conducted in Vietnam above the Ho Chi Minh Trail); and soporifics, which are also called calmatives, sedatives, and hypnotics. "What they used in the Moscow Theatre," Heal says, referring to the occasion, in 2002, when Chechen terrorists took over a theatre, with nearly eight hundred people in it, and were subdued with a chemical delivered through the ventilation system. More than a hundred of the hostages died, some of them as a result of the chemical. Still, Heal says, they are the only weapons that "allow you to intervene in a lethal situation without having to resort immediately to lethal force."

Heal was among the first Americans to use modern non-lethal weapons, as a marine in Somalia in 1995. One was a foam called sticky foam, which was shot from a hose and designed to fix a person's feet to the ground. The problem was that people could move their feet faster than the sticky foam could be applied, although, Heal says, if you hit a person's thighs his legs sometimes stuck together. Heal's orders were to provide a twenty-minute window between the withdrawal of American soldiers and the arrival of "the people with crude weapons and guns on the backs of old trucks who'd rush in to take over." He had his troops scatter caltrops, ancient devices made of spiked rods welded together in such a way that, however they land, a spike faces upward, like a child's jack. The Somalis cast the caltrops aside. Heal had his soldiers lay down more caltrops and cover them with sticky foam; the Somalis picked these up, too, and threw them away, although it took longer. Heal's soldiers then put down sheets of plywood, laid concertina wire over the plywood, laid caltrops on the plywood, and covered everything with sticky foam, which held up the Somalis for about five minutes, sufficient for the troops to retreat. Heal and others think that sticky foam might work in an embassy or at a missile base or a nuclear plant, where the floors could be flooded if someone broke in.

For more than thirty years, Heal, who is fifty-eight, and is known as Sid, divided his career between the Marine reserves and the Los Angeles Sheriff's Department. (The Sheriff's Department acts as the police in parts of Los Angeles County that are not incorporated, and in cities such as Compton, where its services are retained by contract.) He is probably the most knowledgeable figure in America on the civil uses of non-lethal weapons. According to Nicholas C. Nicholas, the lead scientist at the Institute for Non-Lethal Defense Technologies, at Penn State, "There's nobody close to him. I saw him interviewed on TV the other night, and I said to my wife, 'That's Mr. Non-Lethal Weapons as far as the police are concerned.'" Heal has served on the front in four wars—Vietnam, Somalia, Kuwait, and Iraq. When he returned from Somalia, he says, he "ended up on the lecture tour for the Marines in lessons learned." The Los Angeles undersheriff called him into his office and said that if he could specialize in non-lethal weapons for the Marines he could do it for the Sheriff's Department. Heal became the only municipal-law-enforcement figure in America then devoted to non-lethal weapons.

Manufacturers typically produce non-lethal weapons for soldiers, because the military market is larger and the military has more money. To sell weapons to the police, the manufacturers tend to modify, rather than redesign, the military versions. In addition, manufacturers often take advice from retired military officers, who, Heal says, have "no insight into law enforcement." Heal began urging inventors and manufacturers to design non-lethal weapons for policemen rather than soldiers, and whenever they made something he tested it. He assumed that manufacturers would be responsive, because the L.A.S.D. is so big—"Sixteen thousand employees, five thousand vehicles, and I don't know how many boats and planes"—that he thought it could be a market in itself. As an incentive, Heal was willing to provide for free the expertise for which manufacturers paid consultants hundreds of dollars an hour.

Heal had a talent for describing to a manufacturer precisely what a policeman needed and whether or not its product worked well. Over the years, about twenty-five ideas that inventors and manufacturers have approached him with have become products, including a portable robot called a Throwbot, which has wheels and a camera and can go into rooms where someone might be hiding with a gun; the SkySeer, an unmanned aerial vehicle with a camera; the Pepper-Ball, a projectile like a paintball that disperses an irritating powder; and a few repulsive malodorants. Among those that haven't worked out are the Bola Ball, which a policeman would carry on his belt and fling at running suspects (it was too difficult to master), and a device shaped like a pistol which used ultrasound to detect concealed weapons (it worked well on cotton and wool but less reliably on leather or synthetic fabrics). Recently, Heal has attended tests of the Active Denial System, or A.D.S., made for the military by Raytheon, which sends a beam of energy that heats a person's skin to a hundred and thirty degrees within a matter of seconds. It is sometimes called the pain ray. Heal says that being beamed with it is like stepping into a scalding shower. "It's the first non-lethal device in history to provide protection against lethal force, because its range exceeds rifle fire," he says. The military hopes to use the A.D.S. in

Iraq to disperse crowds or stop people at check-points who keep coming after being told to stop. It currently has little use in law enforcement, though. "If they gave it to us for free, we probably couldn't use it," Heal told me. The first police chief to use the pain ray on Americans would become famous overnight.

It isn't so much that the police are uncomfortable about using violence when they feel that their safety is jeopardized; it is that often when they kill people they end up in lawsuits. When a non-lethal weapon is being tested, Heal says, the critical standard is whether it creates a "save"—that is, whether a person who would have been killed was instead apprehended, because the manufacturer can then cite the dollars saved from a lawsuit. The standing of any non-lethal weapon that creates a save advances from speculative to favorable. According to Nicholas, the non-lethal weapon that everyone desires is "the phaser where you can put it on stun."

Non-lethal weapons can force a suspect to declare his intentions, and that sometimes leads to a save. Heal once took part in a gun battle with a man who was shooting at him and his fellow-deputies from behind a barricade. "He had a Winchester .458 calibre," Heal says. "An elephant gun—the bullets are as big as your thumb. He's shooting through cinderblock walls, and we're using the holes to look back at him. Finally, he comes out with his hands in his pockets. We're all yelling, 'Get your hands out of your pockets.' All around me, I can hear the slack coming out of the triggers—they're about to shoot. It's pretty clear he's trying to commit suicide by cop, but what if there's a weapon in his pockets? What gets us killed isn't the ability to apply lethal force; it's the reluctance to use it, and the reason we're reluctant is that we can't make informed decisions. The rules of engagement that allow us to use lethal force mean that we have to tolerate a lot more abuse and risk. With a non-lethal-weapon option, you don't have to accept the conditions offered. What happened was, someone threw a flashbang at this guy, and his hands came out of his pockets, and we jumped him and wrestled him down. The flash-bang enabled us to determine his intentions. That's a save."

HEAL IS ABOUT SIX FEET TALL. His carriage is erect. He has a large nose and sharp, elemental features—he looks a little as if a child had drawn him. He is exceptionally fit—he runs every morning before dawn, and sometimes he rides his bicycle a hundred miles in a day. His manner is emphatic, and his eyes sometimes widen when he speaks. He has blue eyes and brown hair cut short on the sides and a little longer on top. Several times a day, he plants his feet, takes a black comb from his back pocket, and draws it slowly across the front of his head, smoothing his hair with his following hand so that it stands up like a hedge. Commanders in the L.A.S.D. (there are twenty-eight of them) can wear their own clothes, but Heal would always wear a uniform. He was the only commander who did. "I have color-coördination issues," he says. Heal grew up on a farm in Michigan. The trip he made at the age of eighteen, to San Diego, to join the Marines, was the first time he had ever taken a bus or a taxi or a plane. While he was there, he saw his first movie. His hearing was damaged during training, when a soldier stepped on a trip wire that set off a booby trap about a foot from his head.

Heal has been injured more often at work than he was at war. Between 1979 and 1982, he was a deputy sheriff assigned to South Central L.A., where, he says, he couldn't drive down the street without seeing a crime. One year, he drew his gun so many times that the bluing on the barrel wore off. He has surgical pins in his hand from a fight with a glue sniffer. Another drug suspect broke his nose, leaving a scar between his eyes that looks like the flippers on a pinball game. ("It's not pretty," Heal says, "but it's better than what I had.") He was also hurt repeatedly in fights with suspects intoxicated with PCP, which is a dissociative anesthetic. "They'd take off their clothes, because their body temperature was so hot," Heal says. "They'd be slimy hot, and they'd jump into swimming pools and showers, and, for whatever reason, they'd climb onto roofs. If you got a call for a naked man on a roof, that was PCP."

PCP made even small men feel unnaturally strong, and a strong man was nearly impossible to subdue. "The only way to overwhelm them was with weight," Heal told me. "We tried nets, we tried poles, ladders, fire extinguishers." For a while, they tried throwing blankets over them and binding them with ropes. One man, a Samoan, required four officers to bend his arms into handcuffs. "'Non-lethal' was hardly a term in those days," Heal says. "The non-lethal options were a baton, which all it did was get the guy mad, or tear gas, which they didn't feel and tended to work better on us."

Heal's field trials of new weapons last several weeks or months and involve sometimes just a few deputies and sometimes as many as five hundred. In 2000, he tested the TigerLight, a flashlight that also dispersed pepper spray. Deputies carried pepper spray and flashlights on their tool belts; the problem was that fights broke out too quickly for them to get to their pepper spray, whereas they usually had their flashlights in hand. "When a deputy gets in trouble, he's going to hit with his flashlight, and you're going to get stitches, which almost always result in lawsuits," Heal says.

Initially, Heal distributed twenty TigerLights. The deputies didn't like that when the lights were upside down the pepper spray leaked on them. The manufacturer fixed the problem, and in 2005 Heal gave out five hundred TigerLights. "We figured if the option to use the spray in the TigerLight could reduce head strikes by even two or three per cent we're going to recover the money the TigerLights cost," Heal says. The difference was closer to thirty per cent. "It was a real sleeper." He says that at the end of a trial the endorsement he looks for is that deputies complain when he takes the weapon away.

MANUFACTURERS WHO HAVE A PRODUCT that they want Heal to consider tend to bring it to him, but he also travels a lot.

He answers anyone who contacts him, and he has spent a good deal of time driving around Southern California visiting inventors. Recently, I went with him to see David McGill, a retired member of the L.A.P.D., who had written a letter describing a device he calls the Carpoon. McGill and his wife live in Temecula, about seventy miles southeast of L.A. The Carpoon is designed to stop cars that are fleeing the police.

"People have thought of all kinds of harpoon devices," Heal told me on the way to McGill's. "Some shoot out the tires, some lock onto the car, then you drag them to a stop by slamming on the brakes. What we're going to see here is called a running gear-entanglement system. His idea is he fires a probe that hits a tire then rolls a cable around the axle and kills the ability to drive the wheel. It's the release part that's a good idea—being entangled is not attractive. Nobody likes entanglement. You're entangled, he spins out, which makes us spin out; it's like a boa. There's so much civil liability with that. Even if a bad guy's breaking the law, he was safely breaking the law until we spun him out."

Recalling other inventions, Heal mentioned a man who had built a remote-control machine gun. "You looked at a little TV screen that has a crosshair on it, and you fired with a toggle switch," he said. "I put eight rounds through a target, but it had no application in law enforcement that I could think of. Another lab had a sniper-detection system that would locate a sniper by a combination of acoustics and light. They were taking it to the Balkans—this was '97 or '98. I tried to get them to let us borrow one for South Central L.A., but it was classified."

Heal took an exit off the freeway. "One device I really liked was a camera that fit on a dog's head," he continued. "It was just like a little hat, and when the dog searches for a crook you see what the dog sees. There was also a little speaker that fit in the dog's ear. You could talk quietly and the dog would follow your commands. That one, I think, still has potential. The dog handlers were willing to try it; I just wasn't able to get the canine to buy into it. The problem is, it takes about three weeks for the dogs to tolerate it, and until they do they'll scratch their heads and pull at their ears. The guy only wanted to give it to me for a month."

By now, we had arrived in a neighborhood of single-story houses. Heal had brought McGill's letter with him and, reading the address on the back of the envelope, he parked in front of a house where a tall, thin man in a red sweatshirt and jeans waved to us from the lawn—McGill himself. We went into the house and met his wife, Cheryl, then we sat in the living room.

"I might mention that my first pursuit was in 1957," McGill said. "Kid running for nothing, and he ended up hitting a train off Alameda. Knocked the train off the track and didn't do him any good, either." He went on for a while, then said, "Let's change gears and talk about Carpoon."

"How do you envision this?" Heal asked. "It shoots a probe?"

"Powerful mini-barrel air gun mounted on the front bumper of a police car," McGill said. He leaned toward Heal. "The air gun is slaved to a dash-mounted computerized video camera that will project the image of the road in front of the police car. As soon as the officer goes into pursuit mode, the other car's rear tires appear on his computer screen. The officer touches a tire on the screen, crosshairs immediately appear. Another touch on the screen moves the crosshair to any quadrant of the tire he wants, and when he's satisfied he gets an aural tone, like a sidewinder missile. As long as he hears that tone, that crosshair is on the tire, no matter where the guy goes."

McGill waved a hand. "From here on out, everything is automatic," he said. "All the time the officer's driving, he hears the tone. At a predetermined distance, the gun is going to fire. He's just driving."

Heal's BlackBerry began buzzing, and he took it out and read a message. Then he said, "Sorry."

"Air gun shoots a tethered dart into the tire," McGill went on.

"Now the bad guy's got a quarter-inch hole in his tire. In addition, the computer will give him some cable that will wrap around his wheel and cause real havoc. I'm hoping we can engineer something that will break an axle, break a tire shaft."

McGill turned to me. "These guys, Sid and I know, will lose a tire and keep going, but we've taken the hundred-mile-an-hour thing out of it."

"You have no idea on price, though, because you don't have a developer, right?" Heal asked.

"I don't have anything," McGill said. "I need a money partner."

Heal leaned back slightly. "All this stuff is feasible," he said. "Military uses it all the time." He asked if McGill had consulted the National Institute of Justice Office of Science and Technology.

"I haven't looked at anything," McGill said. "I just got the patent."

"You're going to need a working prototype before you have much of a chance," Heal said. "They got to see it, touch it, smell it, watch it work."

He looked hard at McGill and said, "I have to tell you something: Do not mortgage your house. Do not give up your retirement."

McGill looked at his wife. "We're not going to do that," he said. His wife shook her head.

"Perfect is the enemy of good," Heal said. "If you can get to the field-trial stage, you're the only one there. When I first read your letter, it came across as a tether device, and they're almost universally rejected."

Heal said a few more things about how McGill might proceed, then he and McGill shook hands, and we went to Heal's car. As we drove away, McGill waved to us from the lawn.

I asked Heal what chance he thought the Carpoon had. "What we're hoping really is somebody invents a directed-energy device that uses a signal from our car to interrupt the other car's ability to supply fuel or ignition," he said. "It may make the fuel mixture too rich or too thin, and if you can change it even briefly the car will die. That's the Holy Grail. Whoever invents that will be rich from the day he does."

MORE THAN NEW INVENTIONS, Heal sees weapons made for the military and adapted for the police. Traditionally, many adaptations have involved shooting less harmful things at people than metal bullets. In 1958, British colonial police in Hong Kong used bullets made from teak called baton rounds. They would aim the guns at the ground, and the bullets would ricochet—it was called skip-firing—and hit people in the shins, which was very painful. A refinement, rubber bullets—which were lethal often enough to be controversial—was invented by the British in 1970, to be used against the Irish in Northern Ireland. The government wanted some means of striking protesters who were throwing rocks at them from afar.

The Taser, which the police tend to adore and civil-liberties organizations loathe, was patented, in 1974, by a NASA researcher named John Cover. The name Taser is derived from "Tom Swift and His Electric Rifle," a book in a series for adolescents first published in the early twentieth century. Tom Swift was an inventor, and the plots usually involved things he dreamed up to resolve a crisis. (Cover was fond of the books.) The Taser can reach a person thirty-five feet away. The pain it causes is temporarily debilitating. Nevertheless, people have died after being shot with it. Amnesty International believes that the Taser hasn't been tested properly and that it should be withdrawn until more is known about how it affects certain classes of people. Short of that, the organization would like to see it used solely when killing someone is the only alternative. Heal regards the Taser as a valuable tool that should never be used recklessly—merely to subdue a troublesome person, for example.

"In law enforcement, our core value is to have a reverence for human life," Heal told me. "It doesn't mean we can't or won't take it; it means we would avoid taking it if we could. Life-and-death decisions are made in the military and in law enforcement by the least experienced people, just the opposite of business. But they are the ones in harm's way. And therein lies a great irony: even the failure of a non-lethal weapon makes a case for restraint. Let's say a guy's coming with a machete. We hit him with bean bags. He doesn't stop. And we kill him. We went to great efforts. A primitive option is a warning shot."

For policemen, Heal said, "twenty-one feet and a hundred and eighty feet are the two figures your non-lethal weapon has to satisfy. Twenty-one feet is the distance at which you can be killed by a person with an edged weapon or club if the force you use to deter him is not immediately effective, which means right-now lethal. A hundred and eighty feet—less than three per cent of the population can throw an object large enough to cause serious injury beyond that. Golfballs, spark plugs—they'll give you stitches. But a brick—you get hit in the head, helmet or not, it'll put you on your knees. If you have a weapon that has a range shorter than a hundred and eighty feet, while you're approaching them to get into your range you're being pummelled with bricks and bottles. In the middle of the city, where everything's paved, they bring stuff to throw at us—wheel weights, things that are cheap. We had one guy who could throw a golf ball ninety-seven yards. You can buy a bag of golf balls for five bucks and equip everybody in the mob."

One day, I went with Heal to a sheriff's station to meet a salesman from a company in Washington State who had a laser that he wanted Heal to see. The salesman's name was Clint Meyers. From a briefcase he produced a black metal tube that looked like a gunsight, and a larger one that was about the size of a Maglite. He handed the small one to Heal. "This is the military version they're using over in the sandbox right now," he said.

"What's eye safe on this?" Heal asked.

"Eye safe is about eighteen metres," Meyers said.

Heal twisted the device in his hands. "The official term the military gives it is 'to visually dissuade,'" Meyers said for my benefit. "Someone approaching a checkpoint sees this, he knows he's supposed to stop."

"What do you see as your law-enforcement market?" Heal asked.

"Entries," Meyers said. He turned to me. "The reason I wanted the Commander to see this is it's a way to come into a building— you know, the bright lights they have on shields; it does the same kind of job."

"I don't want anyone using shields on entries," Heal said. "You're in a defensive posture, you're sacrificing mobility." He turned the laser in his hands. "Some of it's going to carry through to law enforcement, and some's not," he added. "By shining that light, you're going to make an individual take one of two actions— turn away or fight through."

"The military doesn't care which," Meyers said.

Heal asked how much the device cost.

"I don't really have an answer," Meyers said. "Five thousand for the military one."

Heal told Meyers that he'd like to see the SWAT team test the laser; he thought three to six months would be a sensible period for a trial. "If they like it, they'll fight for it," Heal said.

Then Meyers measured off seventy feet, and we took turns shining the laser at each other. "I've been shot with these many times, so I don't mind," Heal said. When it was shined at me, I couldn't see for several minutes to take notes, and Heal said that this was called the afterburn.

IN JANUARY, Heal gave notice that he would retire from the Sheriff's Department on March 31st. At that point, he had received at least sixteen job offers, including one to teach crowd- and riot-control tactics in China—three days in Canton and three days in Beijing. He has no idea how he came to the attention of the Chinese government. The offer he finds most interesting involves consulting with Raytheon on the Active Denial System—the pain ray. There were also offers to work with a lab that is building a light-emitting diode incapacitator, and another that is working on a means of stopping a car by interfering with its onboard computer.

Heal's first plan was to ride his bicycle across the Mojave and then through the Great Plains, and eventually to Michigan, stopping at every historical site and library he passed. (He left at the end of April.) "I want to continue with my 'calling' and build better non-lethal options and work with developers and law-enforcement agencies," he wrote to me in an e-mail. "But for right now I just want to put my life back in order." So far, he has agreed only to take part in a study in Washington that focusses on what parallels might exist between law enforcement's treatment of gangs and the military's handling of tribes and clans.

Early in April, at a retirement luncheon attended by more than two hundred people, including colleagues from the Sheriff's Department and the Marines, Heal was given the Distinguished Service Award, one of the department's highest honors. He also received proclamations from the California Senate and the Assembly, and the five badges he had worn throughout his career. Heal's place will be taken by the man he worked with the most, Sergeant Brian Muller, who kept a notebook in which he wrote down remarks Heal made.

I ASKED HEAL if he had ever read a letter describing an invention and dropped it in the wastebasket. He shook his head. "I'll listen to everything." Then he said that one of the products he likes best was initially among the least plausible. It is a speaker that broadcasts sound by means of magnets, and he took me to

Costa Mesa to see it. "This guy called me and made these fantastic, wild, incredible claims," he said as we drove. "I talked to him, but the things he was claiming were impossible. There is a law in physics called the inverse square law, which says that as the distance is doubled the sound is quartered, and yet this guy was saying that with his invention we can hear sound with clarity at ranges that we've never seen before, at factors more powerful."

The product, he said, was called MAD, for magnetic audio device. "A guy named Vahan Simidian's the owner, and his chief technical officer's a guy named Dragoslav Colich. Everybody else was making bigger speakers, adding more power, adding longer wave guides, which is the bullhorn part of the speaker; it's like a barrel. Anyway, instead of using a speaker this guy's using magnets, and instead of using an acoustical wave he's using something called a planar wave. I'll let them tell you what it is."

Craning his neck to read a number on a wall, Heal said, "This is it," and pulled into a parking lot outside a low cement building. "When he demonstrated the system, I went a hundred yards down the road, and he's playing a Queen record," he said. "As the drummer is hitting his drum, I can feel it on my chest so tangibly that I look down to see if my shirt is moving. As I'm leaving, he says, 'If you think that's something, I can make the sound go a mile.' So we picked a date, and I brought a sixty-thousand-watt generator. We took a G.P.S. and measured a mile, and I listened to a Frank Sinatra record and everything was there—the lyrics, the orchestra, the cymbal sound, everything. We couldn't even see where the sound was coming from anymore. At three-quarters of a mile, we had trusties from the jail raking leaves, and they were putting in music requests."

Heal started collecting papers beside him on the seat. "We don't even know everything it will do; it's just started the trials," he said. "First thing, though, it replaces conventional hailing devices. Second thing is, it has non-lethal capabilities. I have to give you a little class. All non-lethal agents are debilitating, not incapacitating. They don't force you to leave an area; they just make it difficult for you to remain. Tear gas is weather-dependent, though. If the wind blows the wrong way, it affects everyone in the area; it's dangerous to use around schools and hospitals. The human brain is susceptible to certain frequencies that have nothing to do with volume. Most people cringe when you scrape a fingernail on a blackboard. What if we create a repellent sound? Will it make people avoid an area? We don't have a weather-dependency system, then, we don't have collateral damage, and because we can do it with clarity and be specific in our target we have an advantage.

"The third thing with this is that, after we started working with them, they had a major technical breakthrough. They made it so you can throw a switch and turn it into a microphone. On rescues, we can point it at somebody and have them hear us, and then we can have him talk to us, even though there's a helicopter, say. He can participate in his own rescue."

Heal got out of the car, and I followed him to the company's door. "First time I came here, I thought, My job is to encourage this guy, not crush him," he said.

Vahan Simidian turned out to be tall, with dark curly hair. He took us into a warehouse that had a big garage door at one end which had been raised. On a tripod in the parking lot was a square block of speakers about four feet by four feet. Beside it stood Colich, who was a few inches smaller than Simidian and a little heavier. Simidian said that the membrane, which he called a diaphragm, vibrated like vocal cords. "The difference between our technology and the rest of the world's is that our sound goes out in parallel beams," he said. "It's called a plane sound source."

I asked what that was, and Simidian said, "Drag, how do you explain a plane source?"

"Big surface that vibrates and creates tones that project forward," Colich said. "What you normally have is a single-point source, where everything radiates outward."

"Conically," Simidian said.

"Spherically," Colich said.

It is as if a line of sound had left the magnet speakers and remained intact, Colich explained, instead of a wave in the shape of a V that became wider and weaker as it travelled.

Simidian walked us about a hundred yards across the parking lot and had Colich play a sound that he called a wobble tone, which was a little like a siren. I didn't so much hear it as feel that I was in its way.

"Play the machine gun," Simidian yelled. "The .50 calibre."

The report sounded as if it had come from a weapon the size of a backhoe. All around us, birds took to the air.

Heal was grinning. "Did you hear the brass shells hitting the ground?" he asked.

"If there's crowds around, and they hear that, they're going to disperse," Simidian said.

We walked across the parking lot and into the warehouse. At the far end of the room was a microphone. Simidian gave me a pair of headphones, then he walked outside, so that the microphone was about eighty feet away from him. I stood with my back to him while he crushed a dry leaf, and I heard it as if it were in my own hands and I was holding them against my ear.

"Keeping the good guy away from the bad guy until the good guy knows what he's up to is the point," Simidian said. He told me that two governments—the American and the British—were using the speakers in Iraq to clear neighborhoods and to tell people at checkpoints to stop.

Heal asked Simidian if he could play the dog tape for me, but Simidian said he didn't know where it was. "Everyone's frightened of that," Heal said. A deputy had played the tape outside a junk yard where he thought a gang member was hiding. Then,

Heal said, the deputy announced that he was sending in the dogs, and a stream of gang members came out.

ALEC WILKINSON *has been a writer at* The New Yorker *since 1980. Before that he was a policeman in Wellfleet, Massachusetts, and before that a rock and roll musician. He has published nine books—two memoirs, three biographical portraits, two collections of essays, and two works of reporting, most recently* The Protest Singer, *about Pete Seeger.*

Coda

Sid Heal retired in 2008 and rode his bicycle from Los Angeles to his childhood home in Michigan. "4,163 total miles over sixty-three days, fifty-eight of them pedaling," he wrote me, "78,000-plus feet of ascent. Had more storms than I would have thought possible. Everyone said that this was the worst spring in their memory. Started with windstorms in Arizona and then wind and dust and the Trigo fires in New Mexico. Hit the southern end of the Great Plains at Trinidad, Colorado, and then headed north. Got caught in the hail and thunderstorms all the way through Colorado and Nebraska and then stiff and cold headwinds in the Dakotas and then freezing temps through northern Minnesota and then warm rains through Wisconsin and Michigan. In fact, it rained on me every single day for more than two weeks from Stevens Point, Wisconsin, to Davison, Michigan." He continues to teach at the war colleges and to consult and is working on a handbook for people who use non-lethal weapons.

Hanna Rosin

AMERICAN MURDER MYSTERY

FROM *The Atlantic*

TO GET TO THE OLD ALLEN police station in North Memphis, you have to drive all the way to the end of a quiet suburban road until it turns country. Hidden by six acres of woods, the station seems to be the kind of place that might concern itself mainly with lost dogs, or maybe the misuse of hunting licenses. But it isn't. Not anymore. As Lieutenant Doug Barnes waited for me to arrive one night for a tour of his beat, he had a smoke and listened for shots. He counted eight, none meant for buck. "Nothing unusual for a Tuesday," he told me.

Barnes is white, middle-aged, and, like many veteran cops, looks powerful without being fit. He grew up four miles from the station during the 1960s, he said, back when middle-class whites lived peacefully alongside both city elites and working-class African Americans. After the 1968 riots, Barnes's father taught him the word *curfew* and reminded him to lock the doors. Still, the place remained, until about 10 years ago, a pretty safe neighborhood where you could play outside with a ball or a dog. But as he considered more-recent times, his nostalgia gave way to something darker. "I have never been so disheartened," he said.

He remembers when the ground began to shift beneath him. He was working as an investigator throughout the city, looking into homicides and major crimes. Most of his work was downtown. One day in 1997, he got a call to check out a dead car that someone had rolled up onto the side of the interstate, on the way to the northern suburbs. The car "looked like Swiss cheese," he said, with 40 or 50 bullet holes in it and blood all over the seats. Barnes started investigating. He located one corpse in the woods nearby and another, which had been shoved out a car door, in the parking lot of a hospital a few miles away. He found a neighborhood witness, who gave up everything but the killers' names. Two weeks later, he got another call about an abandoned car. This time the body was inside. "It was my witness," he recalled, "deader than a mackerel."

At this point, he still thought of the stretch of Memphis where he'd grown up as "quiet as all get-out"; the only place you'd see cruisers congregated was in the Safeway parking lot, where churchgoing cops held choir practice before going out for drinks. But by 2000, all of that had changed. Once-quiet apartment complexes full of young families "suddenly started turning hot on us." Instead of the occasional break-in, Barnes was getting calls about armed robberies, gunshots in the hallways, drug dealers roughing up their neighbors. A gang war ripped through the neighborhood. "We thought, *What the hell is going on here?* A gang war! In North Memphis! All of a sudden it was a damn war zone," he said.

As we drove around his beat, this new suburban warfare was not so easy to make out. We passed by the city zoo and Rhodes College, a serene-looking campus on a hill. We passed by plenty of quiet streets lined with ranch houses, not fancy but not falling down, either. Then Barnes began to narrate, street by street, getting more animated and bitter by the block.

Here was the perfectly pleasant-looking Maplewood Avenue, where the old azaleas were just starting to bloom and the local cops were trying to weed out the Chicago drug connection. Farther down the avenue, two households flew American flags, and a third was known for manufacturing "cheese," a particularly potent form of powdered heroin. The Hollywood branch of the local library, long famous for its children's room, was now also renowned for the time thugs stole $1,800 there from a Girl Scout who'd been collecting cookie funds. Finally we came to a tidy brick complex called Goodwill Village, where Barnes had recently chased down some gang members who'd been taking turns having sex with a new female recruit. As we closed in on midnight, Barnes's beat began to feel like the setting of a David Lynch movie, where every backyard and cul-de-sac could double as a place to hide a body. Or like a suburban remake of *Taxi Driver*, with Barnes as the new Travis Bickle. "I'm like a zookeeper now," said Barnes. "I hold the key, and my job right now is to protect the people from all the animals."

On September 27, 2007, a headline in *The Commercial Appeal*, the city's biggest newspaper, announced a dubious honor: "Memphis Leads U.S. in Violent Crime." Local precincts had been seeing their internal numbers for homicide, rape, aggravated assault, and robbery tick up since the late 1990s, starting around the time Barnes saw the first dead car. By 2005, a criminologist closely tracking those numbers was describing the pattern as a crime explosion. In May of 2007, a woman from upscale Chickasaw Gardens was raped by two men, at gunpoint; the assailants had followed her and her son home one afternoon. Outraged residents formed Citizens Against Crime and lobbied the statehouse for tougher gun laws. "People are concerned for their lives, frankly," said one county commissioner, summarizing the city's mood. This March, a man murdered six people, including two young children, in a house a few miles south of Old Allen Station.

Falling crime rates have been one of the great American success stories of the past 15 years. New York and Los Angeles, once the twin capitals of violent crime, have calmed down significantly, as have most other big cities. Criminologists still debate why: the crack war petered out, new policing tactics worked, the economy improved for a long spell. Whatever the alchemy, crime in New York, for instance, is now so low that local prison guards are worried about unemployment.

Lately, though, a new and unexpected pattern has emerged, taking criminologists by surprise. While crime rates in large cities stayed flat, homicide rates in many midsize cities (with populations of between 500,000 and 1 million) began increasing, sometimes by as much as 20 percent a year. In 2006, the Police Executive Research Forum, a national police group surveying cities from coast to coast, concluded in a report called "A Gathering Storm" that this might represent "the front end . . . of an epidemic of violence not seen for years." The leaders of the group, which is made up of police chiefs and sheriffs, theorized about what might be spurring the latest crime wave: the spread of gangs, the masses of offenders coming out of prison, methamphetamines. But mostly they puzzled over the bleak new landscape. According to FBI data, America's most dangerous spots are now places where Martin Scorsese would never think of staging a shoot-out— Florence, South Carolina; Charlotte-Mecklenburg, North Carolina; Kansas City, Missouri; Reading, Pennsylvania; Orlando, Florida; Memphis, Tennessee.

Memphis has always been associated with some amount of violence. But why has Elvis's hometown turned into America's new South Bronx? Barnes thinks he knows one big part of the answer, as does the city's chief of police. A handful of local criminologists and social scientists think they can explain it, too. But it's a dismal answer, one that city leaders have made clear they don't want to hear. It's an answer that offers up racial stereotypes to fearful whites in a city trying to move beyond racial tensions.

Ultimately, it reaches beyond crime and implicates one of the most ambitious antipoverty programs of recent decades.

EARLY EVERY THURSDAY, Richard Janikowski drives to Memphis's Airways Station for the morning meeting of police precinct commanders. Janikowski used to teach law and semiotics, and he still sometimes floats on a higher plane; he walks slowly, speaks in a nasal voice, and quotes from policy books. But at this point in his career, he is basically an honorary cop. A criminologist with the University of Memphis, Janikowski has established an unusually close relationship with the city police department. From the police chief to the beat cop, everyone knows him as "Dr. J," or "GQ" if he's wearing his nice suit. When his researchers are looking for him, they can often find him outside the building, having a smoke with someone in uniform.

One Thursday in March, I sat in on the morning meeting. About 100 people—commanders, beat cops, researchers, and a city councilman—gathered in a sterile conference room with a projector up front. The session had none of the raucous air of precinct meetings you see on cop shows. Nobody was making crude jokes or bragging about the latest run-in with the hood rats.

One by one, the precinct commanders presented crime and arrest statistics in their wards. They broke the information down into neat bar graphs—type of crime, four-week comparison, shifting hot spots. Thanks to Janikowski's influence, the commanders sounded more like policy wonks than police. "It used to be the criminal element was more confined," said Larry Godwin, the police chief. "Now it's all spread out. They might hit one area today and another tomorrow. We have to take a sophisticated look on a daily, hourly basis, or we might never get leverage on it." For a police department facing a volatile situation, the bar graphs imposed some semblance of order.

Janikowski began working with the police department in 1997, the same year that Barnes saw the car with the bullet holes. He initially consulted on a program to reduce sexual assaults citywide and quickly made himself useful. He mapped all the incidents and noticed a pattern: many assaults happened outside convenience stores, to women using pay phones that were hidden from view. The police asked store owners to move the phones inside, and the number of assaults fell significantly.

About five years ago, Janikowski embarked on a more ambitious project. He'd built up enough trust with the police to get them to send him daily crime and arrest reports, including addresses and types of crime. He began mapping all violent and property crimes, block by block, across the city. "These cops on the streets were saying that crime patterns are changing," he said, so he wanted to look into it.

When his map was complete, a clear if strangely shaped pattern emerged: *Wait a minute,* he recalled thinking. *I see this bunny rabbit coming up. People are going to accuse me of being on shrooms!* The inner city, where crime used to be concentrated, was now clean. But everywhere else looked much worse: arrests had skyrocketed along two corridors north and west of the central city (the bunny rabbit's ears) and along one in the southeast (the tail). Hot spots had proliferated since the mid-1990s, and little islands of crime had sprung up where none had existed before, dotting the map all around the city.

Janikowski might not have managed to pinpoint the cause of this pattern if he hadn't been married to Phyllis Betts, a housing expert at the University of Memphis. Betts and Janikowski have two dogs, three cats, and no kids; they both tend to bring their work home with them. Betts had been evaluating the impact of one of the city government's most ambitious initiatives: the demolition of the city's public-housing projects, as part of a nationwide experiment to free the poor from the destructive effects of concentrated poverty. Memphis demolished its first project in

1997. The city gave former residents federal "Section 8" rent-subsidy vouchers and encouraged them to move out to new neighborhoods. Two more waves of demolition followed over the next nine years, dispersing tens of thousands of poor people into the wider metro community.

If police departments are usually stingy with their information, housing departments are even more so. Getting addresses of Section 8 holders is difficult, because the departments want to protect the residents' privacy. Betts, however, helps the city track where the former residents of public housing have moved. Over time, she and Janikowski realized that they were doing their fieldwork in the same neighborhoods.

About six months ago, they decided to put a hunch to the test. Janikowski merged his computer map of crime patterns with Betts's map of Section 8 rentals. Where Janikowski saw a bunny rabbit, Betts saw a sideways horse shoe ("He has a better imagination," she said). Otherwise, the match was near-perfect. On the merged map, dense violent-crime areas are shaded dark blue, and Section 8 addresses are represented by little red dots. All of the dark-blue areas are covered in little red dots, like bursts of gunfire. The rest of the city has almost no dots.

Betts remembers her discomfort as she looked at the map. The couple had been musing about the connection for months, but they were amazed—and deflated—to see how perfectly the two data sets fit together. She knew right away that this would be a "hard thing to say or write." Nobody in the antipoverty community and nobody in city leadership was going to welcome the news that the noble experiment that they'd been engaged in for the past decade had been bringing the city down, in ways they'd never expected. But the connection was too obvious to ignore, and Betts and Janikowski figured that the same thing must be happening all around the country. Eventually, they thought, they'd find other researchers who connected the dots the way they had, and then maybe they could get city leaders, and even national leaders, to listen.

BETTS'S OFFICE IS FILLED with books about knocking down the projects, an effort considered by fellow housing experts to be their great contribution to the civil-rights movement. The work grew out of a long history of white resistance to blacks' moving out of what used to be called the ghetto. During much of the 20th century, white people used bombs and mobs to keep black people out of their neighborhoods. In 1949 in Chicago, a rumor that a black family was moving onto a white block prompted a riot that grew to 10,000 people in four days. "Americans had been treating blacks seeking housing outside the ghetto not much better than . . . [the] cook treated the dog who sought a crust of bread," wrote the ACLU lawyer and fair-housing advocate Alexander Polikoff in his book *Waiting for Gautreaux*.

Polikoff is a hero to Betts and many of her colleagues. In August 1966, he filed two related class-action suits against the Chicago Housing Authority and the U.S. Department of Housing and Urban Development, on behalf of a woman named Dorothy Gautreaux and other tenants. Gautreaux wanted to leave the ghetto, but the CHA offered housing only in neighborhoods just like hers. Polikoff became notorious in the Chicago suburbs; one community group, he wrote, awarded him a gold-plated pooper-scooper "to clean up all the shit" he wanted to bring into the neighborhood. A decade later, he argued the case before the Supreme Court and won. Legal scholars today often compare the case's significance to that of *Brown v. Board of Education of Topeka*.

In 1976, letters went out to 200 randomly selected families among the 44,000 living in Chicago public housing, asking whether they wanted to move out to the suburbs. A counselor went around the projects explaining the new Section 8 program, in which tenants would pay 25 percent of their income for rent and the government would pay the rest, up to a certain limit. Many residents seemed dubious. They asked how far away these places were, how they would get there, whether the white people would let them in.

But the counselors persevered and eventually got people excited about the idea. The flyers they mailed out featured a few stanzas of a Gwendolyn Brooks poem, "The Ballad of Rudolph Reed."

> I am not hungry for berries
> I am not hungry for bread
> But hungry hungry for a house
> Where at night a man in bed
> May never hear the plaster
> Stir as if in pain.
> May never hear the roaches
> Falling like fat rain.

(This was a risky decision. One later stanza, omitted from the flyers, reads:

> By the time he had hurt his fourth white man
> Rudolph Reed was dead.
> His neighbors gathered and kicked his corpse
> "Nigger—" his neighbors said.)

Starting in 1977, in what became known as the Gautreaux program, hundreds of families relocated to suburban neighborhoods—most of them about 25 miles from the ghetto, with very low poverty rates and good public schools. The authorities had screened the families carefully, inspecting their apartments and checking for good credit histories. They didn't offer the vouchers to families with more than five children, or to those that were indifferent to leaving the projects. They were looking for families "seeking a healthy environment, good schools and an opportunity to live in a safe and decent home."

A well-known Gautreaux study, released in 1991, showed spectacular results. The sociologist James Rosenbaum at Northwestern University had followed 114 families who had moved to the suburbs, although only 68 were still cooperating by the time he released the study. Compared to former public-housing residents who'd stayed within the city, the suburban dwellers were four times as likely to finish high school, twice as likely to attend college, and more likely to be employed. *Newsweek* called the program "stunning" and said the project renewed "one's faith in the struggle." In a glowing segment, a *60 Minutes* reporter asked one Gautreaux boy what he wanted to be when he grew up. "I haven't really made up my mind," the boy said. "Construction worker, architect, anesthesiologist." Another child's mother declared it "the end of poverty" for her family.

In 1992, 7-year-old Dantrell Davis from the Cabrini-Green project was walking to school, holding his mother's hand, when a stray bullet killed him. The hand-holding detail seemed to stir the city in a way that none of the other murder stories coming out of the high-rises ever had. "Tear down the high rises," demanded an editorial in the *Chicago Tribune*, while that boy's image "burns in our civic memory."

HUD Secretary Henry Cisneros was receptive to the idea. He spent a few nights in Chicago's infamous Robert Taylor Homes and subsequently spoke about "these enclaves of poverty," where "drug dealers control the stairwells, where children can't go outside to play, where mothers put their infants to bed in bathtubs." If people could see beyond the graffitied hallways of these projects, they could get above that way of life, argued the researchers, and learn to live like their middle-class brothers and sisters. Cisneros floated the idea of knocking down the projects and moving the residents out into the metro area.

The federal government encouraged the demolitions with a

$6.3 billion program to redevelop the old project sites, called HOPE VI, or "Housing Opportunities for People Everywhere." The program was launched in the same spirit as Bill Clinton's national service initiative—communities working together to "rebuild lives." One Chicago housing official mused about "architects and lawyers and bus drivers and people on welfare living together." Wrecking balls began hitting the Chicago high-rises in the mid-1990s. Within a few years, tens of thousands of public-housing residents all over the country were leaving their apartments. In place of the projects, new developments arose, with fanciful names like "Jazz on the Boulevard" or "Centennial Place." In Memphis, the Hurt Village project was razed to make way for "Uptown Square," which the local developer Henry Turley declared would be proof that you could turn the inner city into a "nice place for poor people" to live. Robert Lipscomb, the dynamic director of the Memphis Housing Authority, announced, "Memphis is on the move."

WHEN THE DIXIE HOMES housing project was demolished, in 2006, a group of residents moved to a place called Springdale Creek Apartments in North Memphis, on Doug Barnes's beat. They were not handpicked, nor part of any study, and nobody told them to move to a low-poverty neighborhood. Like tens of thousand s of others, they moved because they had to, into a place they could afford. Springdale Creek is not fancy, but the complex tries to enforce its own quiet order. A sliding black gate separates the row of brick buildings from busy Jackson Avenue, where kids hang out by the KFC. Leslie Shaw was sold when she heard the phrase *gated community* mentioned by the building manager.

When Shaw saw the newly painted white walls, "so fresh and clean," with no old smudges from somebody else's kids, she decided to give away all her furniture. "I didn't want to move in here with any garbage from Dixie," she said. "I said to myself, 'Might as well start over.'" She bought a new brown velour couch and a matching loveseat. She bought a washer and dryer, and a dresser for her 8-year-old grandson, Gerrell, who lives with her. The only thing she kept was a bookshelf, to hold the paperbacks coming monthly from the book club she'd decided to join.

Shaw is 11 years crack-free and, at 47, eager to take advantage of every free program that comes her way—a leadership class, Windows Vista training, a citizen police course, a writing workshop. What drove her—"I got to be honest with you"—was proving her middle-class sisters and brother, "who didn't think I'd get above it," wrong. Just after she moved in, one sister came over and said, "This is nice. I thought they would put you back in the projects or something."

I visited Shaw in February, about a year and a half after she'd moved in. The view outside her first-floor window was still pretty nice—no junk littered the front lawn and few apartments stood vacant. But slowly, she told me, Springdale Creek has started to feel less like a suburban paradise and more like Dixie Homes. Neighborhood boys often kick open the gate or break the keypad. Many nights they just randomly press phone numbers until someone lets them in. The gate's main use seems to be as a sort of low-thrills ride for younger kids whose parents aren't paying attention. They hang from the gate as it slides open; a few have gotten their fingers caught and had to be taken to the emergency room.

When Shaw recounts all the bad things that have happened at Springdale Creek, she does it matter-of-factly (even as a grandma, she says, "I can jump those boys if I have to"). Car thefts were common at first—Shaw's neighbor Laura Evans is one of about 10 victims in the past two years. Thieves have relieved the apartment management company of some of its computers, extra refrigerators, and spare stoves. A few Dixie boys—sons of one of Shaw's friends—were suspected of breaking the windows in vacant apartments. Last year, somebody hit a pregnant woman in the head with a brick. In the summer, a neighborhood kid chased his girl-friend's car, shooting at her as she drove toward the gate; the cops, who are called in regularly for one reason or another, collected the spent shells on the grass. "You know, you move from one place to another and you bring the element with you," said Evans, who stopped by Shaw's apartment while I was there. "You got some trying to make it just like the projects."

In the afternoon, I visited an older resident from Dixie Homes who lives across the way from Shaw. Her apartment was dark, blinds drawn, and everyone was watching Maury Povich. A few minutes after I arrived, we heard a pounding at the door, and a neighbor rushed in, shouting.

"They just jumped my grandson! That's my grandson!"

This was 64-year-old Nadine Clark, who'd left Dixie before it got knocked down. Clark was wearing her navy peacoat, but she had forgotten to put in her teeth. From her pocket she pulled a .38-caliber pistol, which was the only thing that glinted in the room besides the TV.

"There's 10 of them! And I'm gonna go fuck them up! That's my grandson! They took him away in an ambulance!"

Nobody in the house got excited. They kept their eyes on Maury Povich, where the audience was booing a kid who looked just like the thug who'd shot up his girlfriend's car. "She'll calm down," someone said, and after a few minutes, Clark left. I drove down to Northside High, a few blocks away, where the grandson had gotten beaten up. TV crews and local reporters were already gathered outside the school, and a news chopper hovered over-head. There had been two school shootings in the neighborhood that month, and any fresh incidents made big news.

Clark's grandson is named Unique, although everyone calls him Neek. Outside school that day, Neek had been a victim of one of the many strange dynamics of the new urban suburbia. Neek is tall and quiet and doesn't rush to change out of his white polo shirt and blue khakis after school. He spends most of his afternoons in the house, watching TV or doing his homework.

Neek's middle-class habits have made him, unwittingly, a perfect target for homegrown gangs. Gang leaders, cut loose from the housing projects, have adapted their recruiting efforts and operations to their new setting. Lately, they've been going after "smart, intelligent, go-to-college-looking kid[s], without gold teeth and medallions," said Sergeant Lambert Ross, an investigator with the Memphis Police. Clean-cut kids serve the same function as American recruits for al-Qaeda: they become the respectable front men. If a gang member gets pulled over with guns or drugs, he can hand them to the college boy, who has no prior record. The college boy, raised outside the projects, might be dreaming of being the next 50 Cent, or might be too intimidated not to join. Ross told me that his latest batch of arrests involved several kids from two-car-garage families.

Neek generally stayed away from gang types, so some older kids beat him with bats. No one is sure whether a gun was fired. As these things go, he got off easy. He was treated at the emergency room and went back to school after a few days.

IN THE MOST LITERAL SENSE, the national effort to diffuse poverty has succeeded. Since 1990, the number of Americans living in neighborhoods of concentrated poverty—meaning that at least 40 percent of households are below the federal poverty level—has declined by 24 percent. But this doesn't tell the whole story. Recently, the housing expert George Galster, of Wayne State University, analyzed the shifts in urban poverty and published his results in a paper called "A Cautionary Tale." While fewer Americans live in high-poverty neighborhoods, increasing numbers now live in places with "moderate" poverty rates, meaning rates of 20 to 40 percent. This pattern is not necessarily better, either for poor people trying to break away from bad neighbor-

hoods or for cities, Galster explains. His paper compares two sce-
narios: a city split into high-poverty and low-poverty areas, and a
city dominated by median-poverty ones. The latter arrangement is
likely to produce more bad neighborhoods and more total crime,
he concludes, based on a computer model of how social dysfunction spreads.

Studies show that recipients of Section 8 vouchers have tended
to choose moderately poor neighborhoods that were already on
the decline, not low-poverty neighborhoods. One recent study
publicized by HUD warned that policy makers should lower
their expectations, because voucher recipients seemed not to be
spreading out, as they had hoped, but clustering together. Galster
theorizes that every neighborhood has its tipping point—a thresh-
old well below a 40 percent poverty rate—beyond which crime
explodes and other severe social problems set in. Pushing a greater
number of neighborhoods past that tipping point is likely to produce more total crime. In 2003, the Brookings Institution published a list of the 15 cities where the number of high-poverty
neighborhoods had declined the most. In recent years, most of
those cities have also shown up as among the most violent in the
U.S., according to FBI data.

The "Gathering Storm" report that worried over an upcoming
epidemic of violence was inspired by a call from the police chief
of Louisville, Kentucky, who'd seen crime rising regionally and
wondered what was going on. Simultaneously, the University of
Louisville criminologist Geetha Suresh was tracking local patterns of violent crime. She had begun her work years before, going blind into the research: she had just arrived from India, had
never heard of a housing project, had no idea which were the bad
parts of town, and was clueless about the finer points of American
racial sensitivities. In her research, Suresh noticed a recurring pattern, one that emerged first in the late 1990s, then again around
2002. A particularly violent neighborhood would suddenly go
cold, and crime would heat up in several new neighborhoods. In

each case, Suresh has now confirmed, the first hot spots were the neighborhoods around huge housing projects, and the later ones were places where people had moved when the projects were torn down. From that, she drew the obvious conclusion: "Crime is going along with them." Except for being hand-drawn, Suresh's map matching housing patterns with crime looks exactly like Janikowski and Betts's.

Nobody would claim vouchers, or any single factor, as the sole cause of rising crime. Crime did not rise in every city where housing projects came down. In cities where it did, many factors contributed: unemployment, gangs, rapid gentrification that dislocated tens of thousands of poor people not living in the projects. Still, researchers around the country are seeing the same basic pattern: projects coming down in inner cities and crime pushing outward, in many cases destabilizing cities or their surrounding areas. Dennis Rosenbaum, a criminologist at the University of Illinois at Chicago, told me that after the high-rises came down in Chicago, suburbs to the south and west—including formerly quiet ones—began to see spikes in crime; nearby Maywood's murder rate has nearly doubled in the past two years. In Atlanta, which almost always makes the top-10 crime list, crime is now scattered widely, just as it is in Memphis and Louisville.

In some places, the phenomenon is hard to detect, but there may be a simple reason: in cities with tight housing markets, Section 8 recipients generally can't afford to live within the city limits, and sometimes they even move to different states. New York, where the rate of violent crime has plummeted, appears to have pushed many of its poor out to New Jersey, where violent crime has increased in nearby cities and suburbs. Washington, D.C., has exported some of its crime to surrounding counties in Maryland and Virginia.

Much research has been done on the spread of gangs into the suburbs. Jeff Rojek, a criminologist at the University of South

Carolina, issued a report in 2006 showing that serious gang activity had spread to eight suburban counties around the state, including Florence County, home to the city of Florence, which was ranked the most violent place in America the year after Memphis was. In his fieldwork, he said, the police complained of "migrant gangs" from the housing projects, and many departments seemed wholly unprepared to respond.

After the first wave of housing-project demolition in Memphis, in 1997, crime spread out, but did not immediately increase. (It takes time for criminals to make new connections and to develop "comfort zones," Janikowski told me.) But in 2005, another wave of project demolitions pushed the number of people displaced from public housing to well over 20,000, and crime skyrocketed. Janikowski felt there were deep structural issues behind the increase, ones that the city was not prepared to handle. Old gangs—the Gangster Disciples and the LeMoyne Gardens gang—had long since re-formed and gotten comfortable. Ex-convicts recently released from prison had taken up residence with girlfriends or wives or families who'd moved to the new neighborhoods. Working-class people had begun moving out to the suburbs farther east, and more recipients of Section 8 vouchers were taking their place. Now many neighborhoods were reaching their tipping points.

Chaotic new crime patterns in suburbia caught the police off guard. Gang members who'd moved to North Memphis might now have cousins southeast of the city, allowing them to target the whole vast area in between and hide out with relatives far from the scene of the crime. Memphis covers an area as large as New York City, but with one-seventeenth as many police officers, and a much lower cop-to-citizen ratio. And routine policing is more difficult in the semi-suburbs. Dealers sell out of fenced-in backyards, not on exposed street corners. They have cars to escape in, and a landscape to blend into. Shrubbery is a constant headache for the police; they've taken to asking that bushes be cut down so suspects can't duck behind them.

I BEGAN REPORTING THIS STORY because I came across a newspaper article that ranked cities by crime rate and I was surprised to see Memphis at the very top. At first I approached the story literally, the same way a cop on a murder case would: here's the body, now figure out what happened. But it didn't take long to realize that in Memphis, and in city after city, the bodies are just the most visible symptoms of a much deeper sickness.

If replacing housing projects with vouchers had achieved its main goal—infusing the poor with middle-class habits—then higher crime rates might be a price worth paying. But today, social scientists looking back on the whole grand experiment are apt to use words like *baffling* and *disappointing*. A large federal-government study conducted over the past decade—a follow-up to the highly positive, highly publicized Gautreaux study of 1991—produced results that were "puzzling," said Susan Popkin of the Urban Institute. In this study, volunteers were also moved into low-poverty neighborhoods, although they didn't move nearly as far as the Gautreaux families. Women reported lower levels of obesity and depression. But they were no more likely to find jobs. The schools were not much better, and children were no more likely to stay in them. Girls were less likely to engage in risky behaviors, and they reported feeling more secure in their new neighborhoods. But boys were as likely to do drugs and act out, and more likely to get arrested for property crimes. The best Popkin can say is: "It has not lived up to its promise. It has not lifted people out of poverty, it has not made them self-sufficient, and it has left a lot of people behind."

Researchers have started to look more critically at the Gautreaux results. The sample was tiny, and the circumstances were ideal. The families who moved to the suburbs were screened heavily and the vast majority of families who participated in the program didn't end up moving, suggesting that those who did were particularly motivated. Even so, the results were not always sparkling. For instance, while Gautreaux study families who had moved to the suburbs were more likely to work than a control group who stayed in the city, they actually worked less than before they had moved. "People were really excited about it because it seemed to offer something new," Popkin said. "But in my view, it was radically oversold."

Ed Goetz, a housing expert at the University of Minnesota, is creating a database of the follow-up research at different sites across the country, "to make sense of these very limited positive outcomes." On the whole, he says, people don't consistently report any health, education, or employment benefits. They are certainly no closer to leaving poverty. They tend to "feel better about their environments," meaning they see less graffiti on the walls and fewer dealers on the streets. But just as strongly, they feel "a sense of isolation in their new communities." His most surprising finding, he says, "is that they miss the old community. For all of its faults, there was a tight network that existed. So what I'm trying to figure out is: Was this a bad theory of poverty? We were intending to help people climb out of poverty, but that hasn't happened at all. Have we underestimated the role of support networks and overestimated the role of place?"

HOPE VI stands as a bitter footnote to this story. What began as an "I Have a Dream" social crusade has turned into an urban-redevelopment project. Cities fell so hard for the idea of a new, spiffed-up, gentrified downtown that this vision came to crowd out other goals. "People ask me if HOPE VI was successful, and I have to say, 'You mean the buildings or the people?'" said Laura Harris, a HOPE VI evaluator in Memphis. "It became seen as a way to get rid of eyesores and attract rich people downtown." Phyllis Betts told me that when she was interviewing residents leaving the housing projects, "they were under the impression they could move into the new developments on site." Residents were asked to help name the new developments and consult on the architectural plans. Yet to move back in, residents had to meet strict criteria: if they were not seniors, they had to be working, or in school, or on disability. Their children could not be delinquent in school. Most public-housing residents were scared off by the criteria, or couldn't meet them, or else they'd already moved and didn't want to move again. The new HOPE VI developments aimed to balance Section 8 and market-rate residents, but this generally hasn't happened. In Memphis, the rate of former public-housing residents moving back in is 5 percent.

A few months ago, Harris went to a Sunday-afternoon picnic at Uptown Square, the development built on the site of the old Hurt Village project, to conduct a survey. The picnic's theme was chili cook-off. The white people, mostly young couples, including little kids and pregnant wives, sat around on Eddie Bauer chairs with beer holders, chatting. The black people, mostly women with children, were standing awkwardly around the edges. Harris began asking some of the white people the questions on her survey: Do you lack health insurance? Have you ever not had enough money to buy medication? One said to her, "This is so sad. Does anyone ever answer 'yes' to these questions?"—Harris's first clue that neighbors didn't talk much across color lines. One of the developers was there that day surveying the ideal community he'd built, and he was beaming. "Isn't this great?" he asked Harris, and she remembers thinking, *Are you kidding me? They're all sitting 20 feet away from each other!*

In my visits with former Dixie Homes tenants who'd moved around the city, I came across the same mix of reactions that researchers had found. The residents who had always been intent on moving out of Dixie Homes anyway seemed to be thriving; those who'd been pushed out against their will, which was the vast majority, seemed dislocated and ill at ease.

I met 30-year-old Sheniqua Woodard, a single mother of three who'd been getting her four-year degree while living at Dixie. She was now working at a city mental-health clinic and about to start studying toward a master's degree in special education. She'd moved as far out of the city as she could, to a house with a big backyard. She said, "The fact of being in my own home? Priceless."

But I also met La Sasha Rodgers, who was 19 when Dixie was torn down (now she's 21). "A lot of people thought it was bad, because they didn't live there," she told me. "But it was like one big family. It felt like home. If I could move back now, the way it was, I would." She moved out to a house in South Memphis with her mother, and all the little cousins and nieces and nephews who drift in during the day. She doesn't know anyone else on the block. "It's just here," she said about her new house. Rodgers may not see them right out her window, but she knows that the "same dope dealers, the same junkies" are just down the block. The threats are no less real, but now they seem distant and dull, as if she were watching neighborhood life on TV. At Dixie, when there were shots at the corner store, everyone ran out to see what was happening. Now, "if somebody got shot, we wouldn't get up to see."

Rodgers didn't finish high school, although she did get her GED, and she's never had a job. Still, "I know I have to venture out in the world," she said, running through her options: Go back to school? Get a job? Get married? Have a baby? "I want more. I'm so ready to have my own. I just don't know how to get it."

IT'S DIFFICULT to contemplate solutions to this problem when so few politicians, civil servants, and academics seem willing to talk about it—or even to admit that it exists. Janikowski and Betts are in an awkward position. They are both white academics in a city with many African American political leaders. Neither of them is a Memphis native. And they know that their research will fuel the usual NIMBY paranoia about poor people destroying the suburbs. "We don't want Memphis to be seen as the armpit of the nation," Betts said. "And we don't want to be the ones responsible for framing these issues in the wrong way."

The city's deep pride about the downtown renaissance makes the issue more sensitive still. CITY, COOL, CHIC read downtown billboards, beckoning young couples to new apartments. Developers have built a new eight-block mall and a downtown stadium for the Grizzlies, the city's NBA team. In 2003, *The Commercial Appeal* likened downtown Memphis to a grizzly bear "rumbling back into the sun." The city is applying to the federal government for more funds to knock down the last two housing projects and build more mixed-income developments, and wouldn't want to advertise any problems.

Earlier this year, Betts presented her findings to city leaders, including Robert Lipscomb, the head of the Memphis Housing Authority. From what Lipscomb said to me, he's still not moved. "You've already marginalized people and told them they have to move out," he told me irritably, just as he's told Betts. "Now you're saying they moved somewhere else and created all these problems? That's a really, really unfair assessment. You're putting a big burden on people who have been too burdened already, and to me that's, quote-unquote, criminal." To Lipscomb, what matters is sending people who lived in public housing the message that "they can be successful, they can go to work and have kids who go to school. They can be self-sufficient and reach for the middle class."

But Betts doesn't think this message, alone, will stick, and she gets frustrated when she sees sensitivity about race or class blocking debate. "You can't begin to problem-solve until you lay it out," she said. "Most of us are not living in these high-crime neighborhoods. And I'm out there listening to the people who are not committing the crimes, who expected something better." The victims, she notes, are seldom white. "There are decent African American neighborhoods—neighborhoods of choice—that are going down," she said.

In truth, the victims are constantly shifting. Hardly any Section 8 families moved into wealthy white suburbs. In the early phases, most of the victims were working-class African Americans who saw their neighborhoods destroyed and had to leave. Now most of them are poor people like Leslie Shaw, who are trying to do what Lipscomb asks of them and be more self-sufficient. Which makes sorting out the blame even trickier. Sometimes the victim and the perpetrator live under the same roof; Shaw's friend at Springdale Creek wanted a better life for herself and her family, but she couldn't keep her sons from getting into trouble. Sometimes they may be the same person, with conflicting impulses about whether to move forward or go back. In any case, more than a decade's worth of experience proves that crossing your fingers and praying for self-sufficiency is foolish.

So what's the alternative? Is a strained hope better than no hope at all? "We can't send people back to those barricaded institutions, like *Escape From New York*," said Betts. "That's not a scenario anyone wants to embrace." Physically redistributing the poor was probably necessary; generations of them were floundering in the high-rises. But instead of coaching them and then carefully spreading them out among many more-affluent neighborhoods, most cities gave them vouchers and told them to move in a rush, with no support.

"People were moved too quickly, without any planning, and without any thought about where they would live, and how it would affect the families or the places," complains James Rosenbaum, the author of the original Gautreaux study. By contrast, years of public debate preceded welfare reform. States were forced to acknowledge that if they wanted to cut off benefits, they had to think about job training, child care, broken families. Housing never became a high-profile issue, so cities skipped that phase.

NOT EVERY PROJECT WAS LIKE Cabrini-Green. Dixie Homes was a complex of two- and three-story brick buildings on grassy plots. It was, by all accounts, claustrophobic, sometimes badly maintained, and occasionally violent. But to its residents, it was, above all, a community. Every former resident I spoke to mentioned one thing: the annual Easter-egg hunt. Demonizing the high-rises has blinded some city officials to what was good and necessary about the projects, and what they ultimately have to find a way to replace: the sense of belonging, the informal economy, the easy access to social services. And for better or worse, the fact that the police had the address.

Better policing, better-connected to new residential patterns, is a step in the right direction. Janikowski believes the chaos can be controlled with information and technology, and he's been helping the department improve both for several years. This spring he helped launch a "real-time crime center," in the hope of making the department more nimble. Twenty-four hours a day, technicians plot arrests on giant screens representing the city's geography, in a newly built studio reminiscent of CNN's newsroom. *Cops on the dots* is the national buzz-word for this kind of information-driven, rapid-response policing, and it has an alluring certainty about it. The changes seem to be making a difference; recent data show violent-crime rates in the city beginning to inch down.

In the long view—both Betts and Janikowski agree—better policing is of course not the only answer. The more fundamental question is the one this social experiment was designed to address in the first place: What to do about deep poverty and persistent social dysfunction?

Betts's latest crusade is something called "site-based resident services." When the projects came down, the residents lost their public-support system—health clinics, child care, job training. Memphis's infant-mortality rate is rising, for example, and Betts is convinced that has something to do with poor people's having lost easy access to prenatal care. The services remained downtown while the clients scattered all over the city, many of them with no convenient transportation. Along with other nonprofit leaders, Betts is trying to get outreach centers opened in the outlying neighborhoods, and especially in some of the new, troubled apartment buildings. She says she's beginning to hear supportive voices within the city government. But not enough leaders have acknowledged the new landscape—or admitted that the projects are gone in name only, and that the city's middle-class dreams never came true.

AND BEYOND THIS, WHAT? The social services Betts is recommending did not lift masses of people out of poverty in the projects. Perhaps, outside the projects, they will help people a little more. But perhaps not. The problems of poverty run so deep that we're unlikely to know the answer for a generation. Social scientists tracking people who are trying to improve their lives often talk about a "weathering effect," the wearing-down that happens as a lifetime of baggage accumulates. With poor people, the drag is strong, even if they haven't lived in poverty for long. Kids who leave poor neighborhoods at a young age still have trouble keeping up with their peers, studies show. They catch up for a while and then, after a few years, slip back. Truly escaping poverty seems to require a will as strong as a spy's: you have to disappear to a strange land, forget where you came from, and ignore the suspicions of everyone around you. Otherwise, you can easily find yourself right back where you started.

Leslie Shaw is writing a memoir, and it contains more weather than most of us can imagine. At 15, she left home with a boy named Fat, who turned out to be a pimp. She spent the next seven years being dragged from state to state as a street hooker, robbing johns and eventually getting addicted to crack. Once, a pimp locked her in his car trunk. Another time, her water broke in a crack house. This covers only the first few chapters. She works on the memoir endlessly—revising, dividing the material into different files (one is labeled, simply, "Shit"). She still has two big sections to go, and many years of her life left to record. Her next big project is to get this memoir under control, finish it, have it published, and "hope something good can come out of it," for herself and the people who read it.

When I last saw Shaw, in March, she had her plan laid out. About seven months earlier, she had taken in her 2-year-old grand-daughter, Casha Mona, for what was supposed to be a temporary stay. The little girl's mother was getting her act together in Albuquerque, where Casha's father (Shaw's son) was in prison. Shaw's plan was to take Casha Mona back to Albuquerque, then begin a writing workshop at the Renaissance Center in Memphis to get her memoir into shape. And just before Easter, she'd dropped Casha off, come home, and signed up for the class. Two days later, she got a call from an aunt in Albuquerque. Casha had swallowed a few crack rocks at her mother's house; state officials had put her in foster care. More weather. Last I spoke to Shaw, she'd bought another round-trip bus ticket to Albuquerque and was going to get the little girl back.

The writing class would have to wait, or she could do it at night, or . . . "I'm just going to get on that bus," she said, "and pray."

HANNA ROSIN *is a contributing writer for* The Atlantic *and a founding editor of Doublex.com, an online women's site. She has also written for* The New Yorker, The New Republic, GQ, *and the* New York Times. *She lives in Washington, D.C., with her husband,* Slate *deputy editor David Plotz, and their three children.*

John Colapinto

STOP, THIEF!

FROM *The New Yorker*

ON A RECENT MORNING, a dapper man in his fifties with a narrow mustache, dressed in a black Armani suit, strolled past the cosmetics counters on the main floor of a midtown Manhattan department store. He was the store's vice-president of corporate asset protection, second in command in the store's loss-prevention department. Loss prevention is devoted to reducing what retailers call "shrink": the erosion of profits—some forty billion dollars in 2006, according to the University of Florida's National Retail Security Survey—resulting from shoplifting, employee theft, and organized retail crime (professional thieves who steal goods in large volume for resale). Some form of loss prevention exists at every level of retail, from dollar stores and big-box discounters like Wal-Mart and Target to high-end establishments like Bergdorf Goodman, Barneys, and Saks Fifth Avenue. But it is a side of retail that many merchants are reluctant to publicize; hence this store's insistence that neither it nor its personnel be named.

The vice-president grew up in East Harlem and the Bronx, and has worked in loss prevention for thirty years. "I started as a store detective on Long Island," he said. "I had a knack for picking out bad guys. I grew up with them and I knew how they behaved." As he walked past the boutiques on the store's main floor, he saw the place very differently from the way shoppers would. A selection of Dolce & Gabbana handbags on display steps from a street door was an open invitation for a shoplifter (or "booster," in industry parlance) to scoop up a few thousand-dollar purses and run out. The seventy-dollar bottles of Christian Dior perfume on open shelves near the entrance posed a similar risk. "The opportunity is there," the vice-president admitted. "But it's a risk that management is willing to take to create an atmosphere that's relaxed and inviting."

He left the store's polished wood cabinets, marble floors, and Roman columns for a dingy stairway tiled in linoleum. At the bottom, he pushed through a door into the asset-protection complex, a warren of windowless basement offices. He went through a door marked "Camera Room"—a low-ceilinged chamber lit by the glow from twenty television screens stacked floor to ceiling along one wall. The screens showed high-angled views of customers moving through more than two hundred thousand square feet of sales floors, wholly unaware (most of them) that the grapefruit-size mirrored domes attached to the tops of pillars and to the ceilings concealed high-resolution color cameras recording their every move. The several hundred cameras dispersed about the store can be rotated three hundred and sixty degrees with remote-control joysticks; that day, they were being operated by three loss-prevention camera agents who sat, in suits and ties, at small consoles in front of the screens.

Loss-prevention professionals say that they avoid any kind of profiling to single out suspects, since thieves can be male or female and come in all colors, ages, and socioeconomic levels. (Winona Ryder, the movie actress, is one of the standing examples of this tenet: in 2001, she was apprehended at Saks Fifth Avenue in Beverly Hills and later convicted of stealing more than five thousand dollars' worth of designer items, including an Yves Saint Laurent blouse, Donna Karan socks, Frédéric Fekkai hair accessories, a Gucci dress, and a Dolce & Gabbana handbag. In 2006, Claude Allen, then the top domestic-policy adviser to George Bush, pleaded guilty to stealing hundreds of dollars by making fraudulent returns at Target.) Instead, agents are trained to recognize the behaviors that betray a person's intention to steal: selecting merchandise without regard for size or price, feeling carefully along clothing seams for sensor tags, or scanning the ceilings and walls for security cameras. Men shopping alone and carrying any kind of bag always draw a second look from agents, according to the vice-president, because it is assumed that most men will go shopping only when dragged by a wife or girlfriend. One of the store's camera agents showed me a surveillance tape from three weeks earlier, when he had zeroed in on a well-dressed white man with graying hair who was carrying an expensive briefcase. The man was trying on three-hundred-dollar designer sunglasses from a swivel rack. Nothing about his relaxed demeanor suggested that he was a thief. But each time the man took off a pair of glasses, he folded them and placed them on the counter before selecting another pair.

"You don't do that when you're trying on glasses," the camera agent pointed out. "You don't fold down the arms."

It was enough to convince the agent that a camera should be kept on the man, who eventually slid a pair of glasses into an inside pocket of his jacket. He unhurriedly pocketed three more pairs, then took a circuitous route out of the store—riding an elevator up two floors and immediately descending on the escalators—trying to shake any floor detectives who might be following him. But the camera detectives never lost sight of him. At the street door, several loss-prevention agents converged on the man. (They never intervene until a thief has made clear his intention to leave without paying.) He was taken to an interview room for questioning. A search of his belongings revealed that his briefcase contained a "booster bag"—an ordinary shopping bag lined, inside and out, with tinfoil affixed with duct tape, a tactic used by boosters to defeat the electronic alarm systems at store exits. Agents also found a knife and wire cutters, a Ralph Lauren suit that had not been paid for, and a list of other items to steal. Clipped to the man's belt was a Taser gun disguised to look like a cell phone. The man was held in one of the complex's barred lockup cells pending the arrival of police. The vice-president told me that he turned out to be a booster from an organized retail-crime ring run by Russian mobsters.

A walkie-talkie lying beside a pair of handcuffs on a camera console crackled. It was a sales associate in one of the denim boutiques, on an upper floor, radioing, breathlessly, to say that he had detected a strong smell of ink in the fitting rooms—a sign that someone was perhaps trying to remove the ink tags from a pair of jeans. (Ink security tags—small conical plastic units that are clipped to clothing—are designed to release staining pigments when removed by anyone but store employees, who have a special device for disassembling them.) Because it is illegal for stores to install surveillance cameras inside fitting rooms, experienced thieves often use the rooms to remove security devices.

One of the camera agents hit a sequence of keys on his keyboard and brought up an image of the exterior of the boutique fitting rooms.

"We have a thirty-nine as per the forty-five," he said into his radio, giving the department's code for a possible theft in progress. The alert went out over the concealed earpieces of the business-suited guards positioned around the sales floors.

On the monitor, the agents watched as one of the loss-prevention department's dozen plainclothes store detectives—a grandmotherly African-American woman carrying a shopping bag—entered the fitting-room area. She came out seconds later and radioed to confirm that a woman was cutting off security devices in one of the booths, and gave a description of the woman. (The booth's lou-vred doors are designed so that store employees can look in.) She cautioned that she had not seen the woman actually put a pair of jeans into her bag.

A minute or so later, a young woman who fit the suspect's description—leather jacket, white cap, sunglasses—emerged from the fitting-room area carrying a large canvas shoulder bag. "Is that her?" the vice-president asked. "Bring the camera more to the left." The agent moved the joystick on his keyboard and the cam-era swivelled, picking her up as she got into an elevator. The agent hit a few buttons, and an image of the woman from a cam-era concealed in the elevator ceiling came up on his screen. When she stepped out onto the main floor, he tapped his keyboard and brought up an image of her as she sauntered past the perfume dis-plays toward the street doors.

The camera agent picked up his walkie-talkie and radioed the guards near the exit. "Get a twenty on her," he said —code for "get her location."

"We can't arrest her," the vice-president said. "We have to have an eyewitness that actually saw her put something in her bag, or we have to have it on camera. Otherwise, if we're wrong, or have the wrong person, we've got to deal with a rash of shit. A lawsuit can cost tens of thousands of dollars to defend, and you pay more in punitive damages. If we didn't see it, it didn't hap-pen." He watched the woman approach the doors. He bent for-ward to scrutinize the monitor. "There's a little weight to that canvas bag," he said, ruminatively, as if about to change his mind. "But . . ."

The woman went out the door. One of the camera agents used a camera mounted on the store's façade to pick her up as she left the store. He zoomed in to follow her up the block. "Sometimes they double back," he said. She disappeared into the crowd.

"We don't like letting them go," the vice-president said. "But when they're successful they always come back. And now her face is burned in our brains. We'll get her next time."

THE ORANGE COUNTY CONVENTION CENTER occupies a pair of low-slung buildings, each more than a million square feet, set among green lawns on an artificial lake thirteen miles from downtown Orlando, Florida. In June, the center played host to the National Retail Federation's Loss Prevention Conference and Expo, an annual three-day event. A record three thousand attendees roamed throughout the Expo Hall, under banners with the motto "PREDICT. PREVENT. PROTECT," and visited the hundreds of booths exhibiting the latest theft-prevention technologies. Two I.B.M. employees demonstrated a video-analytics software program that allows agents to search video data for specific visual evidence, like license-plate numbers. On display nearby was a device called the LaneHawk, an ankle-height grocery-store scanner that uses visual pattern-recognition technology to detect items hidden in the bottoms of grocery carts. (According to a company rep, grocery stores lose an average of ten dollars per lane every day when shoppers fail to disclose items stuffed into the cart's undercarriage.) Throughout the conference, attendees heard presentations by loss-prevention experts and law-enforcement officers, most of which centered on a topic that has dominated the industry for the past few years: organized retail crime.

No one in loss prevention can say precisely when shoplifters began to organize themselves into professionalized gangs, but there is general agreement that one of the first people to isolate the problem was a man named King Rogers. Rogers retired in 2001 as the head of Target Corporation's asset-protection program and now runs his own consulting firm, the King Rogers Group, in Minneapolis. A short, voluble man, sixty-three years old, he is as close as anyone can come to being the star of an

industry that is virtually defined by its secrecy. Rogers is a fix-
ture at every loss-prevention conference, and is, in the words of
Nate Garvis, the vice-president of government affairs at Target,
"one of the giants on whose shoulders we stand." Rogers worked
for a short time at the National Security Agency before taking a
job, in the late nineteen-sixties, as the head of asset protection at
Strawbridge & Clothier, a regional department store in Philadelphia.

In those days, store security was a decidedly less high-tech venture: no cameras, no live video monitoring. Agents were obliged
to improvise, hiding among racks of clothes or in empty boxes to
conduct surveillance. "I can recall lying in the return-air plenum
of a ceiling—the space between the drop ceiling and the main
ceiling—having poked a hole in the acoustic tile so I could look
through," Rogers told me. "In those days, you often didn't have
radios, so you had to signal to your compatriot somewhere on the
selling floor that the person you were watching just concealed
something. You dropped something gently out of that ceiling—
usually a small piece of paper—and let it waft to the ground. That
was the signal to go pick them up." When security personnel did
spot a thief, they commonly took what Rogers calls a "cops-and-
robbers" approach—pursuing the suspect into the street and trying to tackle or otherwise detain him. "I remember working at
the downtown Philadelphia store at Eighth and Market, chasing
some shoplifter out of the store," Rogers said. "He was running
down the street with an armload of clothing and I'm yelling
'Stop!' and thinking, Do I really want to catch this guy? By then,
we had those big clunky two-way radios, and I do recall seeing
one or two of those being used like a football. They'd bring a
fleeing thief to his knees quick."

Sometimes thieves escaping on foot would run into oncoming
traffic (or into an innocent bystander). Retailers were responsible
for any injuries incurred, and such incidents soon compelled

them to take a more proactive approach. In the late seventies and early eighties, many stores began to install closed-circuit cameras and electronic-article-surveillance technology—known as E.A.S. E.A.S. tags, which can be sewn into garments or slipped between the pages of books, contain a small magnetic coil that triggers an alarm at store exits. The technology is still in wide use despite its questionable effectiveness. The problem is not only that false alarms are so frequent (who hasn't set off an alarm at a store exit and been waved through by a weary security guard?), or that thieves have learned to defeat the system with foil-lined booster bags, but that the alarm sounds only *after* a thief has passed through the security gates. "If they've got a load of goods that they intend to convert to money, they're going to keep going," Rogers says— and, because retailers have forbidden loss-prevention agents to give chase, the merchandise is lost.

In 1980, one of Rogers's detectives at a suburban branch of Strawbridge & Clothier noticed a team of four people stealing men's shirts off racks. Two people acted as lookouts while the other two stuffed clothing, hangers and all, into large black plastic garbage bags. The thieves fled the store before they could be detained, but the detective got their license-plate number and phoned the police. The cops apprehended the thieves, booked them for shoplifting, and soon released them on misdemeanor charges—typical in shoplifting cases. But the volume of the thefts, and the shoplifters' brazenness, made Rogers suspect that something more was going on. The following week, a team of thieves using the same method was observed at a different branch, so Rogers enlisted the help of a colleague at the police department and traced the thieves to a tenement in Providence, Rhode Island. The shoplifters, Rogers told me, turned out to be members of a South American gang who were stealing designer clothing from department stores and specialty stores from Boston to Atlanta. "Ultimately, the police had enough evidence to charge them with some elevated theft-larceny charge, beyond shoplifting," Rogers says. "That caused them to pretty much dissipate."

In 1984, when Rogers joined Target (then part of the Dayton Hudson Corporation) as the vice-president of loss prevention, it was not widely recognized that big-box stores were also victims of organized retail crime. "And it was not obvious to *me* right away," Rogers says. "In department stores, the gangs were hitting brand-name and in some cases designer clothes and accessories, but at Target it was the very popular branded-label goods: over-the-counter analgesics, film, batteries, baby formula, smoking-cessation products, condoms, teeth-whitening strips"— any small, easy-to-resell merchandise. "I couldn't understand how there was an aftermarket for those items," Rogers says. "But there obviously was." Stores like Target, Wal-Mart, and Kmart were favorite stops for retail-theft gangs, who travelled from store to store and state to state, wiping out entire shelves' worth of products. Razor blades remain so difficult for retailers to keep in stock that stores like Duane Reade display them behind the cash registers; CVS has installed elaborate push-dispensing mechanisms that release only one pack at a time. (Most large retailers today also keep baby formula and teeth-whitening products under lock and key, along with Wii game software and MP3 players.)

By the mid-nineteen-nineties, Target was the fifth-largest retailer in the country, with around twenty-one billion dollars a year in sales. (Today, Target has annual sales of sixty-three billion dollars.) Target won't release exact figures, but the average shrink rate for retailers is between one and two per cent of sales, which would conservatively put Target's losses in 1995 at around two hundred and ten million dollars. To combat this loss, King Rogers established a national investigations team to focus on organized retail crime. "We had a dozen agents around the country,"

Rogers says. "They had two roles. One was investigating these professional thieves and professional fraudsters who, also in teams, pass bad checks and use stolen credit cards. The second role was to train asset-protection people how to respond when they identified a possible organized retail gang at work." Rather than detain boosters, agents were told to allow them to think that they had got away undetected, and then tail their vehicles.

In this way, Rogers and his investigation team learned that the stolen goods were entering a highly organized distribution chain that often began with the hundreds of flea markets that had sprung up among the suburban sprawl of cities across the country. Crooked flea-market venders would buy stolen goods from boosters, then put a few samples out on their tables—"as a marketing ploy," Rogers says. "Because the next-level-up buyer, a 'middle buyer'—often ex-cons who had discovered this great opportunity—made a habit of going to flea markets looking for product. When he saw Tylenol on a vender's tabletop, he'd say, 'Can you get me more Tylenol in fifty-count gelcaps?'" The vender, if he did not have the item in stock, would tell his boosters what to go and steal. "We'd catch boosters with lists of stuff to steal all the time," Rogers says. Typically, the middle buyers would sell the products to a "cleaning house"—in most cases, a three-to-five-thousand-square-foot warehouse staffed with undocumented workers whose job was to remove price stickers, E.A.S. tags, and identifying store labels. Often, products such as baby formula would sit in cleaning houses beyond their expiration date, in which case workers changed the dates stamped on the products. (In 2001, authorities in Texas arrested an organized retail-crime gang that had reportedly stored a million dollars' worth of stolen baby formula in rodent-infested garages at an improper temperature.) The cleaned products were shrink-wrapped and put in master cartons to look as if they had been bought from the manufacturer, then sold to corrupt wholesalers who would commingle the stolen goods with legitimately purchased products and sell them back to retailers—often to the same store from which they had been stolen.

In 1998, Target began an investigation of an organized retail-crime ring in Atlanta that was stealing computers, DVDs, stereos, televisions, and clothing, along with over-the-counter medicines and razors. Target's agents learned that the group comprised thirty Pakistani immigrants, most of them illegal, who operated a string of convenience stores. They shipped the stolen goods via UPS to large cleaning and repackaging operations in New York, Maryland, and Pakistan. "We got the Atlanta police department and county sheriff's office involved," Rogers says, "and were finally able to lure the F.B.I. into the situation, because at least one of the insiders in this group was a police officer. Then it became a public corruption case." In October, 1998, the F.B.I. launched Operation American Dream, which resulted in the bust of one of the country's biggest organized retail-crime rings. The gang used more than two hundred professional shoplifters, who stole up to a hundred thousand dollars' worth of merchandise a day from various chain stores—Target, Wal-Mart, Kmart. The bust resulted in eighty-seven arrests, the seizure of four hundred and fifty thousand dollars in cash, and the recovery of more than a million and a half dollars in stolen merchandise. Investigators learned that the gang was also involved in money laundering, illegal-alien smuggling, and car theft.

ROGERS RETIRED FROM TARGET IN 2001 and was succeeded as the head of asset protection by Brad Brekke. A tall, lean man of fifty-two, Brekke worked both as an F.B.I. agent and as a lawyer before being recruited by Rogers, in the late nineties, as an investigator. When he became the head of asset protection, Brekke had the revolutionary idea of creating a crime laboratory inside office headquarters to combat retail-theft gangs. "We're realists here," Brekke told me recently, when I met with him at

Target's main offices, in downtown Minneapolis. "Property crimes generally are not a high priority for law enforcement, nor should they be. So we took the approach that if we could do the front-end work—do the video analysis, the fingerprint and computer analysis—then give it to the law-enforcement agencies, they don't have to spend the time and effort on it."

Target's crime labs are situated on the first floor of a sprawling office complex in an industrial park twenty minutes north of downtown Minneapolis. I was given a tour of the labs by Rick Lautenbach, Target's manager of forensic services. We entered through a series of password-protected doors—Lautenbach punched his personal code into a keypad. "We can't just go into a closet at the back of a Target store and open a crime lab," he explained. "We have to have a facility that measures up to the government's standards for admissibility of evidence."

I was taken to a large, windowless room at the end of the main hallway, where Target operates its latent-fingerprint lab—a facility for detecting and recording fingerprints that are not visible to the naked eye. The room contained a fuming chamber, which resembles a glass-fronted refrigerator. To check for prints, agents place any type of nonporous object—plastic CD cases, metal iPods—in the chamber. A drop of Superglue is put into the chamber in a small tin dish and heated; the heat releases fumes of the glue's active ingredient, cyanoacrylate, which adheres to the moisture secreted by fingertips, creating a visible white print. The prints are then dye-stained with a fluorescent pigment and taken to a small adjoining room with black walls, ceiling, and floors, for photographing and scanning under lights of different wavelengths. "We don't have connectivity to any database with people's criminal history, because we're private," Lautenbach says, "but we can match events together to catch a criminal or criminal gang and we pass that along to law enforcement." Lautenbach told me about a recent case of a man suspected of repeated thefts at Target stores in Arizona. He was captured on a security camera as he picked up several items and put them in a shopping cart. Apparently aware that he was under surveillance, the man abandoned his cart and left the store. Loss-prevention agents retrieved a tissue holder that the man had handled and sent it to the fingerprint lab for analysis. Meanwhile, the investigations team was looking into whether the man was selling stolen items on eBay; recent online sale postings matched his known thefts. The agents made a "controlled purchase" from the eBay seller—a box set of "The Sopranos" on DVD. Lab analysis revealed that the fingerprints on both the tissue holder and the "Sopranos" DVDs were the same. "We turned the fingerprints over to the Maricopa County attorney's office," said Lautenbach. The man was convicted of felony trafficking in stolen property and computer tampering.

Next to the fingerprint lab is the video-analysis laboratory, a small room stocked with desktop computers and video equipment. Two agents sat at a computer and compared security-camera recordings of after-hours "smash and grab" A.T.M. thefts at several Target stores in three states in the South. One video showed thieves backing a Jeep Cherokee through the locked glass entrance doors of a Target, shattering them, then hitching a chain to the A.T.M. and ripping the machine off its moorings as they gunned away. Another tape showed the same crime, involving an S.U.V., at a different location. Though the thieves were masked, and the vehicles were different (the license-plate numbers revealed that both were stolen), the thieves' practiced movements and the precision of their actions suggested to the agents that they were the same crew. Lautenbach explained that, in order to get law enforcement to take on a theft case, Target needs to establish the seriousness of the crimes. "To do that," he says, "we need to establish the scope of the criminal activity across a geographic area, or at least show that a common suspect is involved."

Next, I was shown the computer forensics lab. Here Brent Pack, a burly, bearded man who is Target's senior computer investigator, analyzes digital storage devices seized from suspected retail-crime gangs—BlackBerrys, photo memory cards, cell phones, business servers, and desktop computers. Pack joined Target three years ago, after a stint in the United States Army, where, as part of the Computer Crime Investigative Unit, he analyzed the photographs taken by soldiers at Abu Ghraib prison. ("I had to extract the metadata from inside the pictures and create the time line, because there were multiple cameras taking different photographs and each of them was set to different times," Pack said. "Took about two months to complete and another month to finalize. Then I had to go to court for two years to testify about it.") At the moment, Pack was analyzing a hard drive seized by the police in a phony-check-writing operation that had victimized Target stores. "I'm going through here and looking for any evidence of check-writing software on any of their hard drives," he said, pointing to his computer screen, which showed a JPEG of a bank check. "Drives are so big now—some are five hundred gigabytes—you can't just randomly search," he said. "You've got to be tactical."

Brekke launched Target's crime laboratories, five years ago, with the intention of fighting the "brick and mortar" storefront fences and warehouse repackaging operations that King Rogers had helped to uncover. But since then, Brekke says, the labs have increasingly been used to fight "e-fencing," the resale of stolen goods online through eBay, Craigslist, and other e-commerce sites, where thieves can operate with virtual anonymity. (Sellers on eBay and other sites are not required to post any personal information; eBay says that "such requirements do nothing to effectively prevent the sale of stolen goods and would expose honest online sellers to significant risk for identity theft.")

"Those sites have, overnight, become the world's largest pawnshops," Nate Garvis, Target's vice-president of government affairs, says. "It used to be that you'd rip off a stereo, you'd go to a bad part of town and sell it for ten cents on the dollar, and Mrs. Smith, who'd never be caught dead in that part of town, would never find that product. Now you rip it off in bulk, you put it online, you get sixty to seventy to ninety cents on the dollar—because you've cut out the middleman—and Mrs. Smith is shopping in her slippers at her dining-room table."

Brekke says that the explosion of online selling to well-heeled buyers has changed what boosters steal from stores. Instead of baby formula, razors, and over-the-counter medicines, thieves now go after small electronic items and household appliances. According to Paul Ostenson, a senior investigator for Target, and a specialist in the investigation of e-fencing, Dyson vacuum cleaners, which retail for between three hundred and five hundred dollars, have become one of the hottest theft items for sale on auction sites. Thieves often steal the bulky vacuum cleaners through a tactic called "ticket switching": buying a cheap vacuum cleaner for thirty-nine dollars, then removing the U.P.C. bar code and affixing it to a Dyson that costs ten times as much. Some thieves buy their own U.P.C.-bar-code-making machines—available legally on the Internet—and print their own price stickers.

Last fall, testifying before a congressional subcommittee on organized retail crime, Brekke told lawmakers that Internet auction sites need to make "modest changes" to remove the incentives for criminals to sell stolen goods online. He recommended that people who sell up to a hundred thousand dollars a month of merchandise online be required to identify themselves by name on the sites. Arresting individual sellers is not the answer, Brekke maintains, because of the sheer numbers involved. "In the most recent year, Target alone made approximately seventy five thousand theft apprehensions in its stores. By comparison, the total number of criminal cases in all federal district courts across the country is usually less than sixty thousand in any one year," Brekke told lawmakers. "Even if all the U.S. attorneys across the country stopped prosecuting bank robberies, fraud, drug trafficking, and even terrorism, there would still not be enough capacity to prosecute even the apprehensions made by Target."

IT WAS THREE-TWENTY IN THE AFTERNOON, and the vice-president of corporate asset protection at the midtown Manhattan department store had resigned himself to allowing the suspected denim thief to leave the store. He now went into an adjoining room to greet the store's director of shortage control, a small man in his thirties who wore a well-tailored black suit and had a neatly clipped goatee. His job was to reduce inventory losses due to shoplifting or employee theft. Mounted on one wall were twelve computer screens that showed images of several sales associates as they rang up purchases and moved about the sales floor, straightening clothes on racks and greeting customers. The two men watched the employees on the screens for a moment. "They're persons of interest," the director said. "All of them have been flagged for surveillance."

Despite loss prevention's current focus on organized retail crime and e-fencing, by far the biggest theft problem faced by retailers is internal—the actions of light-fingered employees. Shoplifting accounts for almost thirty-two per cent of shrink; employee, or internal, theft accounts for almost forty-seven per cent—although many experts say that these numbers are skewed, since organized retail-crime rings have begun to recruit store employees as accomplices, and even to send gang members to seek jobs at stores. Whatever the case, in 2006, employees stole about nineteen billion dollars' worth of merchandise from their employers—which is why many loss-prevention departments devote as much time to conducting surveillance on their own employees as they do on customers.

The director of shortage control pointed to one of the screens, on which a salesman in his thirties—I'll call him Jeffrey—was straightening piles of T-shirts and sweaters on an upper floor of the department store. He was a handsome man with close-cropped hair and a perpetual smile. "The first red flag was that he had the highest number of non-receipt returns in his department," the director said. "Everyone else in his department was getting about three returns a week. He was getting five a day."

That was four months earlier, in February. Since then, the loss-prevention team had been monitoring Jeffrey's activities. Using "exception-based reporting" software—a program installed in all the computerized cash registers which looks for irregular transactions—the team learned that Jeffrey was ringing up returns for merchandise that had never left the store, then putting the credit on his own card. He had also been making out E.M.C.s (electronic merchandise credits, more commonly known as gift cards) in amounts of up to five thousand dollars, then giving the cards to accomplices who would come in and shop for merchandise. Camera surveillance revealed that Jeffrey was selecting clothing from the racks, removing electronic security tags, and leaving the clothing in fitting rooms for friends to come and collect at appointed times. In the four months that he had been under surveillance, Jeffrey had apparently stolen and embezzled an estimated hundred thousand dollars' worth of false credit and merchandise from the store.

"The scary thing is that he's coming to work every day," the vice-president of corporate asset protection said. "But he's not working for the *store.*"

The director looked at his watch. It was three-thirty—time to arrest Jeffrey.

Two loss-prevention agents came into the room: a woman in a black skirt and blouse and a man with the bulked-up physique of a bodybuilder. The man went to the screens and panned the camera so that it followed Jeffrey across the sales floor.

"I'm salivating at the mouth to pick him up," he said. "It's been a long time coming."

"Your instinct is to jump the gun," the director told me. "You want to arrest him the first time you catch him stealing. But you've got to be patient." For one thing, the loss-prevention team needed to build a solid criminal case; for another, they needed to find out if he was working in collusion with another crooked sales associate.

"O.K.," the vice-president of corporate asset protection said, addressing the two agents who had volunteered to go get Jeffrey: the muscular man and a bespectacled man in his late twenties who was the store's lead investigator. "You've got to be ready for him to deny everything."

The agents nodded.

"So if he becomes indignant and denies everything what're you gonna do? Because the minute you approach him he knows what it's all about."

The muscular agent replied that he would not be thrown off by Jeffrey's denials.

"Well," the vice-president of corporate asset protection said, "the ones you think are going to be a problem often aren't, and vice versa. Some confess to everything. They say they killed Kennedy."

The two agents headed upstairs to make the apprehension, and the remaining loss-prevention team crowded around the monitor.

"He was a very nice guy," one of the camera agents said. "Always said hello to me."

"That's when you *know*," the female agent said.

On the screen, Jeffrey straightened a pile of clothes on a table, checked his hair in one of the mirrors, then walked across the sales floor. The camera agent picked up a walkie-talkie and radioed the arresting agents. "He's going past fragrances," he said.

Suddenly, the two loss-prevention agents appeared from the right side of the screen. Jeffrey stopped, looked at them, and his eyes briefly widened. Then he smiled and shook both agents' proffered hands. (Later, the lead investigator told his colleagues about the arrest. ("I said, 'Can you please follow me?' He was calm but scared. You could tell by the way his lips turned pale a little bit.") With one agent behind him and one in front, Jeffrey walked to the elevator, then rode down to the asset-protection complex. When they passed the open door of the internal-theft camera room, the woman in the black skirt and blouse left the camera room and followed them. She was the lead interviewer. They disappeared into one of the interview rooms down the hall and shut the door.

The purpose of the interview was not to get Jeffrey to confess—they felt that they had the evidence—but to get him to reveal details of where the stolen merchandise was going, how long he had been stealing and how much, and whether he was working with others in the store. The team was particularly interested in Jeffrey's colleague, a young man I'll call Alex. Many of the customers to whom Jeffrey had issued fraudulent gift cards had gone to Alex to redeem them, and Alex had also been overriding the computer denials on stolen credit cards.

At five o'clock, after an hour and a half of questioning, the woman emerged from the interview and joined the vice-president of corporate asset protection in the camera room. "He admits to the fraudulent E.M.C.s and credit cards," she said. "And he talked about boxing up merchandise for his friends. He was getting four hundred for each item."

"Did you get him to roll over on Alex?" he asked.

"I can't get him to give up Alex," she said.

The vice-president scratched his head. "O.K.," he said at length. "Bring the other schmuck down—Alex. I don't see any reason not to. I wouldn't get him in a headlock." He meant this figuratively; the team uses no form of physical persuasion in interviews, he told me. "I don't want him going back to the sales floor and bitching to H.R. Just ask him, 'Why are these guys coming to you with fraudulent E.M.C.s?' Offer him soda. Water. Whatever he wants."

Two agents were dispatched, and a few minutes later Alex, a tall man in a summer-weight beige jacket, appeared in the hallway, his head hanging low. He was led into a neighboring interview room. (It later turned out that Alex was not involved.)

The director of shortage control dropped into a chair in the hallway. It was now six-thirty. The woman in the black skirt and blouse went back into the first interview room to continue talking to Jeffrey.

"Who knows how long it's going to take?" the director said. "He's got a lot of explaining to do." One thing, he thought, seemed certain. The amount of merchandise involved meant that Jeffrey would probably be charged with a felony. "He's going to jail," the director said, but without relish. "You stare at this expensive stuff all day as an employee—stuff you can't afford to buy. It's a temptation."

"You're on commission selling," the vice-president added. "When times are good, you make a fortune. September through the holiday season, you're raking it in. Then Christmas is over, no one is shopping, gas is four dollars a gallon, and your paycheck went from fifteen hundred to five hundred a week and you have to pay off those bills from that Caribbean vacation you took when the money was rolling in. So you think, I'll credit my card for a thousand dollars and make out a fake return. When it works the first time, you try it again. But next time you load a little more onto your card." He shrugged. "And the way this economy's going?" he added. "We're going to be busy."

JOHN COLAPINTO *was for several years a contributing editor at* Rolling Stone, *where he won a National Magazine Award for a story about a famous case of infant sex change (he expanded the story into a book,* As Nature Made Him: The Boy Who Was Raised as a Girl, *which was a* New York Times *bestseller). In 2001, he published a comic crime novel,* About the Author, *which is in development for the movies with producer Scott Rudin. Since 2006 he has been a staff writer at* The New Yorker.

Coda

The world of loss prevention is a secretive, not to say deeply paranoid, one. I knew that, for this story to really work, I would need to get a retailer to allow me to go "backstage" in a store so that I could watch a loss-prevention team in action. This proved harder than expected. Even a store like Target, which was happy to invite me to its corporate headquarters in Minneapolis for long interviews with its top antitheft people, balked when I asked if I could hang out in one of the stores and watch how they actually catch bad guys. I spent five months romancing various loss-prevention VPs at major chain stores and got nowhere. Folks at *Loss Prevention*, the industry trade magazine, laughed when I told them that I was trying to get inside a store. None of them had ever done so; and they assured me that I wasn't going to, either. And then, in one of those mysterious strokes peculiar to journalism and perhaps homicide detection, I cracked the case with a single random phone call in the eleventh hour before the deadline. I happened to call a big Manhattan department store that I hadn't bothered to call earlier because it was such an obvious long shot, and asked if I might be allowed to come in and watch how they stop thieves from shoplifting. The loss prevention honcho said, without hesitation, "Sure, come on down." The next day, I spent an eye-popping six hours with the store detectives described at the beginning and end of the story—scribbling away madly in my notebook as they revealed one secret after another of the profession. I remember that I had been at the store for about four hours and had not yet brought up the touchiest subject of all: internal theft, shrinkage that results from light-fingered employees. I was trying to summon the courage to raise this embarrassing,

almost taboo subject, when one of the detectives motioned me
into a small, windowless room with a wall of screens that showed
grainy images of employees working on the sales floor. It was several seconds before I realized that he was, spontaneously, inviting
me into the Internal Theft room. And not only that. He was going to let me watch them arrest one of their salespeople. Afterward, I ran home, wrote up the story in a rush of adrenaline, and
everyone was happy. Or so we thought. When *The New Yorker*'s
fact-checkers called the Manhattan department store to run my
facts by them, the loss-prevention people were horrified. They
could hardly believe that I had put everything that I had seen into
the story. They thought I just wanted "background." Whatever
that is. I found myself on the phone trying to calm the detectives
who had been so generous with their time and so open in revealing the tricks of their trade. I felt a little like I'd performed an
act of theft right under their noses. We agreed to obscure all
identifying details about the store and they reluctantly, grudg-
ingly, gave their blessing to the story. But they aren't talking to
me anymore. Which is why, unfortunately, I cannot give a follow-up on the fate of the store employee who was arrested. (I was
never told his full name and thus can't look up his case.) But suf-
fice to say that there is every reason to believe, in the current state
of the economy, that loss-prevention departments are busier than
ever.

Matt McAllester

TRIBAL WARS

FROM *Details*

SHAFI AHMED WAS 5 YEARS OLD, too young to understand
what a tribe was or why the men in these tribes had turned his
city into a war zone where, without warning, you could be pulled
from your car and shot dead. He and his seven siblings could hear
the explosions and crackle of gunfire coming from the streets
outside their house in Mogadishu. His mother was terrified, his
father desperate to protect the family.

It was January 1991 and the Somali civil war, a conflict that
continues to this day, had just started. With the ousting of President Mohamed Siad Barre, Somalia's long-simmering tribal rivalries had erupted into extreme violence—many people were
fleeing Somalia, driving south to the safety of Kenya. Shafi's family was running out of food. So his father decided to make a dash
to the store. He barely made it through the front door. A bullet
tore into his chest, and he bled to death on a dusty street of the
capital, among the first to die in a conflict that, according to Human Rights Watch, has killed hundreds of thousands of people.

Two days later, Shafi, his mother, and his seven siblings fled. As they walked through Mogadishu, some neighbors passed them and offered to give the family a ride out of the city. From there they took a bus to Kenya. Eight years later—most of them spent in refugee camps—Shafi Ahmed and his family made it to America.

Seven years after that, in the early hours of May 29, 2006, Shafi was dead. Like his father, he was gunned down in the street in what appears to have been part of a Somali tribal war. But this time the killer likely came from a new kind of tribe: one of the Somali gangs of Minneapolis and St. Paul.

OFFICER JEANINE BRUDENELL WORKS for the Intelligence Sharing and Analysis Center of the Minneapolis Police Department and has come to know more about Somali gangs in Minnesota than probably anyone else in the Twin Cities law-enforcement community. She strongly believes that the situation needs to be addressed before it escalates.

"It's going to be like when we decided to ignore the African-American gangs when they came into Minneapolis and we pretended we didn't have gangs," she says. "It will grow into a more organized crime syndicate."

While Somalis currently constitute a small percentage of the Twin Cities' gangs (African-Americans make up the largest portion, police sources say), Brudenell believes that if the cities' Somali community—which some Somalis estimate to number as many as 60,000 people—continues to grow and the local authorities don't start paying attention, the problem could spiral out of control.

"A lot of very young people were involved in the civil war," says Shukri Adan, a community leader who was commissioned in 2006 by the city of Minneapolis to write a report on Somali youth issues. "They witnessed extreme violence."

This is confirmed by officials within the justice system. When young Somalis are arrested and enter the juvenile detention center in Minneapolis, they are given a medical examination. "A lot of Somali youth suffer from PTSD [post-traumatic stress disorder]," Chris Owens, the director of Hennepin County's Juvenile Probation Division, tells me. "They've seen a lot of horrible things. [In America] they just jump back to whatever violence they observed in their formative years."

The Minnesota Gang Strike Force, a combined-law-enforcement group that combats gang activity in the Twin Cities, now has 52 Somali gang members listed on its classified roster—but law-enforcement officials and Somali community leaders say that figure is only scratching the surface. One federal agent who has significant experience investigating immigrant gangs says that he has rarely come across a closer-knit, harder-to-penetrate gang culture. Very few ethnicities are structured so strongly along tribal lines.

Somalis, who made up the largest percentage of refugees admitted to the United States in 2004, 2005, and 2006, have turned Minneapolis into the Mogadishu of the Midwest. In 2006, 25 percent of all refugees to come to the United States were Somalis. What worries Brudenell is that the gang problem isn't being addressed. Another 4,000 to 6,000 Somali refugees are expected to show up in the United States during 2008.

Government officials and Somali community leaders estimate that the majority of these new arrivals will head for the Twin Cities because of the area's well-established Somali tribal networks. At first the Somali refugees gravitated toward San Diego, but word spread before long that Minnesota—Minneapolis in particular—was the place to go. Its people were tolerant; the city and state welfare systems were comparatively welcoming; there were lots of good jobs in meat-packing plants and on assembly lines for which you didn't need more than a few words of English; and more and more in the Twin Cities and throughout the state of Minnesota, there were familiar and friendly faces from back home. Only California is the initial home to more Somali refugees than Minnesota—and not by much; the difference is only two percentage points.

Many of the arriving Somalis are expected to be young: In 2006, nearly 42 percent of Somali refugees coming to the United States were age 17 or under—which makes them more likely to be recruited by gangs. And among them are Somalia's very own lost boys—who see violence as the norm.

EVEN THE SOMALI KIDS WHO WERE DEEPLY involved in the closed-ranks violence of the Twin Cities Somali gangs (the Murda Gang, the Hot Boyz, the Somali Outlaws) knew Shafi Ahmed was a good kid. He was proud and studious, a little nerdy. He would memorize the Koran while his Somali classmates were finding other, less safe ways to combat the intimidation and violence they encountered as non-English-speaking refugees in an American city.

It was, to the first wave of refugee kids' surprise, the African-American kids who beat up on them the most. ("Go back to Africa, animals," some of them would say.) The Mexicans and the Asians got their licks in too. Shafi was occasionally beaten up by African-American kids, just like everybody else, his mother says. But he turned to his studies and his religion for succor.

His prom photo, from 2004, shows a good-looking, clean-cut young man. He has a slim face with high cheekbones. He's wearing a gray polo shirt with a white T-shirt underneath. Nothing about him could be described as gangsta, but he was encountering rivalries nonetheless—as do many young Somalis.

"I don't hate blacks," one former Somali gang member tells me. "But for us Somalians, blacks put us through hell. They didn't like how we looked—they never accept us as black like them."

The African-Americans' hostility did not prevent Somali kids from imitating their tormentors. There's nothing more embarrassing to a Somali kid than to be called a "Flight 13" by other Somalis. Flight 13 was a legendary early plane load of Somali refugees. To be a Flight 13 is to be fresh off the boat. Not American, not hip-hop.

SOME PARTS OF THE TWIN CITIES seem like they could be a short subway ride from downtown Mogadishu. The Starbucks on Riverside Avenue and Highway 94 in Minneapolis has been turned into a meeting point for Somali men, many of them elders of different tribes; it is rare to see a non-Somali customer. There are mosques, a community center, restaurants, food stores, and the run-down towers of the Cedar-Riverside projects.

Most Somali of all are the malls. To enter the Village Market mall in south Minneapolis is to step into a bustling corner of Mogadishu, with narrow corridors lined with racks of long, colorful skirts and scarves; barbers and travel agents and restaurants where men play dominoes; and windowless stores that sell everything a Somali home might need.

I have arranged to meet a woman named Kali in one of these stores. There isn't much to see of Kali, just her dark eyes and her hands. The rest is covered by the black and maroon folds of a devout Muslim woman's garb. The voice-mail message on her cell phone is a long sermon by a Muslim preacher.

Kali is 26. She came to the United States when she was 9. That makes her part of the early wave of Somali refugees—and one of the first generation of Somali gang members.

"All I knew is war," she tells me when I ask her what she remembers of Somalia. "It was hell. I saw a lot of death. I saw bodies on the streets."

At her new school in Minneapolis, Kali found herself the target of bullies. They'd call her names, beat her up, steal her money, and threaten to strip her naked or pull her head scarf off, exposing her hair. There was a group of kids at her high school,

Roosevelt, called RTS. Rough Tough Somalis. Kali joined. They would tell their attackers, "We kill our own. You think we care about you?"

Some gang members started routinely carrying weapons, but Kali did not go that far. She had her own tactic, something she'd learned in Africa.

"One day I got jumped, really bad," she says. "And they cut my chest. So I went to the hospital. I was in for a month." Kali was patient as she planned her revenge against the African-American girls who had stabbed her. She waited until she was fully recovered. Then, one winter day after school, she and a friend followed the two girls who Kali says had attacked her onto a bus. The bus stopped and the girls got off.

"Let them beat me all they want, but I'm going to get their face," Kali told her friend.

She carried five razor blades in her mouth. Kali says that they cut a little, but she had numbed the pain with alcohol. She nestled one blade in each cheek, a third under her tongue, a fourth on her tongue, and the last pressed against the roof of her mouth. She used an oil to lubricate the blades and make them easier to spit out.

On the street she confronted the girl she says had stabbed her. "When she tried to hit me I spit at her," Kali says. The blade sliced near the girl's eye, as planned. "She couldn't see. She was like, 'Oh my God, oh my God.'"

Kali caught up with the second girl, who had started running. "I [spit] like four razors in her face."

Both girls were on the sidewalk, blood from the cuts blinding them. "They were crying like a baby bird," Kali says.

She ran before the police came.

Eventually Kali dropped out of high school, and her mother threw her out of the house, she says. She had several troubled years and a couple of kids with a man she's no longer with before she got straight. Now Kali spends as much time as possible talking with younger Somali gang members, persuading them that joining gangs is a big mistake.

"Everywhere in the world, they all have gangs," she says. "But Somalian gangs are more complicated because they go by tribe. There's a D–Block gang, which is Darod, which is a tribe. There's Hot Boyz, which is Hawiye, the ones who are running Somalia right now. There's a lot of different tribes."

And then Kali echoes what I've heard from law-enforcement officials: "What happens in Somalia is going on right here."

Her words foreshadowed a tragic event. Just over a month after I met her last winter, Kali's 27-year-old brother was shot dead in south Minneapolis, along with a distant 25-year-old relative.

Kali is unreachable, but I speak to her sister. I ask if her brother was a gang member. "When he was little—but he changed a lot," she says. "He matured and [wasn't] involved in gangs." There has been no arrest, but police believe her brother's killing was gang-related.

THROUGHOUT HIS TEENAGE YEARS, Shafi remained a good student and respectful son—at least that's what his family observed. But many others I speak to noticed a shift in his behavior a few years ago. They say that he started to drink alcohol and began hanging out with the wrong kinds of people (Shafi's family disputes this). Law-enforcement sources say that he was arrested in April 2005 while smoking marijuana in a parked car. The police gave him a citation and a small fine for possession of the drug. A few days later he was arrested for passing a forged check.

One day about a year later he turned up at a spoken-word event called Nomadic Expression, at the Profile Event Center, a community meeting place on University Avenue in southeast

Minneapolis, with a Dell flat-screen monitor. A community leader who knew and liked Shafi asked him where the monitor had come from. He was selling it for a friend, Shafi said, "for gas money."

"I was like, 'Shafi, you're better than this,'" the community leader says. "'Why are you doing this? If you need gas money you can ask me, you know?'"

A young Somali woman who knew Shafi noticed the change in him in 2006. "He would come and always harass one of the girls that was working [at the Profile] and say, 'Give me something to eat—I have money,' and always yelling," she says.

Shafi lived alone with his mother, who doesn't speak English very well. All seven of his siblings had left home.

In early May 2006, the police investigated Shafi on a charge of indecent conduct—specifically, that he allegedly made lewd comments to an 11-year-old girl.

On Friday, May 26, the community leader from the center sat Shafi down. "I saw the pattern he was following," he says. "The stolen monitor, and then the drink—I knew what was coming next." The man gave Shafi a ride to where he was meeting his friends, taking the opportunity to try to talk some sense into Shafi, who was noticeably drunk.

No one I speak to knows for sure what turned Shafi from a quiet, studious boy into someone constantly on the verge of trouble. "Maybe he was going through hard times, or he wanted to see what life was like other than being in the mosque, being the nice guy," the community leader tells me.

On the night before Memorial Day, there was a party at the Profile. Shafi was there. One room in the center was hosting a traditional Somali concert while a hip-hop show was going on elsewhere in the building.

The Somali who claims she had seen Shafi harassing a woman at the Profile was at the hip-hop party. Later, she heard that Shafi was drunk and had been telling a Somali gang that they were nothing compared with another group.

"When he [was] drunk he [talked] a hell of a lot," she tells me.

PEOPLE AREN'T TELLING THE POLICE much about what happened that night, but what is known is that at about three on Monday morning someone shot Shafi dead on the street outside a local TV station. The shooting was just over the border between the Twin Cities, in St. Paul. Police were called to the scene, where they found a man with gunshot wounds. An employee at the TV station claimed that six shots were fired and that two young men drove away in a white van. Shafi Ahmed was pronounced dead at the scene by St. Paul Fire Department paramedics.

Law-enforcement officials tell me that it's a case they expect will never be solved. "The suspects were never charged in the murder," one official says. "And a lot of that has to do with the sheer fact that witnesses wouldn't come forward. And I don't foresee witnesses coming forward in the future. People in the community know who did it, but nobody wants to be a witness. There's a lot of fear."

TWO YOUNG SOMALIS I SPEAK WITH, Yusuf and Ali (not their real names), say they know what happened to Shafi Ahmed. We talk at a juvenile-probation facility in Minneapolis, in the presence of their probation officers. Yusuf and Ali decline to say what they have done to get in trouble. They insist that they are not in gangs, and that they don't even like to use the term, preferring *groups* or *brotherhoods*. Yusuf, who says that as a child in Mogadishu he was hit in the neck with a piece of shrapnel from a rocket-propelled grenade, is dressed hip-hop-style. Ali is articulate and has a job at Target. I ask them what happened to Shafi.

"It was actually the [gang that] my brother was in," Ali says. He adds that Shafi was a member of the gang. "They were both in it."

So was he killed by a rival gang or members of his own gang? Ali says he doesn't know.

The guys he thinks may have killed him "really hated" Shafi, Ali says, "especially the one that ran away, that we believe pulled the trigger. They really hated each other, them two."

"And did he belong to a different group?" one of the probation officers asks. He's referring to the killer.

"Yeah," Ali says.

Whatever the circumstances, Shafi Ahmed was shot and killed in the street, like his father in Mogadishu; the perpetrator is still at large; and it's unlikely that anyone will be charged with the crime.

DEK NOR, Shafi's half-brother, opens his wallet and pulls out a folded piece of paper. We are in the living room of his mother's house. He unfolds the paper and holds it flat. It's a mug shot. A young Somali man stares impassively at the camera.

Nor reads out the name below the photograph: "Abdiwali Abdirazak Farah." His date of birth: August 26, 1986. Just a few months after Nor's murdered brother's.

Farah is a suspect in Shafi's killing (although he has never been charged), a law-enforcement source confirms. The only problem is that soon after the shooting, authorities believe, he got on a flight back to Somalia, en route to a relatively peaceful, semi-autonomous region called Puntland. No one expects him to return to the United States voluntarily, and the government of Somalia has more pressing matters to attend to than extraditing some kid back to America. Some people say Farah is now in Dubai.

Shafi's family believes Farah was in Puntland, at least temporarily, because they faxed his picture to family members still living in Somalia, and someone in Puntland claimed to have recognized him in a store. If Farah was proved to be guilty, under tribal law, Shafi's family in the United States could have sought redress from Farah's family in Somalia. But, the family says, they held a meeting after Shafi's death to discuss how they should respond to what had happened. They were in America now, they decided, and American laws would apply. They want American justice.

So they grieve, and once or twice a month someone from the family drives to a spot seven miles south of the Mall of America and visits a granite gravestone in the Muslim corner of a mainly Christian cemetery. A bronze plaque on the granite reads: SHAFI AHMED. APR. 29, 1986–MAY 29, 2006.

When I visit the grave it is early morning on a lovely fall day. People in the city are saying that the snow will come soon, and they're bracing themselves for the hard slog through the crushing winter.

Gang members stay inside, like everyone else, during the cold. But when the summer arrives, trouble will follow. And with the influx of Flight 13s, with their limited English, their years in refugee camps, and their memories of violence, there could be a fresh crop of kids trying to prove themselves Flight 13s no longer.

"Most of the things happen in the summer," Ali says. "Everyone comes out; it's hot. There's guns everywhere. It's, like, shootings everywhere. One of these days I'm going to end up dead."

MATT MCALLESTER *was for thirteen years a reporter for* Newsday. *He was part of the paper's Pulitzer Prize–winning team that covered the crash of TWA Flight 800 in 1996. In 1999, he became the newspaper's*

Middle East correspondent, based in Jerusalem. He has covered conflicts in Israel, the Palestinian Territories, Iraq, Afghanistan, Lebanon, Kosovo, Nepal, Nigeria, Macedonia, Pakistan, and Turkey. McAllester has published three books: Beyond the Mountains of the Damned: The War Inside Kosovo *(2002), named one of the best nonfiction books of the year by* Publishers Weekly; Blinded by the Sunlight: Surviving Abu Ghraib and Saddam's Iraq *(2004); and* Bittersweet: Lessons from My Mother's Kitchen *(2009). He has won several awards, including the Asia Society's Osborn Elliott Award for excellence in Asian journalism, the George Plimpton Feature Writing Award, and three Overseas Press Club citations. He lives in Brooklyn, New York, and is a contributing editor at* Details *magazine.*

Coda

Summer didn't need to come for the killing to start again in the Twin Cities. On December 1, 2007, a few weeks after I left town, police found the bodies of two young Somali men at a house in south Minneapolis. One of the dead, Arie Musse Jama, was a rapper with a long criminal record. People called him Snoop. He had been in the Rough Tough Somalis. Snoop's brother, Mohamed, apparently swore revenge, but seven months later, before he could even the score with the guy he believed killed Snoop, he too was shot dead. By that time the killing season had begun in earnest once more: Abdillahi Awil Abdi, aged eighteen, shot dead on April 11, 2008. And then, on September 29, twenty-two-year-old Abdishakur Adan Hassan, whose alleged murderer was Abdillahi Abdi's cousin. That was five dead Somali youths in under a year. There were other shootings that did not result in fatalities.

In early 2009, I asked Jeanine Brudenell, who was now the Somali community liaison officer for the Minneapolis Police Department, if there were any updates on the Shafi Ahmed case.

"He is still gone," she said of Shafi's alleged killer. "I don't see that one closing any time soon."

Brudenell told me that since October 2008 things had been quieter. It was the winter lull again, she said. "I am expecting an increase in the summer," she said. "We shall see over the next few months."

Permissions

GRATEFUL ACKNOWLEDGMENT is made to the following for permission to reprint previously published material:

"The Zankou Chicken Murders" by Mark Arax, first published in *Los Angeles* magazine, April. Copyright © 2008 by Mark Arax. Reprinted by permission of the author.

"Everyone Will Remember Me as Some Sort of Monster" by Mark Boal, first published in *Rolling Stone*, August 21. Copyright © 2008 by Mark Boal. Reprinted by permission of Kuhn Projects as agents for the author.

"Mexico's Red Days" by Charles Bowden, first published in *GQ*, August. Copyright © 2008 by Charles Bowden. Reprinted by permission of the author.

"Stop, Thief!" by John Colapinto, first published in *The New Yorker*,

September 1. Copyright © 2008 by John Colapinto. Reprinted by permission of the author.

"The Fabulous Fraudulent Life of Jocelyn and Ed" by Sabrina Rubin Erdely, first published in *Rolling Stone,* March 20. Copyright © 2008 by Sabrina Rubin Erdely. Reprinted by permission of *Rolling Stone* and the author.

"True Crime" by David Grann, first published in *The New Yorker,* February 11/18. Copyright © 2008 by David Grann. Reprinted by permission of the author.

"Body Snatchers" by Dan P. Lee, first published in *Philadelphia* magazine, April. Copyright © 2008 by Dan P. Lee. Reprinted by permission of the author.

"Tribal Wars" by Matt McAllester, first published in *Details,* March. Copyright © 2008 by Matt McAllester. Reprinted by permission of the author.

"The Day Kennedy Died" by Michael J. Mooney, first published in *D Magazine,* November. Copyright © 2008 by Michael J. Mooney. Reprinted by permission of the author.

"Hate and Death" by R. Scott Moxley, first published in *OC Weekly,* July 18. Copyright © 2008 by R. Scott Moxley. Reprinted by permission of the author.

"Dead Man's Float" by Stephen Rodrick, first published in *New York* magazine, February 18. Copyright © 2008 by Stephen Rodrick. Reprinted by permission of *New York* magazine and the author.

"American Murder Mystery" by Hanna Rosin, first published in

The Atlantic, July/August. Copyright © 2008 by Hanna Rosin. Reprinted by permission of The Wylie Agency, LLC.

"The Color of Blood" by Calvin Trillin, first published in *The New Yorker*, March 2. Copyright © 2008 by Calvin Trillin. Reprinted by permission of the author.

"Breaking the Bank" by L. Jon Wertheim, first published in *Sports Illustrated*, April 14. Copyright © 2008 by L. Jon Wertheim. Reprinted by permission of *Sports Illustrated*.

"Non-Lethal Force" by Alec Wilkinson, first published in *The New Yorker*, June 2. Copyright © 2008 by Alec Wilkinson. Reprinted by permission of the author.

THE BEST AMERICAN CRIME REPORTING SERIES

Otto Penzler and Thomas H. Cook, Series Editors

THE BEST AMERICAN CRIME REPORTING 2009

Jeffrey Toobin, Editor

ISBN 978-0-06-149084-2 (paperback)

"Mixes the political, the macabre, and the downright brilliant." —*Entertainment Weekly*

THE BEST AMERICAN CRIME REPORTING 2008

Jonathan Kellerman, Editor

ISBN 978-0-06-149083-5 (paperback)

"[A] fascinating collection of great crime journalism…You just can't make this stuff up." —*USA Today*

THE BEST AMERICAN CRIME REPORTING 2007

Linda Fairstein, Editor

ISBN 978-0-06-081553-0 (paperback)

"Fans of true crime will want to make this book last, but will likely have trouble putting it down." —*Publishers Weekly* (starred review)

Visit www.AuthorTracker.com
for exclusive information on your favorite HarperCollins authors.

Available wherever books are sold, or call 1-800-331-3761 to order.

ecco *An Imprint of HarperCollinsPublishers*

3 1901 04364 8999